First World War
and Army of Occupation
War Diary
France, Belgium and Germany

37 DIVISION
111 Infantry Brigade
Rifle Brigade (The Prince Consort's Own)
13th Battalion
29 July 1915 - 31 July 1918

WO95/2534/1

The Naval & Military Press Ltd
www.nmarchive.com
Published in association with The National Archives

Published by

The Naval & Military Press Ltd

Unit 10 Ridgewood Industrial Park,

Uckfield, East Sussex,

TN22 5QE England

Tel: +44 (0) 1825 749494

www.naval-military-press.com

www.nmarchive.com

This diary has been reprinted in facsimile from the original. Any imperfections are inevitably reproduced and the quality may fall short of modern type and cartographic standards.

© Crown Copyright

Images reproduced by permission of The National Archives, London, England, 2015.

Contents

Document type	Place/Title	Date From	Date To
Heading	WO95/2534/1 13 Bn Rifle Bde Aug 1915-Feb 1919		
Heading	37th Division 111th Infy Bde 13th Bn Rifle Bde Aug 1915-Feb 1919		
Heading	WO95/2534/1		
Heading	111th Inf. Bde. 37th Div. Battn. Disembarked Havre From England 30.7.15 War Diary 13th Battn. The Rifle Brigade. August And September (29.7.15 To 30.9.15) 1915 Feb 19		
Heading	War Diary Of 13th Battn. Rifle Brigade From July 29th 15 To September 30th 15 (Volume 1)		
War Diary	Windmill Hill Camp, Salisbury	29/07/1915	29/07/1915
War Diary	Havre	30/07/1915	31/07/1915
War Diary	Walten	01/08/1915	01/08/1915
War Diary	Nortebecourt & Mentque	02/08/1915	04/08/1915
War Diary	Campagne	05/08/1915	05/08/1915
War Diary	St. Sylvestre	06/08/1915	07/08/1915
War Diary	St. Sylvestre Cappel	08/08/1915	16/08/1915
War Diary	Bailleul	17/08/1915	17/08/1915
War Diary	Le Bizet	18/08/1915	25/08/1915
War Diary	Bailleul	26/08/1915	27/08/1915
War Diary	Halloy	28/08/1915	01/09/1915
War Diary	St. Amand	02/09/1915	02/09/1915
War Diary	Hannescamps	03/09/1915	10/09/1915
War Diary	Bienvillers	11/09/1915	15/09/1915
War Diary	Humbercamp	16/09/1915	27/09/1915
War Diary	Hannescamps	28/09/1915	30/09/1915
Heading	111th Inf. Bde. 37th Div. War Diary 13th Battn. The Rifle Brigade. October 1915		
Heading	War Diary Of 13th Battn. Rifle Brigade From October 1st 1915 To October 31st 1915 (Volume 2)		
War Diary	Hannescamps.	01/10/1915	03/10/1915
War Diary	Bienvillers	04/10/1915	09/10/1915
War Diary	Berles-Au-Bois	10/10/1915	15/10/1915
War Diary	St. Amand	16/10/1915	21/10/1915
War Diary	Hannescamps	22/10/1915	27/10/1915
War Diary	Bienvillers	28/10/1915	31/10/1915
Heading	111th Inf. Bde. 37th Div. War Diary 13th Battn. The Rifle Brigade November 1915 Attached: Appendix A.		
Heading	13th Battn. Rifle Brigade War Diary From November 1st 1915 To November 30th 1915 (Volume 3)		
War Diary	Bienvillers	01/11/1915	02/11/1915
War Diary	Humbercamps	03/11/1915	14/11/1915
War Diary	Hannescamps.	15/11/1915	17/11/1915
War Diary	Bienvillers	18/11/1915	20/11/1915
War Diary	Hannescamps	20/11/1915	23/11/1915
War Diary	Bienvillers	23/11/1915	29/11/1915
War Diary	Humbercamps	30/11/1915	30/11/1915
Heading	Appendix A.		
Miscellaneous	Special Report On A Patrol Night 20-21 Nov.	20/11/1915	20/11/1915

Heading	111th Inf. Bde. 37th Div. War Diary 13th Battn. The Rifle Brigade. December 1915		
Heading	War Diary Of 13th Battn. Rifle Brigade From 1st December 1915 To 31st December 1915 (Volume 4)		
War Diary	Humbercamps	01/12/1915	08/12/1915
War Diary	Hannescamps	09/12/1915	10/12/1915
War Diary	Bienvillers	11/12/1915	12/12/1915
War Diary	Hannescamps	13/12/1915	16/12/1915
War Diary	Bienvillers	17/12/1915	20/12/1915
War Diary	Humbercamps	21/12/1915	31/12/1915
Heading	111th Brigade 37th Division. 1/13th Rifle Brigade January 1916		
Heading	War Diary Of 13th (S) Battalion Rifle Brigade From January 1st 1916 To January 31st 1916 (Volume 4)		
War Diary	Humbercamps	01/01/1916	01/01/1916
War Diary	Hannescamps	02/01/1916	07/01/1916
War Diary	Bienvillers	08/01/1916	13/01/1916
War Diary	Humbercamps	14/01/1916	27/01/1916
War Diary	Hannescamps	28/01/1916	31/01/1916
Heading	111th Brigade 37th Division 1/2 1/13th Rifle Brigade February 1916		
Heading	War Diary Of 13th (S) Battn. Rifle Brigade From February 1st 1916 To February 29th 1916 (Volume 6)		
War Diary	Bienvillers	01/02/1916	06/02/1916
War Diary	Humbercamps	07/02/1916	12/02/1916
War Diary	Gastineau Berles-Au-Bois	13/02/1916	16/02/1916
War Diary	Bailleulmont	17/02/1916	20/02/1916
War Diary	Gastineau	21/02/1916	24/02/1916
War Diary	Bailleulmont	25/02/1916	28/02/1916
War Diary	Gastineau Berles-Au-Bois	29/02/1916	29/02/1916
Heading	111th Brigade 37th Division. 1/13th Rifle Brigade March 1916		
Heading	13th Battn. The Rifle Brigade War Diary From March 1st 1916 To March 31st 1916 (Volume 6)		
War Diary	Gastineau Berles-Au-Bois	01/03/1916	01/03/1916
War Diary	Bailleulmont	02/03/1916	04/03/1916
War Diary	Gastineau Berles-Au-Bois	05/03/1916	07/03/1916
War Diary	Bailleulmont	08/03/1916	10/03/1916
War Diary	Gastineau	11/03/1916	14/03/1916
War Diary	Bailleulmont	15/03/1916	18/03/1916
War Diary	Halloy	19/03/1916	19/03/1916
War Diary	Occoches	20/03/1916	25/03/1916
War Diary	Auxi-Le-Chateau	26/03/1916	31/03/1916
Heading	111th Brigade 37th Division. 1/13th Rifle Brigade April 1916		
Heading	War Diary Of 13 (S) Battn. The Rifle Brigade From April 1st 1916 To April 30th 1916 (Volume 8)		
War Diary	Auxi-Le-Chateau	01/04/1916	29/04/1916
War Diary	Outrebois	30/04/1916	30/04/1916
Heading	111th Brigade 37th Division. 1/13th Rifle Brigade May 1916		
Heading	War Diary Of 13th (S) Battn. The Rifle Bde. From 1st May 1916 To 31st May 1916 (Volume 8)		
War Diary	Halloy	01/05/1916	01/05/1916
War Diary	Berles-Au-Bois	02/05/1916	03/05/1916
War Diary	Bailleulval	04/05/1916	06/05/1916

War Diary	Trenches In Front Of Ransart	07/05/1916	12/05/1916
War Diary	Bailleulval	13/05/1916	18/05/1916
War Diary	Trenches In Front Ransart	19/05/1916	24/05/1916
War Diary	Bailleulval	25/05/1916	30/05/1916
War Diary	Trenches In Front Of Ransart	30/05/1916	31/05/1916
Heading	111th Brigade 37th Division. Battalion Attached To 34th Division 5th July-Rejoined 37th Division 21.8.16 1/13th Rifle Brigade June 1916		
Heading	War Diary Of 13th Battalion The Rifle Brigade From June 1st 1916 To June 30th 1916 (Volume 9)		
War Diary	Trenches Opposite Ransart	01/06/1916	05/06/1916
War Diary	Bailleulval	06/06/1916	11/06/1916
War Diary	Trenches Opposite Ransart	12/06/1916	16/06/1916
War Diary	Bailleulval	17/06/1916	22/06/1916
War Diary	Trenches Opposite Ransart	23/06/1916	29/06/1916
War Diary	Bailleulval	30/06/1916	30/06/1916
Heading	111th Brigade. 37th Division. 34th Division From 5.7.16. Transferred With 111th Brigade From 37th To 34th Division 5th July 1916. 1/13th Battalion The Rifle Brigade July 1916		
War Diary	Bailleulval	01/07/1916	03/07/1916
War Diary	Humbercourt	04/07/1916	05/07/1916
War Diary	Bresle	06/07/1916	06/07/1916
War Diary	Albert	07/07/1916	07/07/1916
War Diary	Old British Front Line Trenches S Of La Boisselle	08/07/1916	10/07/1916
War Diary	Trenches E of La Boisselle	10/07/1916	12/07/1916
War Diary	Usna-Tara Line	13/07/1916	15/07/1916
War Diary	Trenches S.E. of La Boisselle	16/07/1916	19/07/1916
War Diary	Albert	20/07/1916	20/07/1916
War Diary	Bresle	21/07/1916	31/07/1916
Heading	111th Brigade 34th Division Rejoined 37th Division 22.8.16. Battalion Rejoined From 34th Division 22nd August 1916 1/13th Rifle Brigade August 1916		
War Diary		01/08/1916	31/08/1916
Heading	111th Brigade 37th Division. 1/13th Rifle Brigade September 1916		
Heading	War Diary Of 13th Battn. The Rifle Brigade From 1st September 1916 To 30th September 1916 (Volume 12)		
War Diary	Verdrel	01/10/1916	10/10/1916
War Diary	Fosse.10	11/10/1916	11/10/1916
War Diary	Cite Calonne	12/10/1916	15/10/1916
War Diary	Front Line	16/10/1916	20/10/1916
War Diary	Bully-Grenay	21/10/1916	26/10/1916
War Diary	Front Line	27/10/1916	30/10/1916
Heading	111th Brigade 37th Division. 1/13th Rifle Brigade October 1916		
Heading	War Diary of 13th Battn. The Rifle Brigade From October 1st 1916 To October 31st 1916 (Volume 13)		
War Diary	Calonne	01/10/1916	02/10/1916
War Diary	Calonne Village	03/10/1916	09/10/1916
War Diary	Maroc	10/10/1916	17/10/1916
War Diary	Barlin	18/10/1916	18/10/1916
War Diary	La Thieuloye	19/10/1916	20/10/1916
War Diary	Houvin-Houvigneul	21/10/1916	21/10/1916
War Diary	Gezaincourt	22/10/1916	22/10/1916
War Diary	Puchevillers	23/10/1916	30/10/1916

War Diary	Longuevillette	31/10/1916	31/10/1916
Heading	111th Brigade 37th Division. 1/13th Battalion Rifle Brigade November 1916		
Heading	War Diary Of 13th Battalion The Rifle Bde. From November 1st 1916 To November 30th 1916 (Volume 14)		
War Diary	Longuevillette	01/11/1916	11/11/1916
War Diary	Puchevillers	12/11/1916	12/11/1916
War Diary	Hedauville	13/11/1916	20/11/1916
War Diary	Englebelmer	21/11/1916	24/11/1916
War Diary	Louvencourt	25/11/1916	26/11/1916
War Diary	Puchevillers.	27/11/1916	30/11/1916
Heading	111th Brigade. 37th Division. 1/13th Battalion Rifle Brigade December 1916		
War Diary	Puchevillers.	01/12/1916	13/12/1916
War Diary	Authieule.	14/12/1916	14/12/1916
War Diary	Noeux.	15/12/1916	15/12/1916
War Diary	Oeuf.	16/12/1916	16/12/1916
War Diary	Heuchin.	17/12/1916	17/12/1916
War Diary	Auchy.	18/12/1916	18/12/1916
War Diary	Calonne.	19/12/1916	20/12/1916
War Diary	Paradis.	21/12/1916	21/12/1916
War Diary	Croix	22/12/1916	26/12/1916
War Diary	Barbee.	26/12/1916	27/12/1916
War Diary	Neuve Chapelle Trenches	28/12/1916	31/12/1916
Heading	War Diary of 13th (S) Battn. The Rifle Bde. From January 1st 1917 To January 31st 1917 (Volume 16)		
War Diary	Neuve Chapelle Trenches.	01/01/1917	02/01/1917
War Diary	Paradis.	03/01/1917	15/01/1917
War Diary	Croix Barbee	16/01/1917	21/01/1917
War Diary	Neuve Chapelle Trenches.	22/01/1917	27/01/1917
War Diary	La Fosse	28/01/1917	31/01/1917
Heading	War Diary Of 13th (S) Battn. The Rifle Brigade From February 1st 1917 To February 28th 1917 (Volume 17)		
War Diary	La Fosse	01/02/1917	01/02/1917
War Diary	Robermetz.	02/02/1917	10/02/1917
War Diary	Bethune	11/02/1917	11/02/1917
War Diary	Philosophe	12/02/1917	12/02/1917
War Diary	Hulluch Left Sector	12/02/1917	28/02/1917
Heading	War Diary Of 13th (S) Battn. The Rifle Bde. From 1st March 1917 To 31st March 1917 (Volume 18)		
War Diary	Hulluch Left Sector	01/03/1917	01/03/1917
War Diary	Mazingarbe	02/03/1917	02/03/1917
War Diary	Chocques	03/03/1917	04/03/1917
War Diary	Fontes.	05/03/1917	09/03/1917
War Diary	Pernes	10/03/1917	10/03/1917
War Diary	Maisnil-St Pol.	11/03/1917	31/03/1917
Heading	War Diary of 13th (S) Bn. The Rifle Brigade From April 1st 1917 To April 30th 1917 (Volume 19)		
War Diary	Maisnil St. Pol	01/04/1917	05/04/1917
War Diary	Villers. Sir-Simon.	06/04/1917	07/04/1917
War Diary	Agnez.	08/04/1917	08/04/1917
War Diary	Wagnonlieu	09/04/1917	10/04/1917
War Diary	In Front of Monchy-Le-Preux	10/04/1917	12/04/1917
War Diary	Arras	13/04/1917	13/04/1917
War Diary	Agnez.	14/04/1917	17/04/1917

War Diary	Habarcq.	18/04/1917	19/04/1917
War Diary	Agnez.	20/04/1917	20/04/1917
War Diary	Blangy.	21/04/1917	23/04/1917
War Diary	Nr. Village Of Gavrelle.	23/04/1917	23/04/1917
War Diary	Right Of Gavrelle	23/04/1917	30/04/1917
Miscellaneous	Account of "Arras 1917". Action of 13th Rifle Brigade. By Lieut. L.S. Chamberlen.	07/04/1917	07/04/1917
Miscellaneous	13th (Service) Battn. The Rifle Brigade. Winchester District. Daily casualty List d/-16.4.1917	16/04/1917	16/04/1917
Miscellaneous	13th (Service) Battn. The Rifle Brigade. Winchester Record Office. Daily Casualty List D/-17.4.1917	17/04/1917	17/04/1917
Miscellaneous	13th (Service) Battn. The Rifle Brigade. Winchester Record Office. Daily Casualty List D/-18.4.17	18/04/1917	18/04/1917
Miscellaneous	13th (Service) Battn. The Rifle Brigade. Winchester Record Office Daily Casualty List Dated 20.4.17	20/04/1917	20/04/1917
Miscellaneous	13th (Service) Battn. The Rifle Brigade. Winchester Record Office. Daily Casualty List D/-20.4.1917	20/04/1917	20/04/1917
Miscellaneous	13th (S) Battn. The Rifle Brigade. Winchester Record Office. Daily Casualty List. D/-20-4-17	20/04/1917	20/04/1917
Miscellaneous	13th (Service) Battn. The Rifle Brigade. Winchester Record Office. Daily Casualty List Dated 20.4.17	20/04/1917	20/04/1917
Miscellaneous	13th (Service) Battn. The Rifle Brigade. Winchester Record Office. Daily Casualty List D/-24.4.17	24/04/1917	24/04/1917
Miscellaneous	13th (Service) Battn. The Rifle Brigade. Winchester Casualty List D/-24.4.1917	24/04/1917	24/04/1917
Miscellaneous	13th (Service) Battn. The Rifle Brigade. Winchester Record Office. Daily Casualty List D/-21.4.17	21/04/1917	21/04/1917
Miscellaneous	13th (Service) Battn. The Rifle Brigade. Winchester Record Office. Daily Casualty List D/-25.4.17	25/04/1917	25/04/1917
Miscellaneous	13th (Service) Battalion The Rifle Brigade. Winchester Record Office. Daily Casualty List D/-26.4.17	26/04/1917	26/04/1917
Miscellaneous	13th (Service) Battalion The Rifle Brigade. Winchester Record Office. Daily Casualty List D/-28.4.1917	28/04/1917	28/04/1917
Miscellaneous	13th (Service) Battn. The Rifle Brigade. Winchester Record office. Daily Casualty List D/-28.4.1917	28/04/1917	28/04/1917
Miscellaneous	13th (Service) Battalion The Rifle Brigade. Winchester Record Office. Daily casualty List D/-30.4.1917	30/04/1917	30/04/1917
Miscellaneous	13th (Service) Battalion The Rifle Brigade. Winchester Record Office. Daily Casualty List D/-30.4.17	30/04/1917	30/04/1917
Heading	13th Rifle Brigade January To December 1917		
Heading	Subject.		
Heading	War Diary Of 13th Battn. Rifle Brigade From May 1st To May 31st 1917 (Volume 21)		
War Diary	Villers-Sir-Simon.	01/05/1917	18/05/1917
War Diary	Berneville	19/05/1917	19/05/1917
War Diary	Arras.	20/05/1917	20/05/1917
War Diary	Tilloy.	21/05/1917	21/05/1917
War Diary	Monchy-Le-Preux.	28/05/1917	31/05/1917
Miscellaneous	Casualties. 13th (S) Rifle Brigade.	01/05/1917	01/05/1917
Miscellaneous	13th (Ser) Battn. The Rifle Brigade. Winchester Record Office. Daily Casualty List D/-1.5.17	01/05/1917	01/05/1917
Miscellaneous	13th (Service) Battalion The Rifle Brigade. Winchester Record Office. Daily Casualty List D/-1.5.1917	01/05/1917	01/05/1917
Miscellaneous	13th (Service) Battn. The Rifle Brigade. Winchester Record Office. Daily Casualty List D/-3.5.1917	03/05/1917	03/05/1917

Miscellaneous	13th (Service) Battn. The Rifle Brigade. Winchester Record Office. Daily Casualty List D/-3.5.17	03/05/1917	03/05/1917
Miscellaneous	13th (Service) Battn. The Rifle Brigade. Winchester Record Office. Daily Casualty List D/-4.5.17	04/05/1917	04/05/1917
Miscellaneous	13th (Service) Battn. The Rifle Brigade. Winchester Record office. Daily Casualty List D/-5.6.19170	05/05/1917	05/05/1917
Miscellaneous	13th (Service) Battalion The Rifle Brigade. Winchester Record Office. Daily Casualty List D/-6.5.1917	06/05/1917	06/05/1917
Miscellaneous	13th (Service) Battn. The Rifle Brigade. Winchester Record Office. Daily Casualty List D/-6.5.17	06/05/1917	06/05/1917
Miscellaneous	13th (Service) Battalion The Rifle Brigade. Winchester Record Office. Daily Casualty List D/-6.5.17	06/05/1917	06/05/1917
Miscellaneous	13th (Service) Battalion The Rifle Brigade. Winchester Record Office. Daily Casualty List D/-7.5.1917	07/05/1917	07/05/1917
Miscellaneous	13th (Service) Bn. The Rifle Brigade. Winchester Record Office. Daily Casualty List D/-8.5.17	08/05/1917	08/05/1917
Miscellaneous	13th Battalion The Rifle Brigade. Winchester Record Office Daily Casualty List D/ 9.5.17	09/05/1917	09/05/1917
Miscellaneous	13th. (S) The Rifle Brigade Winchester Record office Casualty List D/-13.5.17	13/05/1917	13/05/1917
Miscellaneous	13th. (S) Bn. The Rifle Brigade. Winchester Record Office. Daily List D/-13.5.17	13/05/1917	13/05/1917
Miscellaneous	13th. (S) Bn. The Rifle Brigade. Winchester Record Office Daily Casualty List D/-13.5.17	13/05/1917	13/05/1917
Miscellaneous	13th (Service) Battalion The Rifle Brigade. Winchester Record Office. Daily Casualty List D/-16.5.17	16/05/1917	16/05/1917
Miscellaneous	13th (Service) Battalion The Rifle Brigade. Winchester Record Office. Daily Casualty List D/-17.5.1917	17/05/1917	17/05/1917
Miscellaneous	13th (Service) Battn. The Rifle Brigade. Winchester Record Office. Daily Casualty List D/-17.5.17	17/05/1917	17/05/1917
Miscellaneous	13th (Service) Battalion The Rifle Brigade. Winchester Record Office. Daily Casualty List D/-23.5.1917	23/05/1917	23/05/1917
Miscellaneous	13th (Service) Battalion The Rifle Brigade. Winchester Record Office. Daily Casualty List D/-24.5.1917	24/05/1917	24/05/1917
Miscellaneous	13th (Service) Battalion The Rifle Brigade. Winchester Record Office. Daily Casualty List D/-26.5.17	26/05/1917	26/05/1917
Miscellaneous	13th (Ser) Battn. The Rifle Brigade. Winchester Record Office. Daily Casualty List D/-31.5.17	31/05/1917	31/05/1917
Miscellaneous	111th Inf Brigade	31/05/1917	31/05/1917
Miscellaneous Heading	War Diary of 13th Bn. The Rifle Brigade. From June 1st 1917 To June 30th 1917 (Volume 21)		
War Diary	Monchy Le-Preux	01/06/1917	02/06/1917
War Diary	Berlencourt.	03/06/1917	06/06/1917
War Diary	Sachin	07/06/1917	07/06/1917
War Diary	Erny-St Julien.	08/06/1917	23/06/1917
War Diary	Guarbecque	24/06/1917	24/06/1917
War Diary	La Kreule	25/06/1917	25/06/1917
War Diary	Locre.	26/06/1917	28/06/1917
War Diary	Wytschaete	29/06/1917	30/06/1917
Miscellaneous	13th (Service) Battalion The Rifle Brigade. Winchester Record Office. Daily Casualty List D/-1.6.17	01/06/1917	01/06/1917
Miscellaneous	13th (Service) Battalion The Rifle Brigade. Winchester Record Office. Daily Casualty List D/-6.6.17	06/06/1917	06/06/1917
Miscellaneous	13th (Service) Battalion The Rifle Brigade. Winchester Record Office. Daily Casualty List Dated 6.6.17	06/06/1917	06/06/1917

Type	Description	From	To
Miscellaneous	Battalion The Rifle B. 13th (Service) Battalion The Rifle Brigade. Winchester Record Office. Daily Casualty List dated 9.6.17	09/06/1917	09/06/1917
Miscellaneous	13th (Service) Battalion The Rifle Brigade. Winchester Record Office. Daily Casualty List D/-11.6.17	11/06/1917	11/06/1917
Miscellaneous	13th (Service) Battalion The Rifle Brigade. Winchester Record Office. Daily Casualty List D/-13.6.17	13/06/1917	13/06/1917
Miscellaneous	13th (Service) Battalion The R Brigade. Winchester Record Office. Daily Casualty List Dated 19.5.1917	19/06/1917	19/06/1917
Miscellaneous	13th (Service) Battn. The Rifle Brigade. Winchester Record Office. Daily Casualty List Dated 20.6.1917	20/06/1917	20/06/1917
Miscellaneous	13th. (Service) The Rifle Brigade. Winchester Record Office. Daily Casualty List dated 21-6-1917	21/06/1917	21/06/1917
Miscellaneous	13th (Service) Battalion The Rifle Brigade. Winchester Record Office. Daily Casualty List Dated 29.6.17	29/06/1917	29/06/1917
Heading	War Diary Of 13th (S) Battn. The Rifle Brigade. From 1st July 1917 To 31st July 1917 (Volume 22)		
War Diary	Torreken Farm (O.20.d.2.3.)	01/07/1917	07/07/1917
War Diary	Front Left Sector.	08/07/1917	11/07/1917
War Diary	Dranoutre	12/07/1917	26/07/1917
War Diary	Oostaverne Left Sector.	27/07/1917	29/07/1917
War Diary	Kemmel Hill	30/07/1917	31/07/1917
Miscellaneous	13th. (S) Bn. The Rifle Brigade. Winchester Record Office. Daily Casualty List D/-3.7.17	03/07/1917	03/07/1917
Miscellaneous	13th (Service) Battn. The Rifle Brigade. Winchester Record Office. Daily Casualty List D/-6.7.17	06/07/1917	06/07/1917
Miscellaneous	Winchester Record Office. Daily Casualty List D/-10.7.17	10/07/1917	10/07/1917
Miscellaneous	13th (Service) Battn. The Rifle Brigade. Winchester Record Office. Daily Casualty List D/-11.7.17	11/07/1917	11/07/1917
Miscellaneous	13th. (S) Bn. The Rifle Brigade. Winchester Record Office. Daily Casualty List D/-14.7.17	14/07/1917	14/07/1917
Miscellaneous	13th (S) Battn. The Rifle Brigade. Winchester Record Office. Daily Casualty List D/-16.7.17	16/07/1917	16/07/1917
Miscellaneous	13th (Service) Battn. The Rifle Brigade. Winchester Record Office. Daily Casualty List D/-16.7.17	16/07/1917	16/07/1917
Miscellaneous	13th (S) Bn. The Rifle Brigade. Winchester Record Office. Daily Casualty List Dated 18-7-17	18/07/1917	18/07/1917
Miscellaneous	N/8/185	11/07/1917	11/07/1917
Miscellaneous	13th (S) Bn. The Rifle Brigade. Winchester Record Office. Daily Casualty List D/-19.7.17	19/07/1917	19/07/1917
Miscellaneous	13th (Service) Battn. The Rifle Brigade. Winchester Record Office. Daily Casualty List dated 21-7-17	21/07/1917	21/07/1917
Miscellaneous	13th (Service) Battn. The Rifle Brigade. Winchester Record Office. Daily Casualty List Dated 20.7.17	20/07/1917	20/07/1917
Miscellaneous	13th (Service) Battn. The Rifle Brigade. Winchester Record Office. Daily Casualty List dated 2-7-17	24/07/1917	24/07/1917
Miscellaneous	13th (Ser) Bn. The Rifle Brigade. Winchester Record Office. Daily Casualty List D/-24.7.17	24/07/1917	24/07/1917
Miscellaneous	13th (Service) Battalion The Rifle Brigade Winchester Record Office. Daily Casualty List Dated 27-7-17	27/07/1917	27/07/1917
Heading	13th (Service) Battalion The Rifle Brigade War Diary From 1st August 1917 To 31st August 1917 Volume No. 23		
Miscellaneous			
War Diary	Wytschaete	01/08/1917	06/08/1917

Type	Description	Date From	Date To
War Diary	Kemmel	07/08/1917	07/08/1917
War Diary	Locre	08/08/1917	25/08/1917
War Diary	Rossignol Wood.	26/08/1917	26/08/1917
War Diary	Denys Wood	27/08/1917	31/08/1917
Miscellaneous	13th (Service) Battalion The Rifle Brigade. Winchester Record Office. Daily Casualty List dated 1-8-17	01/08/1917	01/08/1917
Miscellaneous	13th (Service) Battn. The Rifle Brigade. Winchester Record Office. Daily Casualty List Dated 1.8.17	01/08/1917	01/08/1917
Miscellaneous	13th (Service) Battn. The Rifle Brigade. Winchester Record Office. Daily Casualty List D/-1-8-17	01/08/1917	01/08/1917
Miscellaneous	13th (Service) Battalion The Rifle Brigade. Winchester Record Office. Daily Casualty List D/-3.8.17	03/08/1917	03/08/1917
Miscellaneous	13th (Service) Battn. The Rifle Brigade. Winchester Record Office. Daily Casualty List Dated 3.8.17	03/08/1917	03/08/1917
Miscellaneous	13th (Service) Battn The Rifle Brigade. Winchester Record Office. Daily Casualty List Dated 7.8.17	07/08/1917	07/08/1917
Miscellaneous	Brigade. Winchester Record Office Daily Casualty List Dated 9-8-17	09/08/1917	09/08/1917
Miscellaneous	13th (Service) Battalion The Rifle Brigade. Winchester Record Office. Daily Casualty List dated 10.8.17	10/08/1917	10/08/1917
Miscellaneous	Winchester Record Office Daily Casualty List Dated 11.8.17	11/08/1917	11/08/1917
Miscellaneous	13th (Service) Battalion The Rifle Brigade. Winchester Record Office. Daily Casualty List dated 11.8.1917	11/08/1917	11/08/1917
Miscellaneous	13th (Service) Battn. The Rifle Brigade. Winchester Record Office. Daily Casualty List Dated 13.8.17	13/08/1917	13/08/1917
Miscellaneous	(Service) Battn. The Rifle Brigade. Winchester Record Office. Daily Casualty List dated 14.8.17	14/08/1917	14/08/1917
Miscellaneous	13th (Service) Battn. The Rifle Brigade. Winchester Record Office. Daily Casualty List D/-16.8.17	16/08/1917	16/08/1917
Miscellaneous	13th (Service) Battn. The Rifle Brigade. Winchester Record Office. Daily Casualty List Dated 16.8.17	16/08/1917	16/08/1917
Miscellaneous	13th (Service) Battn. The Rifle Brigade. Winchester Record Office. Daily Casualty List Dated 17-8-17	17/08/1917	17/08/1917
Miscellaneous	13th (Service) Bn. The Rifle Brigade. Winchester Record Office. Daily Casualty List Dated 18-9-17	18/08/1917	18/08/1917
Miscellaneous	13th (Ser) Battn. The Rifle Brigade. Winchester Record Office. Daily Casualty List Dated 23.8.17	23/08/1917	23/08/1917
Miscellaneous	13th (S) Bn. The Rifle Brigade. Winchester Record Office. Daily Casualty List D/-24-8-17	24/08/1917	24/08/1917
Miscellaneous	Winchester Record Office. Daily Casualty List Dated 25.8.17	25/08/1917	25/08/1917
Miscellaneous	13th (S) Bn. The Rifle Brigade. Winchester Record Office. Daily Casualty List D/-125.8.17	25/08/1917	25/08/1917
Miscellaneous			
Miscellaneous	Denys Wood.	01/09/1917	01/09/1917
War Diary	Irish House	02/09/1917	02/09/1917
War Diary	Spoil Bank.	07/09/1917	07/09/1917
War Diary	Beaver Corner	11/09/1917	11/09/1917
War Diary	Ypres-Comines Canal.	14/09/1917	14/09/1917
War Diary	Wakefield Huts.	18/09/1917	18/09/1917
War Diary	Menin Road.	27/09/1917	27/09/1917
Miscellaneous	13th (Service) Battalion The Rifle Brigade. Winchester Record Office. Daily Casualty List D/-3.9.1917	03/09/1917	03/09/1917
Miscellaneous	13th (S) Bn. The Rifle Brigade. Winchester Record Office. Daily Casualty List Dated 5.9.17	05/09/1917	05/09/1917

Miscellaneous	13th (S) Battn. The Rifle Brigade. Winchester Record Office. Daily Casualty List dated 6-9-17	06/09/1917	06/09/1917
Miscellaneous	13th (S) Bn. The Rifle Brigade. Winchester Record Office. Daily Casualty List dated 12-9-17	12/09/1917	12/09/1917
Miscellaneous	Winchester Record Office Daily Casualty List Dated 14.9.17	14/09/1917	14/09/1917
Miscellaneous	Winchester Record Office Daily Casualty List Dated 15.9.17	15/09/1917	15/09/1917
Miscellaneous	13th (Service) Battalion The Rifle Brigade. Winchester Record Office Daily Casualty list dated 17.9.17	17/09/1917	17/09/1917
Miscellaneous	13th (S) Battalion The Rifle Brigade.	20/09/1917	20/09/1917
Miscellaneous	13th (S) Battalion The Rifle Brigade. District rifled records Winchester. Daily Casualty Report.	20/09/1917	20/09/1917
Miscellaneous	District, Rifle Records, Winchester. Daily Casualty Report.	22/09/1917	22/09/1917
Miscellaneous	District. Rifle Records, Winchester. Daily Casualty Report.	26/09/1917	26/09/1917
Miscellaneous	District. Rifle Records, Winchester. Daily Casualty Report.	27/09/1917	27/09/1917
Heading	13th Bn. The Rifle Brigade War Diary From 1st Oct. 1917 To 31st Oct., 1917 (Volume 25)		
Miscellaneous			
War Diary	Menin Road.	01/10/1917	01/10/1917
War Diary	Willibeke Camp.	05/10/1917	05/10/1917
War Diary	Mont Sorrel.	07/10/1917	07/10/1917
War Diary	Dead Dog Farm.	11/10/1917	11/10/1917
War Diary	Locrehof Farm.	15/10/1917	15/10/1917
War Diary	St. Jean.	22/10/1917	22/10/1917
War Diary	Strazeele.	29/10/1917	29/10/1917
Miscellaneous	District, Rifle Records, Winchester. Daily Casualty Report.	02/10/1917	02/10/1917
Miscellaneous	13th (Service) Battn. The Rifle Brigade. Winchester Record Office. Daily Casualty List Dated 5-10-1917	05/10/1917	05/10/1917
Miscellaneous	13th Rifle Brigade.	06/10/1917	06/10/1917
Miscellaneous	Winchester Record Office Daily Casualty List D/-7.10.1917	07/10/1917	07/10/1917
Miscellaneous	13th (S) Battn. The Rifle Brigade. Winchester Record Office. Daily Casualty List dated	07/10/1917	07/10/1917
Miscellaneous	Winchester Record Office Daily Casualty List Dated 10.10.17	10/10/1917	10/10/1917
Miscellaneous	13th (Service) Battalion The Rifle Brigade. Winchester Record Office. Daily Casualty List dated 10.10.17	10/10/1917	10/10/1917
Miscellaneous	13th (S) Battalion The Rifle Brigade.	11/10/1917	11/10/1917
Miscellaneous	District, Rifle Records, Winchester. Daily Casualty Report.	11/10/1917	11/10/1917
Miscellaneous	13th (S) Battalion The Rifle Records. District Rifle Records, Winchester Daily Casualty Report.	11/10/1917	11/10/1917
Miscellaneous	13th (S) Battalion The Rifle Brigade.	12/10/1917	12/10/1917
Miscellaneous	District, Rifle Records, Winchester. Daily Casualty Report.	14/10/1917	14/10/1917
Miscellaneous	District, Rifle Records, Winchester. Daily Casualty Report.	16/10/1917	16/10/1917
Miscellaneous	13th (S) Battn. The Rifle Brigade. District Rifle Records, Winchester. Daily Casualty report.	18/10/1917	18/10/1917
Miscellaneous	13th Battalion The Rifle Brigade.	22/10/1917	22/10/1917

Miscellaneous	District, Rifle Records, Winchester. Daily Casualty Report.	22/10/1917	22/10/1917
Miscellaneous	District, Rifle Records, Winchester. Daily Casualty Report.	24/10/1917	24/10/1917
Miscellaneous	Winchester Record Office Daily Casualty List, Dated 30.10.1917	30/10/1917	30/10/1917
Heading	13th Bn. The Rifle Brigade War Diary From 1st Nov., 1917 To 30th Nov., 1917 Vol. No. 26		
Miscellaneous			
War Diary	Strazeele	01/11/1917	01/11/1917
War Diary	Kemmel Shelters.	08/11/1917	08/11/1917
War Diary	Kleine Zillebeke.	17/11/1917	18/11/1917
War Diary	Ridge Wood.	25/11/1917	26/11/1917
Miscellaneous	Winchester Record Office Daily Casualty List Dated 1.11.1917	01/11/1917	01/11/1917
Miscellaneous	Winchester Record Office. Daily Casualty List Dated 2.11.1917	02/11/1917	02/11/1917
Miscellaneous	13th (Ser) Battalion The Rifle Brigade. Winchester Record Office. Daily Casualty List dated 12.11.17	12/11/1917	12/11/1917
Miscellaneous	13th (Ser) Battalion The Rifle Brigade. Winchester Record Office. Daily Casualty List Dated 13.11.17	13/11/1917	13/11/1917
Miscellaneous	Officer i/c Reg. Inf. Les" No. 2 Base.	06/11/1917	06/11/1917
Miscellaneous	13th (Service) Battalion The Rifle Brigade. District Record Office. Winchester Daily Casualty List.	14/11/1917	14/11/1917
Miscellaneous	O.C. 13th Rifle Brigade.	11/10/1917	11/10/1917
Miscellaneous	13th (Service) Battalion The Rifle Brigade. Winchester Record Office. Daily Casualty List dated 23.11.17	23/11/1917	23/11/1917
Miscellaneous	13th (Service) Battalion The Rifle Brigade. Winchester Record Office. Daily Casualty List dated 24.12.1917	24/12/1917	24/12/1917
Miscellaneous	13th (Service) Battalion The Rifle Brigade. Winchester Record Office. Daily Casualty List dated 27.11.1917	27/11/1917	27/11/1917
Miscellaneous	Winchester Record Casualty List	27/12/1917	27/12/1917
Miscellaneous	13th (S) Bn. The Rifle Brigade. Winchester Record Office. Daily Casualty List dated. 28-11-17	28/11/1917	28/11/1917
Heading	13th Battalion The Rifle Brigade War Diary From 1/12/1917 To 31/12/1917 (Volume No. 27)		
War Diary	Ridge Wood.	01/12/1917	04/12/1917
War Diary	Curragh Camp, Locre.	05/12/1917	13/12/1917
War Diary	Front Line.	13/12/1917	22/12/1917
Miscellaneous			
War Diary	Ridge Wood.	01/12/1917	04/12/1917
War Diary	Curragh Camp, Locre.	05/12/1917	13/12/1917
War Diary	Front Line.	13/12/1917	22/12/1917
War Diary	Ridge Wood.	21/12/1917	29/12/1917
War Diary	Curragh Camp.	29/12/1917	31/12/1917
Heading	13th Rifle Brigade January to December 1918		
Miscellaneous	Inf. Bde.		
Heading	13th (S) Battn. The Rifle Brigade War Diary From 1st Jan., 1918 To 31st Jan., 1918 Vol. 28		
Miscellaneous			
War Diary	Locre	01/01/1918	01/01/1918
War Diary	Curragh Camp.	01/01/1918	05/01/1918
War Diary	Bulgar & Bitter Woods.	05/01/1918	31/01/1918
Miscellaneous	13th (Ser) Battn. The Rifle Brigade. Winchester Record Office. Daily Casualty List dated 31.1.1918	31/01/1918	31/01/1918

Heading	13th Battalion The Rifle Brigade War Diary From February 1st 1918 To February 28th 1918 Vol: 29		
War Diary		01/02/1918	31/03/1918
Miscellaneous			
Heading	111th Inf. Bde. 37th Div. War Diary 13th Battn. The Rifle Brigade. April 1918 Attached Casualty Lists. Attached: Casualty Lists.		
Heading	13th (Service) Battn. The Rifle Brigade War Diary From 1st April 1918 To 30th April 1918 Vol. No. 31		
Miscellaneous			
War Diary	Marieux	01/04/1918	01/04/1918
War Diary	Gommecourt	05/04/1918	12/04/1918
War Diary	Hebuterne	13/04/1918	17/04/1918
War Diary	Coigneux	17/04/1918	17/04/1918
War Diary	Louvencourt	20/04/1918	24/04/1918
War Diary	Ablainzevelle	28/04/1918	30/04/1918
Heading	Casualty Lists.		
Miscellaneous	Winchester Record Office. Daily Casualty List Dated 2.4.1918	02/04/1918	02/04/1918
Miscellaneous	Winchester Record Office. Daily Casualty List Dated 2.4.18	02/04/1918	02/04/1918
Miscellaneous	Winchester Record Office Daily Casualty List Dated 4.4.1918	04/04/1918	04/04/1918
Miscellaneous	13th (Service) Battalion The Rifle Brigade. Winchester Record Office. Daily Casualty List Dated 4.4.18	04/04/1918	04/04/1918
Miscellaneous	Winchester Record Office. Daily Casualty List Dated 5.4.18	05/04/1918	05/04/1918
Miscellaneous	Winchester Record Office Daily Casualty List Dated 10-4-1918	10/04/1918	10/04/1918
Miscellaneous	13th (Ser) Battalion The Rifle Brigade. 13th (Service) Battalion Daily Rifle Records.	10/04/1918	10/04/1918
Miscellaneous	Winchester Record Office Daily Casualty List Dated 11-4-1918	11/04/1918	11/04/1918
Miscellaneous	Winchester 13th Record Office Daily Casualty List Dated 11-4-1918	11/04/1918	11/04/1918
Miscellaneous	13th (Ser) Battalion The Rifle Brigade. Winchester Record Office. Daily Casualty List dated 12.4.1918	12/04/1918	12/04/1918
Miscellaneous	Winchester Record Office Daily Casualty List Dated 15-4-1918	15/04/1918	15/04/1918
Miscellaneous	13th (Ser) Battalion The Rifle Brigade. D.A.G. Base	18/04/1918	18/04/1918
Miscellaneous	13th (Service) Battalion The Rifle Brigade. Winchester Record Office. Daily Casualty List D/-	18/04/1918	18/04/1918
Miscellaneous	Winchester Record Office Daily Casualty List Dated 19.4.1918	19/04/1918	19/04/1918
Miscellaneous	13th (Service) Battalion The Rifle Brigade. Winchester Record Office. Daily Casualty List Dated 20.4.18	20/04/1918	20/04/1918
Miscellaneous		22/04/1918	22/04/1918
Miscellaneous	Winchester Record Office. Daily Casualty List Dated 23.4.1918	23/04/1918	23/04/1918
Miscellaneous	Winchester Record Office. Daily Casualty List Dated 27.4.1918	27/04/1918	27/04/1918
Heading	13th (Service) Battn. The Rifle Brigade. War Diary From 1st May 1918 To 31st May 1918 Vol.32		
War Diary	Bucquoy	01/05/1918	10/05/1918
War Diary	Souastre	10/05/1918	13/05/1918
War Diary	Essarts	13/05/1918	18/05/1918

War Diary	Authie	18/05/1918	30/05/1918
War Diary	Sailly-Au-Bois	30/05/1918	31/05/1918
Heading	13th (Service) Battalion The Rifle Brigade War Diary From 1/6/18 To 30/6/18 Vol.33		
Miscellaneous			
War Diary	Sailly Au Bois.	01/06/1918	01/06/1918
War Diary	Authie.	04/06/1918	05/06/1918
War Diary	Bouvelles.	06/06/1918	06/06/1918
War Diary	Guinemicourt.	06/06/1918	09/06/1918
War Diary	Rumigny	10/06/1918	10/06/1918
War Diary	Sains-En-Amienois.	15/06/1918	16/06/1918
War Diary	Nampty.	19/06/1918	20/06/1918
War Diary	Henu.	21/06/1918	22/06/1918
War Diary	Bucquoy.	24/06/1918	01/07/1918
Heading	War Diary July 1918. Volume 34. 13: Bn. The Rifle Brigade.		
War Diary	Bucquoy	01/07/1918	01/07/1918
War Diary	Souastre	03/07/1918	03/07/1918
War Diary	Bucquoy	08/07/1918	08/07/1918
War Diary	Essarts	14/07/1918	14/07/1918
War Diary	Pigeon Wood	21/07/1918	21/07/1918
War Diary	Bucquoy	31/07/1918	31/07/1918
Heading	War Diary August 1918 Volume 35. 13th Battalion The Rifle Brigade.		
Miscellaneous	13th. Battn. The Rifle Brigade War Diary August 1918	00/08/1918	00/08/1918
Miscellaneous	Appendix 'A'	23/08/1918	23/08/1918
Miscellaneous	Urgent Operations Priority. Handed in at Ruje. Appendix 'B'	25/08/1918	25/08/1918
Miscellaneous	Appendix "B"	25/08/1918	25/08/1918
Miscellaneous	The 13th. Battn. The Rifle Brigade. Appendix "C"	25/08/1918	25/08/1918
Miscellaneous	13th Battalion, The Rifle Brigade. Winchester Record Office Daily Casualty List.	02/09/1918	02/09/1918
Heading	13th Battalion The Rifle Brigade. War Diary For September 1918. Volume No. 36		
Miscellaneous	13th Battalion The Rifle Brigade. War Diary.	03/10/1918	03/10/1918
Miscellaneous	13th Battalion The Rifle Brigade.	11/09/1918	11/09/1918
Miscellaneous	13th Battalion, The Rifle Brigade. Winchester Record Office Daily Casualty List	23/09/1918	23/09/1918
Miscellaneous	13th Battalion. The Rifle Brigade. Winchester Record Office. Daily Casualty List.	24/09/1918	24/09/1918
Miscellaneous	13th Battalion, The Rifle Brigade. Winchester Record Office. Daily Casualty List.	25/09/1918	25/09/1918
Miscellaneous	13th Battalion, The Rifle Brigade. Winchester Record Office. Daily Casualty List.	27/09/1918	27/09/1918
Heading	13th. Battalion The Rifle Brigade. War Diary For Month Of October 1918 Volume 37		
Miscellaneous	13th. Battalion The Rifle Brigade. War Diary-October 1918	02/11/1918	02/11/1918
Miscellaneous	13th Battalion. The Rifle Brigade. Winchester Record Office. Daily Casualty List.	19/10/1918	19/10/1918
Miscellaneous	13th Battalion, The Rifle Brigade. Winchester Record Office. Daily Casualty List.	02/11/1918	02/11/1918
Operation(al) Order(s)	13th Battalion The Rifle Brigade Order No. 29	22/10/1918	22/10/1918
Miscellaneous	13th Battn. The Rifle Brigade. War Diary November 1918	00/11/1918	00/11/1918

Miscellaneous	13th Battalion, The Rifle Brigade. Winchester Record Office. Daily Casualty List.	15/11/1918	15/11/1918
Miscellaneous	13th Battalion, The Rifle Brigade. Winchester Record Office. Daily Casualty List.	13/11/1918	13/11/1918
Heading	War Diary Of 13th (S) Battn. Rifle Brigade From Dec. 1st To Dec. 31st, 1918 (Volume 40)		
Miscellaneous	13th Battalion, The Rifle Brigade. War Diary December 1918	01/01/1919	01/01/1919
Heading	13th Rifle Brigade January & February 1919		
Miscellaneous	8th Inf. Bde. Nov.1919		
Miscellaneous	Messages Form. 13 Rifle Bde vol 41		
Miscellaneous	13th Battalion The Rifle Brigade. War Diary January 1919	06/01/1919	06/01/1919
Miscellaneous	13th Battalion The Rifle Brigade. War Diary February 1918	03/03/1919	03/03/1919

WO 95/2534/1
13 Bn Rifle Bde Aug 1915 – Feb 1919

37TH DIVISION
111TH INFY BDE

13TH BN RIFLE BDE
AUG 1915-FEB 1919

37TH DIVISION
111TH INFY BDE

13th (Service) Battalion The Rifle Brigade.

WO 95/25341

111th Inf. Bde.
37th Div.

Battn. disembarked
Havre from England
30.7.15.

WAR DIARY

13th BATTN. THE RIFLE BRIGADE.

AUGUST AND SEPTEMBER

(29.7.15 to 30.9.15)

1 9 1 5

111th Inf.Bde.
37th Div.

Battn. disembarked
Havre from England
30.7.15.

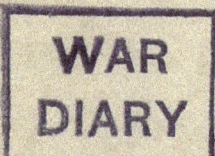

13th BATTN. THE RIFLE BRIGADE.

AUGUST AND SEPTEMBER

(29.7.15 to 30.9.15)

1 9 1 5

Feb 19

Confidential.

War Diary
of
13th Battn. Rifle Brigade.

From   July 29th '15

To   September 30th '15

(Volume 1)

WAR DIARY
or
INTELLIGENCE SUMMARY.

(Erase heading not required.)

Army Form C. 2118.

Instructions regarding War Diaries and Intelligence Summaries are contained in F. S. Regs., Part II. and the Staff Manual respectively. Title pages will be prepared in manuscript.

Place	Date	Hour	Summary of Events and Information	Remarks and references to Appendices
Bulford Camp				
Camp Salisbury	29/7/15	10 a.m.	The Battalion left Camp & marched to Southampton. Sailed on "Mononian" to Havre.	
Havre	30/7/15	9 a.m.	Disembarked, marched (Rest Camp) No. 1 (Ph. Newhaven) where sick & officer	
			Hospital there. Remained in Camp for night.	
"	31/7/15 10.15 a.m.		Entrained at Havre, left at 3 pm & journeyed station via Rouen Boulogne.	
			Havre (Ph. Burnier) taken sick & remained behind at St. Omer.	
Watten	1/8/15	7.00 a.m.	Arrived & marched to Billets. 2nd Lieut. Bellew & Mulgan Br. Capt. Hughes	
			Billets at NORTBECOURT. (nigh to HAZEBROUCK)	
Nortbecourt & Moulgue	2/8/15	all day	Remained in Billets.	
"	3/8/15	"	do. do. Battn. Route March by R. on to Bettypunet Billets &	
			commenced studies.	
"	4/8/15	7 am	Left Billets & marched to Campagne where Billets. Route via St. Omer & Arques.	
Campagne	5/8/15	7am	Left Billets & marched to St. Sylvester. Logged via Hazebrouck Fletre & F.H.	
			Eunston taken sick on march & removed to Hospital.	
St Sylvestre	6/8/15	all day	Remained in Billets.	
"	7/8/15	"	do. do.	

A.H. Mason
Captain & Adjutant,
18th Battalion Rifle Brigade.

WAR DIARY or INTELLIGENCE SUMMARY

Army Form C. 2118.

Place	Date	Hour	Summary of Events and Information	Remarks and references to Appendices
St. Sylvestre Cappel	8/8/15	All day.	Remained in Billets. Inspection of Brigade by Gen. Sir Herbert Plumer, Comndg. 2nd Army. Digging party left for Kruisstraat area. N.C.O.'s being changed as follows. Lieutenant La Touche Reynard. Major in charge of Kruisstraat. Medical Officer. 9 officers. 259 other ranks 2nd Bn. 246 other ranks. C & B Coy. The party marched to BAILLEUL where billeted for night.	
"	9/8/15	"	Remained in Billets. F.G.C.M. on Pte Parker B Coy. for "Scandalously using his Rifle" finding of Court "Guilty". Sentence 42 days F.P. No. 2. but recommended for mercy.	
"	10/8/15	"	Remained in Billets. Battalion took musketry.	
"	11/8/15	"	do. Two Squadrons to musketry. 4 men wounded slightly from digging party.	
"	12/8/15	"	do. Battalion took musket. Report from digging party dated 12/8/15	
"	13/8/15	"	Bn. resumed digging at 6.50 a.m. Shelled by German Artillery not previously used. 1 man Sergeant wounded treated by M.O. Returned 1 man cut by pick (also returned to duty after treatment by M.O. at 1.30 p.m. (these men are included in the wounded of September at 1.30 p.m. Returned) 6.30 p.m. Remained in Billets.	
"	14/8/15		Remained in Billets. Musketry.	

A. Warren
Captain & Adjutant,
18th Battalion Rifle Brigade.

Army Form C. 2118.

WAR DIARY
or
INTELLIGENCE SUMMARY.
(Erase heading not required.)

Instructions regarding War Diaries and Intelligence Summaries are contained in F. S. Regs., Part II. and the Staff Manual respectively. Title pages will be prepared in manuscript.

Place	Date	Hour	Summary of Events and Information	Remarks and references to Appendices
St. Sylvestre Cappel	18/6/15	All day	Remained in Billets.	
	19/6/15	11 a.m.	Left Billets & marched to BAILLEUL where billeted for night (map 36 Belgium & France)	
BAILLEUL	20/6/15	5.30 am	Left Billets & marched to LE BIZET. put outside PIONEERS. Took over M.E.122.	
LE BIZET	20/6/15	All day	A&B Coys went into trenches at 5 a.m. for instructional purposes under 6th Bucks 2 6th Buffs Regt. (Relieved 37th Inf Bde) C & D Coys digging at 9 a.m. & returned at 6 p.m.	
	21/6/15		A&B Coys. leave trenches 5 a.m. C&D Coys into trenches at 6 a.m. about 19.25 34	
			A/M. W.M. C.H. "D" Coy. killed in action. F&B Coys digging as letters from 3pm to 6pm	
	22/6/15	"	C&D Coys left trenches at 6 am. A&B Coys into trenches at 6 am. C&D Coys digging in afternoon 3pm till 6pm. Twice counted up full area of Trench of Strength.	
	23/6/15	"	A&B Coys leave trenches at 6 am. C&D Coys digging in morning. S. till 12 noon. Brought all officers attend relief of trenches between 6th Queens & 6th Buffs & 7th E. Surreys & 6th R.W. Kent Regts.	
	23/6/15	"	C&D Coys entered trenches at 5 am. 7 & B Coys digging in morning.	
	24/6/15	"	C&D Coys left trenches at 5 am. A&B Coys digging in morning. D coy enter trenches & took over lower Off from 9th E Surry Regt. & B Coy take over trenches 99,100	

Army Form C. 2118.

WAR DIARY
or
INTELLIGENCE SUMMARY.
(Erase heading not required.)

Instructions regarding War Diaries and Intelligence Summaries are contained in F.S. Regs., Part II. and the Staff Manual respectively. Title pages will be prepared in manuscript.

Place	Date	Hour	Summary of Events and Information	Remarks and references to Appendices
LE BIZET.	23/8/15	all day	9.10 am Bn. Hd. Qrs. at 6.30 pm Bn. SCALES "F" Coy. reports from Bde. sent to England & struck off strength. Memo from 111th Bde. Office notifying that the Brigade will be moving on WEDNESDAY Aug 25/8	
"	24/8/15	"	Coy. Coys. digging in morning. F & B Coys. have Trenches at 9 am.	
"	25/8/15	"	F.G.C.M. on Rfn. RAYBOURNE A Coy. Charged with Staying at his post whilst on Sentry. Case Reviewed. Prisoner found "NOT GUILTY".	
"	24/8/15	"	F.G.C.M. on Rfn. MOORE "D" Coy. Charged with "Insolence to an Officer". Prisoner found "GUILTY". & Sentenced to 42 days F.P. No.1.	
	25/8/15	8.10am	Battalion left LE BIZET and marched to CRILLEUR	
BAILLEUL	26/8/15	all day	Remained in Billets. Thorough inspection of arms, Equipment etc.	
"	27/8/15	9am	Battalion left BAILLEUL & marched to SOLEMPREEGNEELDE & entrained to DOULLENS which was reached 8.0pm. Route via HAZEBROUCK, ST. POL. Marched to Billets at MALLOY.	
HALLOY	28/8/15	all day	Remained in Billets	
"	29/8/15	"	do	
"	30/8/15	"	Inspection of Division by Army Commander.	

R.M. Warren
Captain & Adjutant
12th Battalion Rifle Brigade

WAR DIARY or INTELLIGENCE SUMMARY

Army Form C. 2118.

(Erase heading not required.)

Instructions regarding War Diaries and Intelligence Summaries are contained in F.S. Regs, Part II. and the Staff Manual respectively. Title pages will be prepared in manuscript.

Place	Date	Hour	Summary of Events and Information	Remarks and references to Appendices
HALLOY	3/8/15	all day	Parade for musketry, drill etc. 1st Reinforcement arrived, mustering 6 N.C.O's and men	
	1/9/15	10 a.m.	Left HALLOY and marched to ST AMAND via PAS.	
ST AMAND	2/9/15	8.30 a.m.	All Coys & Platoon Sergts. visited trenches at HANNESCAMPS and made an inspection of same. Bath parade at 9 a.m. for musketry etc.	
"	2/9/15	9.30 p.m.	Battn. left BELLEU to relieve French troops in trenches at HANNESCAMPS, BOISDEAU, PAMMEO and BIENVILLERS. Relief carried out successfully.	
HANNESCAMPS	3/9/15	all day	Battn. in trenches all day. Lt. FOWLER & Bty. Sgt. MAJOR took up position at FONCQUEVILLERS. Recommended M/Gun. No other casuals.	
"	4/9/15	"	do do do Very quiet.	
"	5/9/15	"	do do do (1 man slightly wounded)	
"	6/9/15	"	do do do	
"	7/9/15	"	do do do	
"	8/9/15	"	do do do One man shot through head. Corpl. DENT died.	
"	9/9/15	"	do do do Corpl. DENT shot dead guards.	
"	10/9/15	"	do do do Battalion relieved from trenches by 13th Battn. R.R.R.C. Relief carried out successfully. Batt. moved into billets at BIENVILLERS.	
BIENVILLERS	11/9/15		Battalion remained in billets morning parties supplied for fatigues	

[Signature]
Captain & Adjutant
16th Battalion Rifle Brigade

Army Form C. 2118.

WAR DIARY
or
INTELLIGENCE SUMMARY.
(Erase heading not required.)

Instructions regarding War Diaries and Intelligence Summaries are contained in F. S. Regs., Part II. and the Staff Manual respectively. Title pages will be prepared in manuscript.

Place	Date	Hour	Summary of Events and Information	Remarks and references to Appendices
BIENVILLERS.	all day 12/9/15		Battalion resting in Billets. Working parties supplied	
"	13/9/15		do. do. do.	
"	14/9/15		do. do. A few shells dropped into village. No damage done	
"	7.30 pm 15/9/15		Battn. relieved by 6th B. Bedfordshire Regt. & cos of Batt to at HUMBERCAMP	
HUMBERCAMP	16/9/15		Remained in Billets. Physical Drill early morning. Musketry &c.	
"	17/9/15		do. do.	
"	18/9/15		do. Digging party 300 strong supplied under R.E. at ST. AMAND.	
"	19/9/15		do. Musketry &c.	
"	20/9/15		do. do.	
"	21/9/15		do. Route March.	
"	22/9/15		do. do.	
"	23/9/15		do. Musketry Bombing etc.	
"	24/9/15		do. Heavy rain	
"	25/9/15		do. Practice attack carried out.	
"	26/9/15		do. do.	
"	27/9/15	5.0 p.m.	The Battalion relieved the 6th Bedfordshire in Trenches HANNESCAMPS. Relief carried out successfully	

1/4th Battalion Rifle Brigade.

Army Form C. 2118.

WAR DIARY
or
INTELLIGENCE SUMMARY.
(Erase heading not required.)

Instructions regarding War Diaries and Intelligence Summaries are contained in F.S. Regs., Part II. and the Staff Manual respectively. Title pages will be prepared in manuscript.

Place	Date	Hour	Summary of Events and Information	Remarks and references to Appendices
HOUPLINES.	28/8/15	all day	Battalion remained in trenches. Very quiet on front.	
"	29/8/15	"	do. do.	
"	30/8/15	"	do. do.	

A.W. Irwin
Captain & Adjutant,
13th Battalion Rifle Brigade.

111th Inf.Bde.
37th Div.

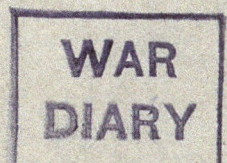

13th BATTN. THE RIFLE BRIGADE.

O C T O B E R

1 9 1 5

Confidential.

War Diary
of
13th Battn. Rifle Brigade

From October 1st 1915

To October 31st 1915

(Volume 2)

Instructions regarding War Diaries and Intelligence Summaries are contained in F. S. Regs., Part II. and the Staff Manual respectively. Title pages will be prepared in manuscript.

INTELLIGENCE SUMMARY.

(Erase heading not required.)

Place	Date	Hour	Summary of Events and Information	Remarks and references to Appendices
HANNESCAMPS.	1/10/15	all day	Battalion in trenches. Very quiet all day. Robert sent out at night & met strong enemy patrol. 1 Officer wounded & 1 man MISSING. 1 Man Killed during day.	
"	2/10/15	"	Battalion in trenches. Very quiet.	
"	3/10/15 6.30pm		Battalion relieved by 13th Bn. K.R.R.C. Relief carried out successfully. Battalion to go Billets at BIENVILLERS.	
BIENVILLERS.	4/10/15	"	Battalion in Billets. Digging parties under R.E.	
"	5/10/15	"	do	
"	6/10/15	"	do	
"	7/10/15	"	do	
"	8/10/15	"	do	
"	9/10/15 4pm		Relieved by 6th Bn. Bedf. Regt. & marched to Billets at BERLES-AU-BOIS.	
BERLES-AU-BOIS	10/10/15 all day		Battalion remained in Billets. Capt & Adjt. Patterson admitted hospital.	
"	11/10/15	"	Lieutn. J. Cruse's. & Wimberley.	
"	12/10/15	"	Major Margus of Winchester's Leaves Battalion to take up appointment as O.C. No. 2. Base Depot. ROUEN.	
"	13/10/15	"	Battalion in Billets. Digging under R.E.	

A McCracken Taylor

INTELLIGENCE SUMMARY.

(Erase heading not required.)

Instructions regarding War Diaries and Intelligence Summaries are contained in F.S. Regs., Part II. and the Staff Manual respectively. Title pages will be prepared in manuscript.

Place	Date	Hour	Summary of Events and Information	Remarks and references to Appendices
BERLES-AU-BOIS	14/6/15	All day	Battalion Route March.	
"	15/6/15	3.0 p.m.	Battalion relieved by 13th Bn. K.R.R.C and took up billets at ST. AMAND.	
ST. AMAND.	16/6/15	all day	Battalion remained in billets. Inspection of musketry. Supplies or range.	
"	17/6/15	"	600 men digging on topo line near R.E.	
"	18/6/15	"	Inspection of Arms etc. Supplying on range during afternoon.	
"	19/6/15	"	Battalion practice attack.	
"	20/6/15	"	600 men digging on topo line near R.E.	
"	21/6/15	3.0 p.m.	Battalion relieved the 6th Regt. in trenches at HANNESCAMPS. Relief carried out successfully.	
HANNESCAMPS.	22/6/15	all day	Battn. in trenches. Very quiet in front.	
"	23/6/15	"	" " 1 man wounded by Shrapnel Bullet (6/Arnold). Asking Reconnaissance was made. A few rounds fired were sent into the enemy lines aiming casualties amounted to 1 man wounded and 2 missing. (Capt + 8 men) The general patrol [illegible] [illegible] ...	
"	24/6/15	"	Battalion in trenches. Very quiet on front. ...	
"	25/6/15	"	do. do.	

A.N. [illegible] Jackson

INTELLIGENCE SUMMARY.

or

(Erase heading not required.)

Instructions regarding War Diaries and Intelligence Summaries are contained in F. S. Regs., Part II. and the Staff Manual respectively. Title pages will be prepared in manuscript.

Place	Date	Hour	Summary of Events and Information	Remarks and references to Appendices
HANNESCAMPS	26/9/15	all day	Battalion in trenches. Enemy Artillery very active during morning, but very little damage to trenches and no casualties.	
	27/9/15	5 pm	Battalion relieved by 8th Batt. King's Royal Rifles. Relief carried out successfully and Battalion marched to Billets at BIENVILLERS.	
BIENVILLERS	28/9/15	day	Battalion in Billets. Inspector of Arms Equipment Etc. Inspected parties of supplies under Capt. Edwards.	
"	29/9/15	"	Battalion in Billets. do	
"	30/9/15	"	do. Enemy Artillery very active & shelled cottage at various altitudes, no casualties. Very distressing.	
"	31/9/15	"	Battalion in Billets. Inspection of Arms etc. Digging under R.E.	

111th Inf.Bde.
37th Div.

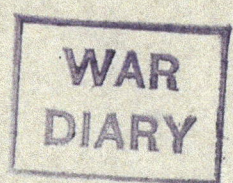

13th BATTN. THE RIFLE BRIGADE.

N O V E M B E R

1 9 1 5

Attached:

Appendix A.

CONFIDENTIAL.

13th Battn. Rifle Brigade.

War Diary

From November 1st 1915

To November 30th 1915

(Volume 3)

WAR DIARY or INTELLIGENCE SUMMARY.

Army Form C. 2118.

Place	Date	Hour	Summary of Events and Information	Remarks and references to Appendices
BIENVILLERS	1/11/15	all day	Battalion in Billets at BIENVILLERS (Rif. Sheet 11 LENS N.E.) Inspection of Arms. Reconnaissance took Kindes 6. Digging parties appeared under R.E.	
	2/11/15	3.9 p.m.	The 6th Battalion Bedfordshire Reg. relieved Battalion and Bath marched to HUMBERCAMPS (Rif. Sheet 11 LENS 9.4) in Brigade Reserve	
HUMBERCAMPS	3/11/15	all day	Battalion at HUMBERCAMPS. General tidying up Billets. Inspection of Equipment &	
	4/11/15	"	do. Baggage etc etc supplied under R.E. Rouvroy Bn.	
	5/11/15	"	marched to pits for Baths.	
	6/11/15	"	Bath in Billets. Inspection of Equipment &c.	
	7/11/15	"	Battalion digging all day under R.E. in Pipeline.	
	8/11/15	"	Church Parade	
	9/11/15	"	Inspection of Arms etc. 200 men digging under R.E.	
	10/11/15	"	Practice Attack with bombing party.	
	11/11/15	"	Heavy rain all day. Battln. remained in Billets.	
	12/11/15	"	Typical morning early morning. Battln. moving in open line alley	
	13/11/15	"	Inspection of Arms etc. Later (blank trial)	
	14/11/15	"	turning Kindesday	

Anstrose Jackson
Captain & Adjutant,
18th Battalion Rifle Brigade.

Army Form C. 2118.

WAR DIARY
or
INTELLIGENCE SUMMARY.
(Erase heading not required.)

Instructions regarding War Diaries and Intelligence Summaries are contained in F. S. Regs., Part II. and the Staff Manual respectively. Title pages will be prepared in manuscript.

Place	Date	Hour	Summary of Events and Information	Remarks and references to Appendices
HINGES CHATS	14/11/15	5.0 p.m.	The Battalion relieved the 1st Bn Bedfordshire Regt. in the trenches at HANNESCAMPS. Relief carried out successfully by 7.0 p.m. Trenches knee deep in mud sniper going to be troublesome.	
HANNESCAMPS	15/11/15	all day	Rather in trenches all day. Enemy Artillery very active (more shells by 1 section of battery) at 1 wounded. Patrol sent out at night (8 p.m.) but returned at 8.35 p.m. as report of enemy.	
"	16/11/15		Battalion in trenches all day. Very quiet in front.	
"	17/11/15	5.0 p.m.	Battalion was relieved by 12th K.R.R.C. and marched back to BIENVILLERS.	
BIENVILLERS	18/11/15		General tidying up of billets in morning. Rigging and R.E. in afternoon.	
"	19/11/15		Inspection of arms etc. Day very quiet. R.E. & important line trenches improving same to Billets etc.	
"	20/11/15	7 a.m.	The Battalion relieved the 13th Kings Royal Rifles in the trenches at HANNESCAMPS. Relief carried out successfully by 8.30 a.m. On our left are 2 Coys. 13 Bn R. Fusiliers and on our right are 2 Coys. 10th R. Fusiliers. On night 20/11/15 are actively in trenches at FONQUEVILLERS. Enemy Artillery active during	

Andrew E. Hilton...... Captain & Adjutant,
13th Battalion Rifle Brigade.

WAR DIARY or INTELLIGENCE SUMMARY.

Army Form C. 2118.

(Erase heading not required.)

Instructions regarding War Diaries and Intelligence Summaries are contained in F.S. Regs., Part II. and the Staff Manual respectively. Title pages will be prepared in manuscript.

Place	Date	Hour	Summary of Events and Information	Remarks and references to Appendices
HANNESCAMPS	20/11/15	all day	morning but were soon silenced with our guns.	
		4.30 pm	A patrol was sent out. (See Report attached)	See report
"	21/11/15	all day	Battalion in trenches. Very quiet in front.	
"	22/11/15		do	
"	23/11/15	4.30 pm	A patrol went out, but seeing no signs of enemy returned at 7.30 p.m.	
		7 am	Battalion was relieved by 13th Bn. K.R.R.C. Relief carried out successfully.	
BERNEUIL	24/11/15	5 pm	Working parties supplied under R.E. at 9pm.	
"		all day	Inspection of Arms. Ammunition etc. Working parties under R.E. at night.	
"	25/11/15	"	A few stalls were dropped into village during afternoon but caused no damage.	
			Inspection of Arms etc. Working parties under R.E. all day.	
"	26/11/15	3 pm	Battalion relieved by 6th Bn. Bedfordshire Regt. Relief carried out successfully and Bn. marched to HUMBERCAMPS (Sq. Map Sheet 11.5N5 G4.)	
"	27/11/15	all day	General tidying up of Billets & repairing same.	
"	28/11/15	"	Battalion digging all day under R.E.	
"	29/11/15	"	Laying of Ry. Inspection of Arms etc.	

A.M.Wade Julton
Captain & Adjutant,
18th Battalion Rifle Brigade.

Army Form C. 2118.

WAR DIARY
or
INTELLIGENCE SUMMARY.
(Erase heading not required.)

Instructions regarding War Diaries and Intelligence Summaries are contained in F.S. Regs., Part II. and the Staff Manual respectively. Title pages will be prepared in manuscript.

Place	Date	Hour	Summary of Events and Information	Remarks and references to Appendices
HUMBERCAMPS	30/11/15	all day	Physical Exercises early morning. 50 men & 1 Officer digging under R.E. in Corps Line. Inspection of treasury equipment.	

Arthur To. Jackson
Captain & Adjutant,
12th Battalion Rifle Brigade.

A P P E N D I X   A.

Copy.   Special Report on a Patrol   "A"
              Night 20-21 Nov.   13'RB

A Patrol of the 13th Batln. the Rifle
Brigade under 2° Lt D.F Bruce, consisting
of a Sergt + 23 men left T.66. at 5pm
on 20' Nov. proceeding up the HANNESCAMPS
ravine with the intention of lying in
wait for any enemy patrol.

Simultaneously a similar Patrol under
Lt J. Morris left T.65 & proceeded up
the ESSARTS ROAD. The intention was
that should one patrol drive the enemy
back the other was to intercept their retreat.
Mr Bruce's patrol took up their final
position in the bed of the Ravine at 5.52p.
at 6.10 pm the first German was seen coming
on the sky line by S'end of OSIERAIE from
E 18 a 6½ 2 on 1/10000 map.
The enemy Patrol had 3 single men in line
at 40 yds interval as a point & R & L flankers
Following were 5 parties of 10-12 in file
at 60yds from each other with 2 connecting files
between. The patrol numbered about 70: It made
straight for the embankment on N of ravine.
and closed up on reaching that point.
Our Patrol had meanwhile crawled into a
fighting position & on the word of command

(11)

gave a fine burst of rapid fire. Many cries and shouted orders were heard & the Germans replied with Bomb & Rifle Fire. A German was then seen running towards the OSERAIE, he was brought down but another got back unhurt. Mr Bruce sent back one man for reinforcements. At 7pm 2nd Lt C. Rowlatt with 14 men came up in support. At this moment the Germans began to retire. Mr Rowlatt and his party were told off to protect the flank & Mr Bruce got his men together and charged. The Germans broke up completely and ran in all directions towards the OSERAIE. Simultaneously our Artillery opened fire on the OSERAIE and Mr Bruce is of opinion that a great many casualties resulted from their action. The course of the enemy's retirement unfortunately did not take them sufficiently close to Mr Morris to enable him to come into action. Mr Bruce's patrol had no casualties: Mr Rowlatt's Patrol had two wounded: one badly (since proved fatal) & the other slightly. The patrols returned carrying with them one dead German shot through the head, at 7.45pm. His effects were forwarded to B.H.Q.....

                                B.W. Bentinck Capt.

The Div General gave Mr Bruce a Red Ticket. The C.O. congratulated Mr Rowlatt on the way in which he handled the supports.

The Patrol received the congratulations & appreciation of the G.O.C. VIIth Corps as well as that of the G.O.C. 37th Div

                   A N Strode Jackson Captain & Adjutant

111th Inf.Bde.
37th Div.

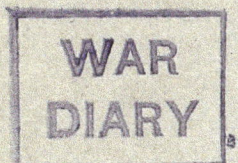

13th BATTN. THE RIFLE BRIGADE.

D E C E M B E R

1 9 1 5

Confidential

War Diary

of

13th Battn. Rifle Brigade

From 1st December 1915

To 31st December 1915.

(Volume 4)

Army Form C. 2118.

WAR DIARY
or
INTELLIGENCE SUMMARY.
(Erase heading not required.)

Instructions regarding War Diaries and Intelligence Summaries are contained in F. S. Regs., Part II. and the Staff Manual respectively. Title pages will be prepared in manuscript.

(Orderly Room stamp: 13TH BATTN RIFLE BRIGADE)

Place	Date	Hour	Summary of Events and Information	Remarks and references to Appendices
HUMBERCAMPS	1/12/15	all day	Battalion in billets. Marched to PAS for baths.	
"	2/12/15	"	Whole Batn. digging under R.E. 2 on Corps line.	
"	3/12/15	"	Running Physical drill early morning. Bath parade (a.m.) for reserve Coy. Boxing groups. Signing Officer and 41 men	
			Issued stores with Coy. Boxing groups. Signing Officer and men attended lecture by Captain Storr Picton.	
"	4/12/15	"	Practice of Riot formations and musketry.	
"	5/12/15	"	Divine Service.	
"	6/12/15	"	Battalion digging under R.E. on Corps line.	
"	7/12/15	9 a.m.	Practice on Miniature range behind billet etc.	
"	9/12/15	3.30 p.m.	Battalion relieved 6th Berkshires Regt. in the trenches (Ref. map Sheet 51 bis 44) Relief carried out successfully.	
HANNESCAMPS	9/12/15	all day	Battalion in trenches. Trenches waist deep in liquid mud & most of them fallen in owing to very wet weather.	
"	10/12/15	4 p.m.	Battalion relieved by 13th K.R.R.C. and marched back to BIENVILLERS.	
BIENVILLERS	11/12/15	all day	Battalion in billets. 175 men working on communication trenches & for shells sent into the village but no damage done.	

WAR DIARY or INTELLIGENCE SUMMARY.

Army Form C. 2118.

Instructions regarding War Diaries and Intelligence Summaries are contained in F.S. Regs., Part II. and the Staff Manual respectively. Title pages will be prepared in manuscript.

(Erase heading not required.)

Place	Date	Hour	Summary of Events and Information	Remarks and references to Appendices
BIENVILLERS	12/12/15	4 p.m.	Battalion relieved 13th Bn. K.R.R.C. in trenches at HANNESCAMPS & BIENVILLERS	
			Relief carried out successfully by 6 p.m. (Ref. Maps Sheet 11. LENS & 4.)	
HANNESCAMPS	13/12/15	all day	Battalion in trenches. Enemy Artillery rather active and shelled	
			HANNESCAMPS – BIENVILLERS ROAD but no damage caused.	
"	14/12/15	"	Very quiet in front. 13 Bn. R. Fus. on our left (2 coys) & the Gloucester Regt.	
			10th Bn. R. Fus. (2 coys) on our right & then 4th Division.	
"	15/12/15	"	Artillery very active on both sides, the enemy firing a number of pieces	
			onto HANNESCAMPS and BIENVILLERS.	
"	16/12/15	4.30 p.m.	Battalion relieved by the 13th Bn. K.R.R.C. and marched to Billets at BIENVILLERS.	
BIENVILLERS	17/12/15	all day	Inspection. Several fatigue & Billets for Artillery caused cost – a	
			few exchanged but chiefly on the enemy's part, but communication	
			trenches. The enemy replied very heavily on HANNESCAMPS and BIENVILLERS. Our	
			few working parties were caught by shell fire & 1 bugler killed & 6 wounded.	
			Night working party supplied to 13th K.R.R.C.	
"	18/12/15	"	General Inspection etc. do. do.	
"	19/12/15	"	Divine Service in morning. Working parties supplied to 13th Bn. K.R.R.C.	

Army Form C. 2118.

WAR DIARY
or
INTELLIGENCE SUMMARY.
(Erase heading not required.)

Instructions regarding War Diaries and Intelligence Summaries are contained in F. S. Regs., Part II. and the Staff Manual respectively. Title pages will be prepared in manuscript.

Place	Date	Hour	Summary of Events and Information	Remarks and references to Appendices
RENNVILLE R.S.	20/7/15	1.30pm	Battalion relieved by 6? Reg? & Rifle Reg? and marched to HUMBERCAMPS	
			(Ref. map. Sheet. 11 2.05.)	
HUMBERCAMPS	21/7/15	all day	Inspection of Billets, Arms etc. Bombing practice.	
"	22/7/15	"	Bombing practice etc. Working parties supplied to 110? Inf? Bde.	
"	23/7/15	"	do.	
"	24/7/15	"	do.	
"	25/7/15	"	Divine Service.	
"	26/7/15	"	Inspection of Arms etc. Visit of ?? Army General Officer Comp? Rifle	
"	27/7/15	"	" (RB.)	
"	28/7/15	"	Inspection of Battery by C.O. Bombing practice & rifle silent drill	
"	29/7/15	"	" (C.Co.) do.	
"	30/7/15	"	" (D.Co.) Coy Commd? Attack by B Coy. Coy? ?? ??	
"	31/7/15	"	Coy. Shell defence Attack.	
"	"	"	do.	

C J Freeton ??
Captain & Adjutant,
Commanding 13th Battalion Rifle Brigade.

111th Brigade
37th Divison.

1/13th RIFLE BRIGADE

JANUARY 1916

Confidential

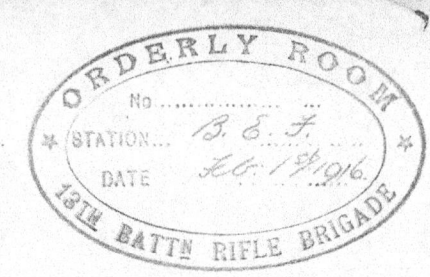

War Diary

of

13th (S) Battalion Rifle Brigade

From January 1st 1916

To January 31st 1916.

(Volume 4)

Army Form C. 2118.

WAR DIARY
or
INTELLIGENCE SUMMARY.
(Erase heading not required.)

Instructions regarding War Diaries and Intelligence Summaries are contained in F.S. Regs., Part II. and the Staff Manual respectively. Title pages will be prepared in manuscript.

Place	Date	Hour	Summary of Events and Information	Remarks and references to Appendices
HUMBER-CAMPS.	1/1/16	10 am	General tidying up of Billets and preparing for trenches.	
		4-5pm	Battalion relieved 6th Bedfordshire Regt. in trenches 3 Coys at HANNESCAMPS and 1 Coy at FONQUEVILLERS. (Ref. Rect. 11 LENS 44.75). Relief successfully completed.	
HANNESCAMPS	2/1/16	Day	Battalion in trenches. Very quiet, no fire.	
"	3/1/16	"	do	
"	4/1/16	"	do	
"	5/1/16	"	Our Artillery bombarded enemy front lines with good effect, enemy made no reply as our front line battalions were reconnoitering right new test. At 3.30 a.m. no enemy seen in good condition but few were still staying.	
	6/1/16		Very quiet as afore. Raining heavily and roads and cultivated areas almost impassable.	
	7/1/16	noon	Enemy Artillery shelled BIENVILLERS heavily during morning. Got guns retaliated briefly on enemy front line trenches and MONCHY and surroundings. The Battalion was relieved by 13th KRRC Relief carried out successfully and	
		4.30pm	Batt. marched back to billets at BIENVILLERS.	
BIENVILLERS.	8/1/16	day	Enemy Artillery shelled village during morning but did no damage.	

Army Form C. 2118.

WAR DIARY
or
INTELLIGENCE SUMMARY.
(Erase heading not required.)

Instructions regarding War Diaries and Intelligence Summaries are contained in F. S. Regs., Part II. and the Staff Manual respectively. Title pages will be prepared in manuscript.

Place	Date	Hour	Summary of Events and Information	Remarks and references to Appendices
BIENVILLE R.S.	8/1/16	1.30pm	Working parties supplied to R.E.	
"	9/1/16	all day	Inspection of arms and musketry	
"	10/1/16	"	do	
"	11/1/16	"	do	
"	12/1/16	"	do	
"	13/1/16	2.30pm	The Battalion was relieved by 6th Bn. Bedfordshire Regt. and marched to HENENCAMPS (Ref. Map Sheet 11 4x5 9.4.)	
HENENCAMPS	14/1/16	all day	General Tidying up of Billets &c. Bombing practice.	
"	15/1/16	"	100 men supplied work on trenches at HENENCAMPS. Musketry by Coys. Ceased remainder of Bn.	
"	16/1/16	"	380 men supplied work for 112 Inf. Bde. Divce. Grrce.	
"	17/1/16	"	100 men supplied work on trenches at HENENCAMPS. Musketry by other Coys. Helmet Drill. Inspection by C.O. Coy attack on trenches. Remainder Bathing &c.	
"	18/1/16	"	100 men supplied work on trenches at HENENCAMPS. 1 Coy inspected by C.O. Short Route March. Musketry. Drill. Helmet Drill. Grenadiers at Trenches.	
"	19/1/16	"	100 men working at HENENCAMPS. 30 men at Rifle Range STANDARD Test. Route March.	

T2134. Wt. W708—776. 500000. 4/15. Sir J. C. & S.

Army Form C. 2118.

WAR DIARY
or
INTELLIGENCE SUMMARY.
(Erase heading not required.)

Instructions regarding War Diaries and Intelligence Summaries are contained in F. S. Regs., Part II. and the Staff Manual respectively. Title pages will be prepared in manuscript.

Place	Date	Hour	Summary of Events and Information	Remarks and references to Appendices
MMBERCAMPS	20/1/16		380 men supplied to work for 112th Lg. Bde. Remainder Coy Bell Drill, Musketry and Tube Rifle Drill and Grenade Practice.	
"	21/1/16		100 men supplied to work on trenches at HANNESCAMPS. Coy Bell, Musketry, Tube Rifle Shoot 2.O.O. L Platoon Musketry on ST AMAND Range.— Musketry Practical. Message went at 3.30 pm Battalion all must and ready to move off at 5.30 pm. Strength 23 Officers and 763 Other Ranks.	
"	22/1/16		100 men supplied to work on trenches at HANNESCAMPS. 1 Coy supplied to C.O. Coy Drill, Musketry Tube Rifle Shoot, Bell, Grenade Practice, Transport inspected by C.O.	
"	23/1/16		100 men working on trenches at HANNESCAMPS. Inspection Coy & Bell Musketry.	
"	24/1/16		380 men supplied to work for 112th Lg. Bde. Remainder Coy Drill. F.G.C.M. on No.9379 Pte. O'Neill for negligently wounding himself.	
"	25/1/16 4.45 p.m.		The Battalion relieved the 6th Bedfordshire Regt. in the trenches at HANNESCAMPS. (Ref. Map. Sheet 11 SENS H4.) Relief carried out successfully.	
"	26/1/16 all day		Battalion in trenches. Very quiet report.	
"	27/1/16 "		Enemy Artillery Whizz banged our front line during afternoon but no damage.	

T2134. Wt. W708—776. 500000. 4/15. Sir J. C. & S.

Army Form C.2118

WAR DIARY
or
INTELLIGENCE SUMMARY.

(Erase heading not required.)

Instructions regarding War Diaries and Intelligence Summaries are contained in F.S. Regs., Part II. and the Staff Manual respectively. Title pages will be prepared in manuscript.

Place	Date	Hour	Summary of Events and Information	Remarks and references to Appendices
HANNESCAMPS	28.1.16		Very quiet in front. At 7.30 p.m. the Gas Alarm was sounded on our own reported from 18th Division on our right. No Gas however reached us and after standing to for an hour Alarm was blown off.	
"	29.1.16		Enemy Artillery shelled our trenches & direct hits being obtained. No casualties occurred and only slight damage to trenches. Our Artillery replied. German front line was mostly quiet. 10 Very weel rockets and red signal flares were seen. Very quiet in front. Patrol left Trenches at 4.30 pm returned 6 am. accomp. scout Pte as connector were ready to do so.	
"	30.1.16			
"	31.1.16		German Artillery shelled our (Capt Lees (Middx Regt)) a Battery officer attached to this Bn as Captain seized a Artillery officer of the R.F.C. when his Battalion and so reached such as supposed to.	
	6.15pm		The 13 Bn R.R.C. relieved 16 Battalion DIENNEBES	

(signed) C.F.N.M. Pinney
Commanding 18th Battalion Rifle Brigade. Lt. Colonel

111th Brigade
37th Division.

1/13th RIFLE BRIGADE

FEBRUARY 1 9 1 6

Confidential

War Diary

of

13th (S) Batn. Rifle Brigade.

From February 1st 1916
To February 29th 1916

(Volume 6)

WAR DIARY or INTELLIGENCE SUMMARY.

Army Form C. 2118.

(Erase heading not required.)

Instructions regarding War Diaries and Intelligence Summaries are contained in F. S. Regs., Part II. and the Staff Manual respectively. Title pages will be prepared in manuscript.

Place	Date	Hour	Summary of Events and Information	Remarks and references to Appendices
BIENVILLERS	1/3/16		General tidying up of Billets. Inspection of Arms &c.	
"	2/3/16		Musketry & Inspection. Working Parties supplied to 93rd Reg. R.E. and 13th R.B.	
"	3/3/16		do. do.	
"	4/3/16		do. do.	
"	5/3/16		do. do.	
"	6/3/16	2 p.m	The Battalion was relieved by 6 Bn. Staffords Regt and marched to Billets at HUMBERCAMPS. Relief successfully carried out by 5.30 p.m.	
HUMBERCAMPS	7/3/16		General tidying up of Billets. Inspection of Arms & Tate Helmets. Musketry.	
"	8/3/16		Inspection of Arms & Bombing exercises. 2 Platoons Range at M.M. MAND.	
"	9/3/16		do. 20 men Syndicat Ground under O.C. 13th Coy.	
"	10/3/16		do. Tate Helmets Issued.	
"	11/3/16		Inspection of Arms. Tate Helmets &c. Bombing Exercise.	
"	12/3/16		The Battalion supplied NUMEROUS Working Parties over both over & part of Lea Ruck Line.	
GASTINEAU REALES AU BOIS.	13/3/16		on M.W. of BEALES AU BOIS. (Ref. High Sheet 45 N.N.C.S.W. 11 & 12)	
"	14/3/16		Very quiet on front. Reaving trenches & tidying up shine. do.	

WAR DIARY
or
INTELLIGENCE SUMMARY.
(Erase heading not required.)

Army Form C. 2118.

Instructions regarding War Diaries and Intelligence Summaries are contained in F. S. Regs., Part II. and the Staff Manual respectively. Title pages will be prepared in manuscript.

Place	Date	Hour	Summary of Events and Information	Remarks and references to Appendices
HASTINGS (SERIES-70 BDS)	15/7/16		Very quiet on front. 50 men supplied from 13 R. Irs employed in carrying material to front line. Twenteen casual evacuation.	
"	16/7/16		Enemy Artillery shelled our front line during morning but did no damage. 6 casualties. 3 men very slightly hit.	
		6 pm	13th Bn. Royal Fusiliers relieved 8th Bn. during evening. Relief carried out successfully and Bn marched to billets at BAILEUL. Ref Map Sheet 57c SE N.2.8	
BAILEUL	17/7/16		Inspection of arms. Tide baths.	
"	18/7/16		50 men supplied to 67th Coys R.E. at BRUAY SUD.	
"	19/7/16		50 men supplied to 67th Bgg. R.S. 100 men supplied to work under 11th & 112th Coys R.E.	
"	20/7/16	9.35 am	The Battalion relieved the 10th Royal Fusiliers in the trenches at the HOSTINEUX. SERIES-70 BDS. Relief carried out successfully.	
HASTINGS	21/7/16		Very quiet on front. Billets of men in front line employed in cleaning revolvers. Trench mortar guns carrying fire 16.30 etc.	
"	22/7/16		do. do.	
"	23/7/16		do. do.	
"	24/7/16	5.30 pm	The Battalion was relieved by 13th Bn. Royal Fusiliers and marched into billets	

WAR DIARY
or
INTELLIGENCE SUMMARY.
(Erase heading not required.)

Army Form C. 2118.

Instructions regarding War Diaries and Intelligence Summaries are contained in F. S. Regs., Part II. and the Staff Manual respectively. Title pages will be prepared in manuscript.

Place	Date	Hour	Summary of Events and Information	Remarks and references to Appendices
BAILLEULMONT			at BAILLEULMONT.	
	25/3/16	22nd Army	Batln. in Billets. Inspection of Arms. Tea Ke 160616.	
	26/3/16	do.	20 men supplied to 13th Royal Irish as working party for trenches.	
	27/3/16		30 men supplied to 13 Bn Royal Irish as working party. One 2nd Lieut supplied with Pioneers Batn in case of retaliation on our left. (1st Bn Royal Irish.)	
			1st Battalion relieved the 13th Bn. Royal Irish Rifles in trenches. Relief commenced at 1pm B. Coy Officers in trenches and recognised with 10. K. B. R. R. Rifle. Reached Regt. Quart. Sept 1216.	
GASTINEHEM	29/3/16		very quiet in front. hardly all men in trenches employed in pumping	
ASYLES N 20 13			water in trenches which were very wet and muddy.	

C. A. F... ..A. Colonel,
Commdg. 13th Batn. Rifle Brigade.

111th Brigade
37th Division.

1/13th RIFLE BRIGADE

MARCH 1 9 1T6

Confidential.

13th Battn. The Rifle Brigade

War Diary

From March 1st 1916.

To March 31st 1916.

(Volume 6.)

WAR DIARY
or
INTELLIGENCE SUMMARY.
(Erase heading not required.)

Army Form C. 2118.

Instructions regarding War Diaries and Intelligence Summaries are contained in F.S. Regs., Part II. and the Staff Manual respectively. Title pages will be prepared in manuscript.

13TH BATTN RIFLE BRIGADE

Place	Date	Hour	Summary of Events and Information	Remarks and references to Appendices
S. ASTINERY BERLES-AU-BOIS	1/3/16		Battalion in trenches. Employed collecting from trenches etc. 50 men supplied from 13th Bn. Royal Fusiliers carrying material to front line	
"		5.30	Battalion relieved in trenches by 3 Bn Royal Fusiliers and marched to Billets at BAILLEULMONT (Ref. map Sheet 51C W.2.C.)	
BAILLEULMONT	2/3/16		General cleaning up of billets. 2 Coys at Baths	
"	3/3/16		Inspection of arms etc. 50 men supplied to 3 Bn. Royal Fusiliers in front line	
"	4/3/16		do. 2 Coys at Baths	
"	5/3/16		Bn. relieved 3 Bn Royal Fusiliers in the trenches. Relief successfully carried out by 9 p.m. (Ref. Map 51C W.2.C. II.C.) 10th Bn R Fusiliers on our left and 7th Bn Leicester Regt 110th Bde on our Right.	
S.ASTINERY BERLES-AU-BOIS	6/3/16	Day	Bn. in trenches. Very quiet on front.	
"	7/3/16		Cleaning up trenches etc. Working parties supplied by 3 R Fus. 50 men on our front	
"		6 p.m.	do. Occupatory front	
"			Battn relieved by 3 Bn. Royal Fusiliers and marched to Billets at BAILLEULMONT Inspection of arms etc. Return to 13 Bn R Fusiliers for 50 men supplied	
BAILLEULMONT	8/3/16		evening at 5.30 p.m. 2 coys bathing	

WAR DIARY or INTELLIGENCE SUMMARY

Army Form C. 2118.

(Erase heading not required.)

Instructions regarding War Diaries and Intelligence Summaries are contained in F. S. Regs., Part II. and the Staff Manual respectively. Title pages will be prepared in manuscript.

Place	Date	Hour	Summary of Events and Information	Remarks and references to Appendices
BAILLEULMONT.	9/3/16		50 men supplied to 3.R.Fus. in front line. 50 men supplied to 3.R.Cy. B.Sa. wiring. 2 coys at Bailts Square Practice of 1 coy during afternoon.	
	10/3/16	5 p.m.	From the Bastes relieved the 3/Bn. Royal Fusiliers in the trenches. Relief successful.	
GASTINEAU.	11/3/16		Battalion in trenches. Very quiet in front.	
"	12/3/16		do.	
"	13/3/16		do.	
"	14/3/16		The Enemy bombarded nearly Batln. H.Q. in Gastineau. Bismarck & G. Long force support trenches also heavily shelled, no injury—falling in enemy. 2 killed and 4 wounded. Our Artillery opened out Field Guns on front German line and Heavy Batteries on MANSART.	
	15/3/16	6 p.m.	3/Bn. Royal Fusiliers relieved Bn. in trenches and Bn. marched to BAILLEUMONT. Trying on Helets and Inspection of Arms. Tube Helmets etc.	
BAILLEULMONT.	16/3/16		Inspection of Arms and 50 men supplied to 3R Fus. for work in front line.	
	17/3/16		do. Same dummy display was attacked by 10 other Bns. and all officers who with danger by Flammenwerfer use by Germans to Battalion was observed by the 2nd Br. Genrs. Inslow & Lt. 41 Divsn.	

Army Form C. 2118.

WAR DIARY
or
INTELLIGENCE SUMMARY.
(Erase heading not required.)

Instructions regarding War Diaries and Intelligence Summaries are contained in F. S. Regs., Part II. and the Staff Manual respectively. Title pages will be prepared in manuscript.

Place	Date	Hour	Summary of Events and Information	Remarks and references to Appendices
HALLOY.	19/3/16		and marched to Halloy via LA HERIERE and AIRPINCOURT. (Ref. Map Sheet 11 LENS 9B, F4, & F3.) Remained in Halloy for night.	
		11.30am	The Battalion marched to OCCOCHES via BEAUREPAIRE and DOULLENS and went into Corps Reserve. (Ref. Map Sheet 11 LENS E4.)	
OCCOCHES.	20/3/16		Inspection of arms etc	
"	21/3/16		do	
"	22/3/16		Musketry & Tate Helmet Inspection	
"	23/3/16		Battalion route march	
"	24/3/16		Inspection of arms, equipment etc	
"	25/3/16		The Battalion marched to AUXI-LE-CHATEAU and were billeted in the Three Army School of Instruction. March via MEZEROLLES, WAVANS.	
AUXI-LE-CHATEAU.	26/3/16		Inspection of arms. Squad drill + saluting practice.	
"	27/3/16		do 140 men supplied to R.E.	
"	28/3/16		Coy. drill, arm drill + saluting.	
"	29/3/16		do	
"	30/3/16		do	

Army Form C. 2118.

WAR DIARY
or
INTELLIGENCE SUMMARY.
(Erase heading not required.)

Instructions regarding War Diaries and Intelligence Summaries are contained in F. S. Regs., Part II. and the Staff Manual respectively. Title pages will be prepared in manuscript.

Place	Date	Hour	Summary of Events and Information	Remarks and references to Appendices
HUM-LE-CHATEAU	3/4/16.		By Rail. Arms & Equipment Inspection. 140 men supplied G.P.S.	

(Sd.) W. A. Curry Lt.
Commdg. 11th Battn N.Z.

T2134. Wt. W708-776. 500000. 4/15. Sir J. C. & S.

111th Brigade
37th Division.

1/13th RIFLE BRIGADE

APRIL 1916

Confidential.

War Diary
of
13(S) Battn. The Rifle Brigade.

From April 1st 1916.
To.   April 30th 1916.

(Volume 8)

WAR DIARY or INTELLIGENCE SUMMARY.

Army Form C. 2118.

(Erase heading not required.)

Instructions regarding War Diaries and Intelligence Summaries are contained in F.S. Regs., Part II. and the Staff Manual respectively. Title pages will be prepared in manuscript.

Place	Date	Hour	Summary of Events and Information	Remarks and references to Appendices
Rocar le Chateau N/b	1/4/16		Coy. Drill, Arms Drill etc. 140 men supplied to R.E.	
"	2/4/16		do. Lewis Guns shooting on the range	
"	3/4/16		do. Snipers shooting on Range	
"	4/4/16		do. Heavy Transport etc. 1st Inspection	
"		2.30 p.m.	The Battalion was inspected by Major General Count Gleichen Comdg 37th Div. The General expressed his approval of the appearance and steadiness of the Battn.	
"	5/4/16		2 Coys paraded for the Enlist scheme to demonstrate field Systems of Wire Entry School of Instruction. 1 Coy digging under R.E.	
"	6/4/16		2 Coys to Corps at fighting & demonstrating first three stages of attack to School. 2 Coy at Baths during afternoon	
"	7/4/16		2 Coys. demonstrated last three stages of attack to school. 2 Platoons Bayonet fighting. 1 Platoon Bombing. 2 Coys. at Baths during afternoon.	
"	8/4/16		2 Coys digging under R.E. of 1st Indian Car. Divn. 1 Platoon Bombing Fighting and 1 Platoon Bayonet	
"	9/4/16	10-45 am	Divine Service for Battalion	

Army Form C. 2118.

WAR DIARY
or
INTELLIGENCE SUMMARY.
(Erase heading not required.)

Instructions regarding War Diaries and Intelligence Summaries are contained in F. S. Regs., Part II. and the Staff Manual respectively. Title pages will be prepared in manuscript.

Stamp: ORDERLY ROOM, STATION B.E.F., DATE April 1916, 13TH BATT. RIFLE BRIGADE

Place	Date	Hour	Summary of Events and Information	Remarks and references to Appendices
Aux-le-Château	10/4/16		2 Coys. working under R.E. 2 Coys. Bayonet fighting. 1 Coy. Drill & bombing attack.	
"	11/4/16		do. 2 Coys. at Baths during afternoon.	
"	12/4/16		do. 1 Platoon shooting on range. 1 Platoon bombing.	
"	13/4/16		2 Coys practising attack. Bathing during afternoon. 2 Coys working under R.E. 1 Platoon shooting on range. 1 Platoon bombing.	
"	14/4/16		50 men under instruction in the Lewis Guns. Bathing in afternoon. 1 Coy. practising Extension to attack. 1 Coy. coop scheme. Order drill. 1 Platoon bombing and 1 Platoon shooting on range. Bayonet fighting.	
"	15/4/16		2 Coys. demonstrating the attack formed for field army school of Instruction. 2 " " " " Trench attack	
"	16/4/16		Divine Service at 10·30 a.m.	
"	17/4/16		2 Coys. demonstrating Fire control Scheme. 1 Platoon bayonet fighting. 1 Platoon bombing. 1 Platoon Shooting on Range. 1 Coy. working under R.E.	
"	18/4/16		2 Platoons shooting on Range. 2 Coys. demonstrating the Attack. 1 Coy under R.E. in morning and afternoon. 2 Coys. bathing during afternoon.	
"	19/4/16		2 Coys demonstrating the Attack. 2 Platoons shooting on Range. 1 Platoon	

Army Form C. 2118.

WAR DIARY
or
INTELLIGENCE SUMMARY.
(Erase heading not required.)

Instructions regarding War Diaries and Intelligence Summaries are contained in F.S. Regs., Part II. and the Staff Manual respectively. Title pages will be prepared in manuscript.

Place	Date	Hour	Summary of Events and Information	Remarks and references to Appendices
Rue C. Carbon	19/4/16		Bombing. 1 Coy under R.E. in morning and afternoon.	
"	20/4/16		2 Coys. demonstrating the attack. 2 Platoons shooting on the Range. 1 Platoon Bombing. 1 Coy. digging under R.E. in morning, afternoon Bathing in afternoon.	
"	21/4/16		do.	
"	22/4/16		Battalion 1st Inspection by C.O.	
"	23/4/16		Coy. Drill. 1 Platoon Bombing. 1 Platoon shooting on Range. do.	
"	23/4/16		Divine Service at 10·45 a.m.	
"	24/4/16		3 Coys. and Transport in full marching order inspected by C.O. 1 Platoon R.E.	
"	25/4/16		3 Coys. demonstrating the attack. 2 Platoons Bayonet fighting. 1 Platoon Bombing. 1 Platoon shooting on range. 2 Coys under R.E. in afternoon.	
"	26/4/16		3 Coys. demonstrating TRENCH ATTACK. 2 Platoons Bayonet fighting. 1 Platoon Bombing and 1 Platoon shooting. 150 men bathing during afternoon.	
"	27/4/16		3 Coys. demonstrating TRENCH ATTACK. 2 Platoons Bayonet fighting and 1 Platoon Bombing. Bathing during afternoon. do.	
"	28/4/16		do.	
"	29/4/16 9am		The Battalion marched to OUTREBOIS and Billeted for night. Route via MAURIS – MEZEROLLES. Ref. Map Sheet. 11. 1/E.H.S.	

WAR DIARY
or
INTELLIGENCE SUMMARY.
(Erase heading not required.)

Army Form C. 2118.

Station: B.E.F.
Date: April 1916
13TH BATTN RIFLE BRIGADE

Place	Date	Hour	Summary of Events and Information	Remarks and references to Appendices
OUTREBOIS	30/4/16	9am	The Battalion marched to HALLOY and Billeted for night. Route via DOULLENS and DOULLENS-ARRAS ROAD.	

G.F.A Read Major
Comndg. 13th Battn. Rifle Brigade.

111th Brigade
37th Division.

1/13th RIFLE BRIGADE

M A Y 1 9 1 6:

Confidential

War Diary

of

13th (S) Battn. The Rifle Bde.

From 1st May 1916. To 31st May 1916.

(Volume 8)

Army Form C. 2118.

WAR DIARY
or
INTELLIGENCE SUMMARY.
(Erase heading not required.)

Instructions regarding War Diaries and Intelligence Summaries are contained in F.S. Regs., Part II. and the Staff Manual respectively. Title pages will be prepared in manuscript.

Stamp: 13th BATT RIFLE BRIGADE, Date ...

Place	Date	Hour	Summary of Events and Information	Remarks and references to Appendices
HALLOY	1/5/16	10 p.m	The Battalion marched to BERLES-AU-BOIS via WARLINCOURT - LA HERLIERE - BAILLEULMONT and were in support to 10th Bn Royal Fusiliers who were in front line (R.B.) (Map 51 SE 5000 & 21)	
BERLES-AU-BOIS	2/5/16		Battalion remained in BERLES all day	
"	3/5/16	11.30 p.m	Battalion was relieved by 13th Bn Kings Royal Rifles and marched to billets at BAILLEUVAL (51.c M29.05, 25.b a00 & 33-34 & N.9.B) and accn: from G 3rd Res Bde	
BAILLEUVAL	4/5/16		Battn: remained at BAILLEUVAL in Divisional Army Reserve. Billets were not up to std. 2/Bns were sent up to occupy Support Trenches (FOSTWAY,TORPEDO,FORT 147(Map 57 SE Supersheet) W.N.13. and vicinity w.16.B.	
"	5/5/16	7.30 p.m	The Battalion relieved 3rd Bn Royal Irish in trenches line W.16.C. by H.m BRITISH. Relief was successfully carried out from ANNETTE 51.SE. RANSART trc/(pm)(pars 13D) W.15.C. by H.m BRITISH. Relief was successfully carried out	
Trenches from RANSART	6/5/16		Bath in Trenches. Work kept up as usual	
"	7/5/16		do. do.	
"	8/5/16		do. 1 Off. and 2 men patrolled enemy's line	

Army Form C. 2118.

WAR DIARY
or
INTELLIGENCE SUMMARY.
(Erase heading not required.)

Instructions regarding War Diaries and Intelligence Summaries are contained in F.S. Regs., Part II. and the Staff Manual respectively. Title pages will be prepared in manuscript.

Place	Date	Hour	Summary of Events and Information	Remarks and references to Appendices
Vimy Sect. 13th S.Att.	9/5/16		At 9 p.m. and again all day quiet on hostile trenches	
"	10/5/16		Very quiet on front.	
"	11/5/16	9pm	The enemy deliberately shelled Neath Cyrs & Nissau & 5.9 shells. Patrols found enemy's wire somewhat. One Artillery officer killed & 10 men. Enemy's front line entirely free of shell P.P.M.S.P.T, included artillery used heavy.	
"	12/5/16	5pm	Explosion in our line 205 caused by 2nd Royal Fusiliers, and reported rich a crater at entrance. Chief successful.	
"	13/5/16		Explosion of front line by Engineers at Horsement R.E. from 8.30 to 11.00pm	
"	14/5/16		40 men received R.E. from 8.30 am to 1/0 a.m. 2.30 noon " 5.5pm to 11.5pm	
"	15/5/16		Work force at 2.30 p.m. 50 men worked R.E. from 8.30 to 1 p.m. 2.0 to 7.0 made the Explosion of Tunes Engineers Sunday service Explosion Ridge 2 foot holes	
"	16/5/16		Working parties as for S.P.C at Bellows-Explosion Ridge - 1 Coy. Rowling - 16y. la Forge 2 Coys.	

Army Form C. 2118.

WAR DIARY
or
INTELLIGENCE SUMMARY.
(Erase heading not required.)

Instructions regarding War Diaries and Intelligence Summaries are contained in F. S. Regs., Part II. and the Staff Manual respectively. Title pages will be prepared in manuscript.

Place	Date	Hour	Summary of Events and Information	Remarks and references to Appendices
BAILLEUL	18/5/16	6.30pm	The Battalion relieved the 8th R. Sussex in the Trenches near St Eloi successfully, nothing to report.	
Trenches in nearby Trenches	19/5/16		Battalion in trenches. Day quiet — nothing to report.	
	20/5/16		do	
	21/5/16		do. Very quiet day. Our Artillery	
	22/5/16		Our artillery ranging at I.33.d.30.95. Artillery 10g Artillery Reply. Rs return of enemy shelling this morning.	
	23/5/16		Hostile aeroplane over our lines this morning very low. Brought down.	
	24/5/16		do	
	25/5/16		At 9.30 a.m. and 9.40 a.m. we were came into a trench. Heavy Stokes Guns in conjunction at a rate to 37.b.25.50	
	26/5/16	9.30pm	Battalion was relieved by the 8th R. Sussex and was en route to Bulford to Tabarge up 88 more supplies to the men drawing up front line Suspicion of Gases etc. etc.	

T2134. Wt. W708-776. 500000. 4/15. Sir J. C. & S.

WAR DIARY
or
INTELLIGENCE SUMMARY.
(Erase heading not required.)

Army Form C. 2118.

Place	Date	Hour	Summary of Events and Information	Remarks and references to Appendices
BRUNEMONT	27/3/18		Coy. deep. musketry. 2 Coys at Bullies Snipers on Range. 1 Coy. Bombing	
	28/3/18		350 men supplied to dig new trench in rear of present front line. Musketry. Inspection of Coys. in Coy. H.Q. 2 Coys. at Bullies 1 Coy. Bombing 30 men supplied for working parties. B.H.Qrs.	
	29/3/18		do.	
	30/3/18 pm		The Battalion moved into Bullecourt trenches on the Reserve successfully executed. Quiet. Occasional enemy S.O.S. signals all quiet on front.	
	31/3/18		Very quiet on front. 1 Officer & men went on patrol to get touch & to ascertain enemy's wire. They came under considerable M.G. fire, enemy jumpy sent up a covering party to some trenches where troops were observed. No touch with enemy who were ordered to fire a flare(?) by way of signal if not met. Flare was seen to N. of Coy. H.Qrs.	

C.F.R. Pinney, Lt. Colonel,
Comdg. 12th Battn. Rifle Brigade.

111th Brigade
37th Division.

Battalion attached to 34th Division
5th July - rejoined 37th Division 21.8.16.

1/13th RIFLE BRIGADE

JUNE 1916

Confidential

War Diary

of

13th Battalion The Rifle Brigade

From: June 1st 1916

To: June 30th 1916

(Volume 9)

WAR DIARY or INTELLIGENCE SUMMARY.

Army Form C. 2118.

Instructions regarding War Diaries and Intelligence Summaries are contained in F. S. Regs., Part II. and the Staff Manual respectively. Title pages will be prepared in manuscript.

(Erase heading not required.)

Place	Date	Hour	Summary of Events and Information	Remarks and references to Appendices
Trenches opposite RANSART.	1/6/16		Battalion in Trenches. Very quiet on front.	
"	2/6/16		do.	
"	3/6/16		do.	
"	4/6/16		do. Heavy shelling during night in retaliation for our bombardment to cover raid by 13th Bn. Royal Fusiliers.	
"	5/6/16	5.15pm	An officers patrol under 2/Lt W. N. B. NOTHARD carried a point N. 18. D. 0. 4. in Belles Ravine (Refm.50 SE (3rd pret 3/f) at 9pm Shortly after our S.P. party of the enemy about 10 strong was seen approaching, when nothing to gain any information, except fire and consequently charged, when upon the enemy fired, leaving two casualties. Carter was fought in our front. (Colony 10th & 76th Regt.	
"	6/6/16 8-9pm		The Battalion was relieved by the 10th Bn. Royal Fusiliers in the Trenches and marched to Billets at BAILLEULVAL.	
BAILLEULVAL.	6/6/16		General Tidying up.	
"	7/6/16		Brigade in Reserve. Brushing & respirator spring practice.	
"	8/6/16		do.	
"	9/6/16		do.	

WAR DIARY
or
INTELLIGENCE SUMMARY.
(Erase heading not required.)

Army Form C. 2118.

Instructions regarding War Diaries and Intelligence Summaries are contained in F. S. Regs., Part II. and the Staff Manual respectively. Title pages will be prepared in manuscript.

Place	Date	Hour	Summary of Events and Information	Remarks and references to Appendices
BAILLEUL RL.	10/6/16		Troops on Range. Smoking and vapour fires reported 300 men occupying in advanced area trench from 9 am to 1 am.	
"	11/6/16	5:30 am	The Bn. relieved the 13 Bn. Royal Fusiliers in trenches. Observer Offr.	
			13 S. Lanes Regt 83rd Division (7 F) and 13 Bn. Kings Royal Rifles observed Bn.	
Trenches opposite RANSART.	12/6/16		Both in the Trenches. Enemy very quiet	
"	13/6/16		do do	
"	14/6/16		do do	
"	15/6/16	7:30 pm	The Bn. was relieved by the 13th L. Fusiliers and marched to Bill Tent BAILLEUL.	
BAILLEUL RL.	16/6/16		General Tidying up and Inspection of Arms &c.	
"	"	9 am	10 Officers and 670 men supplied ready for trenches to front line.	
"	17/6/16	"	7 " and 500 do	
"	18/6/16	"	6 " Detachments to shooting in Range.	
"	19/6/16		Gas Defence + Rifle Exercises + drum Drill.	
"	20/6/16		do do	
"	"	8:45 pm	500 men digging or new entrance trench from 9:30 pm to 1:30 am	
"	21/6/16		Boys paraded for Inspector Reeve Trumpeter under Signal Officer	
"	22/6/16	9:30 pm	The Bn. relieved the 13 Bn. Royal Fusiliers in the Trenches	

WAR DIARY
or
INTELLIGENCE SUMMARY.
(Erase heading not required.)

Army Form C. 2118.

Place	Date	Hour	Summary of Events and Information	Remarks and references to Appendices
Tranchiepheck				
RANSART	23/9/16		Battalion in Trenches. Very quiet day as usual.	
"	24/9/16		do Thunderstorm during afternoon	
"	25/9/16		do do	
"	26/9/16		do A Strong patrol under Corpl N.B. Simpson - Pte DE BRUCE and Pte WESTWARD and 2 other ranks was dispatched to reconnoitre a German Listening Post south of RANSART. Our wire challenged as they were crossing the wire, and Pte WESTWARD moved in the fire and a bomb was thrown. Germans ran, having been heard to leave the post in response to the first bomb.)	
	27/9/16 2.45pm		Gas was discharged from Battalion front on our right and on our left. Coys to the N of the NOVELTY Salient as complete lines stand by in support of the hostile systems. No retaliation was very feeble. In accordance with Corps Instructions, the Bns continued to occupy their usual outposts during the night and after. That the bombt had been to used to hold in the usual strength, and the enemy's enemy relief. Enemy working parties were reported on our fronts and were effectively stopped by Stokes mortar and our Lewis guns.	

WAR DIARY
or
INTELLIGENCE SUMMARY.
(Erase heading not required.)

Army Form C. 2118.

Instructions regarding War Diaries and Intelligence Summaries are contained in F. S. Regs., Part II. and the Staff Manual respectively. Title pages will be prepared in manuscript.

Place	Date	Hour	Summary of Events and Information	Remarks and references to Appendices
Trenches opposite				
MARTINPUICH	27/9/16	10 p.m.	A second volume of fire was opened on our line, the enemy's fire from guns, rifle and machine guns, was heavy, so so much that pretty	
			well every one of our offensive patrols from my Coy. received one thing or another.	
	28/9/16		Very quiet on front.	
"	29/9/16	4 a.m.	There was again considerable firing on our right. Capt Rowland was before MONCHY. Enemy Battery opened fire from our front line from the R.S.F. front	
			trenches. Four Guns two Capt B.R. worked the movements to I managed other. 2 Lt. H.A.C was making visual contact during night. We kept up intermittent Rifle on Gun fire from	
			the position as observed by 13th. Royal Fusiliers and engaged by R.F.A.'s	
		at 8PM	at MARTINPUICH.	
BAILLEUL VAL	30/9/16		General Tidying up and inspection by Capt.	

C. F. Pretor-Pinney ..... Colonel,
Commdg 10th ..... Brigade.

111th Brigade.
37th Division.
34th Division from 5.7.16.

Transferred with 111th Brigade from
37th to 34th Division 5th July 1916.

1/13th BATTALION

THE RIFLE BRIGADE

JULY 1916

Instructions regarding War Diaries and Intelligence
Summaries are contained in F. S. Regs., Part II.
and the Staff Manual respectively. Title pages
will be prepared in manuscript.

INTELLIGENCE SUMMARY.

(Erase heading not required.)

Place	Date	Hour	Summary of Events and Information	Remarks and references to Appendices
Bailleulval	1/7/16		Batt^n in Billets. Posted gam for Church, fighting, Physical Drill, Rapid Fire Exercises, Manual	
	2/7/16		do Parades 10-30 a.m. for Divine Service	
	3/7/16		Batt^n was ordered to move to Humbercourt and reached there about 11-30 p.m.	
Humbercourt	4/7/16		The Batt^n paraded for Manual Fire Exercises and The Inspection	
	5/7/16		Brigade Holiday observed. At 5 p.m. orders were received to be ready to move at once, by motor bus to Bresle (Ref. Map 62 P.N.E. D.S.A.) about 4½ miles W. of Albert. During the night of 5-6th the movement was carried out, Bresle being reached about 5 a.m. on the 6th. The Transport marched in during the afternoon.	
Bresle	6/7/16		At 5 p.m. the Battalion received orders to march to billets at Albert to act as a reserve to the 56th Inf. Bde. to which it was temporarily attached. Billets in Albert were reached about 8 p.m.	
Albert	7/7/16		At 5 a.m. the Batt^n was warned to hold itself in readiness to occupy the Tara-USNA line across the Albert-Bapaume Rd. (about 1 mile N.E. of Albert). At 9 a.m. orders were received to reach this point at 10 a.m. The B^n marched by platoons, the last coming into position at 11 a.m. The Batt^n remained halted during the whole of the day. The bombardment of	

Army Form C. 2118.

Instructions regarding War Diaries and Intelligence Summaries are contained in F.S. Regs., Part II. and the Staff Manual respectively. Title pages will be prepared in manuscript.

INTELLIGENCE SUMMARY.
(Erase heading not required.)

Place	Date	Hour	Summary of Events and Information	Remarks and references to Appendices
	7/1/16		The enemy's lines was heavy & continuous from 5am reaching its greatest intensity about 7.30 am when troops of the 19th Div and the corps on its right & left crowned the enemy's line – on the whole with good results. The 13th Bn Royal Fusiliers made good progress to the W. of La Boisselle. The enemy's infantry with the important exception of their machine guns, made a very poor resistance. The Division in the course of the stay sending in about 600 prisoners. Constant heavy rain storms fell during the day and the major following. At 8 p.m. the Battn was ordered to move at 10.15 p.m. to relieve the 7th Loyal N Lancs Regt in the old British Front line trench S. of La Boisselle [Sheet 57 D. SE X.20 a.3] about 100 yds in rear of the great craters. The march was rendered slow and difficult by the state of the track, and the fact that the whole of the Battn had to move by one and in single file. H.Q. were not reached until after 1 am – whilst crossing Tara Hill the column was shelled O'Coy losing 10 NCOs men and 1 Officer wounded. B Coy 1 man killed and 1 man wounded. The state of trench was wet and ruinous. The Battn had no connection with the 9th on its right and left.	

WAR DIARY
or
INTELLIGENCE SUMMARY.

(Erase heading not required.)

Army Form C. 2118.

Instructions regarding War Diaries and Intelligence Summaries are contained in F.S. Regs., Part II. and the Staff Manual respectively. Title pages will be prepared in manuscript.

Place	Date	Hour	Summary of Events and Information	Remarks and references to Appendices
Old British Front Line Trench Sept La Boisselle	8/7/16		The Batt'n remained in position. Shelling in the neighbourhood was continuous during the day and was particularly heavy during the late afternoon and at intervals during the night. The bulk of the enemy shells fell in La Boisselle, in front of the Barn and in the valley and slopes to the left and along the Albert – Bapaume Rd., and also top of the trench also occupied by ourselves, with the result that B. Coy. had 9 casualties during the day and the night of July 8–9. Some progress was made in repairing the trench and in clearing it of the bodies of those who had fallen 6 days before between the British & Enemy lines. Lachrymator shells were used by the enemy, but the use of goggles rendered their effect very slight. During the night the 13th R. Fusiliers again were in support.	
"	9/7/16		The Battalion remained in the same position. Were shelled intermittently the day.	
		6 p.m.	The Batt'n relieved the 8th Batt'n N. Staffs in frontline Relief carried out with 10 Bouglets.	
	10/7/16		The Batt'n in the front line as follows. 2 Coys in front line and one in support.	

WAR DIARY
or
INTELLIGENCE SUMMARY.
(Erase heading not required.)

Army Form C. 2118.

Place	Date	Hour	Summary of Events and Information	Remarks and references to Appendices
Trenches E. of La Boisselle	10/7/16	9 a.m.	"C" Coy in the front line were sent back to the supporting line as the congestion of troops was too great in the front line. Taken at 10 a.m. — D Coy on left of Trenches line, "A" Coy on right, "C" Coy supporting "D" Coy, "B" Coy supporting "A" Coy. From 3.30 p.m. to 7.30 p.m. we were very heavily shelled, casualties amounting to 2 officers and about 60 other Ranks.	
		8.45 p.m.	Orders were received to attack German front line at 8.45 p.m. "C" & "B" Coys left the supporting line and took Paris Trench into the front line. As soon as the supporting line was in the front line, "D" and "A" Coys left the front line for the objective followed by "C" & "B" Coys. The 1st two Coys had not gone 200 yds. when a message came from 10th Bn. Royal Fus. asking you to send a message that the attack was cancelled. The C.O. gave the order to retire, and the Bn. retired to its original front line, having penetrated to the enemy's 2nd line, inflicted severe losses to the enemy and capturing 100 prisoners. Our casualties amounted to 20 Officers and about 380 other Ranks, included in those Casualties were C.O. 2nd in Command, Adjutant and the 4 O.C. Coys.	

T2134. Wt. W708—776. 500000. 4/15. Sir J. C. & S.

Army Form C. 2118.

WAR DIARY
or
INTELLIGENCE SUMMARY.
(Erase heading not required.)

JULY

Instructions regarding War Diaries and Intelligence Summaries are contained in F. S. Regs., Part II. and the Staff Manual respectively. Title pages will be prepared in manuscript.

Place	Date	Hour	Summary of Events and Information	Remarks and references to Appendices
Tincourt S.E. of LA BOISSELLE	1/7/16	9am	The Bath. was relieved by the 10th Br. Royal Fusiliers and moved back to the 2nd line. During the day casualties amounting to 14 O.R. were caused by hostile shelling.	
"		1pm	The Bath. was relieved by 13th Br. R.F.F.C. and moved back to the original German 2nd Line just beyond the Crater.	
"	2/7/16	3pm	The Battalion were relieved by the 13th. R.Fus. and moved back to the USNA-TARALINE.	
USNA-TARA LINE	3/7/16		Quiet day. General Tidying up.	
"	4/7/16		do	
"	5/7/16		At 1 a.m. orders were received to take up the Old German Support Line being USNA-TARA at 9.30pm this was successfully carried out without casualty.	
Trenches S.E. of LA BOISSELLE	6/7/16		All quiet. Batt. remained in same line	
"	7/7/16		do	
"	8/7/16		do	
"	9/7/16		The Batt. left trenches and returned to ALBERT billets (Billets for night)	
ALBERT	10/7/16	6pm	The Batt. marched to BRESLE (Ref map 57D N.E. DIST H.)	
BRESLE	11/7/16		Batt. at BRESLE. General Tidying up.	

WAR DIARY
or
INTELLIGENCE SUMMARY.
(Erase heading not required.)

Army Form C. 2118.

Place	Date	Hour	Summary of Events and Information	Remarks and references to Appendices
BRESLE	20/7/16		Bath & Coy Drill. Bombing & M.G. courses continued	
	21/7/16		do	in camp. 283 O/R Reinforcements
	22/7/16		Revised and carried out Extra Regimental	Joined from Base & Coy the Regimental
	23/7/16		do	do
	24/7/16		do	in charge of the Brigade
	25/7/16		Bath & Coy Drill. Short Route March. Musketry on carrier Range	
	26/7/16		Field Musketry. Bombing & Lewis Gun Instruction	
	27/7/16		do	
	28/7/16		Battalion marched to BUIRE and billeted in the Ecole	
	29/7/16		Battn. marched to the Trenches in Reserve line S.E. of MAMETZ WOOD and relieved the 7th Bn. R. Sussex Regt. 9th Division having gone through	

J. Puckerm Smio-
Major
LT COL
COMMANDING 12th Bn THE RIFLE BRIGADE

111th Brigade
34th Division
rejoined 37th Division 22.8.16.

Battalion rejoined from 34th Division
22nd August 1 9 1 6

1/13th RIFLE BRIGADE

AUGUST 1 9 1 6

2340

WAR DIARY
or
INTELLIGENCE SUMMARY

Army Form C. 2118.

Date AUGUST 1916
16th BATT RIFLE BRIGADE

Place	Date	Hour	Summary of Events and Information	Remarks and references to Appendices
	1.8.16		The Batn was holding a line of Reserve trenches between BOTTOM WOOD and SHELTER WOOD — The Battn remained in this line of Res	
	3.8.16 4pm		The Battn moved forward to the N. end of MAMETZ WOOD in support of line which had been held by 8th Bn Rifle Brigade in the Bn were to support the 8 R.B. if the night of 6.7 and 8. The Battn on the night of 6.7 and 8. The Battn suffered shelling from about 10 a.m. to 4 pm of the 4th casualties.	
	8.8.16 5.30pm		The Bn moved forward to take up a position of deployment N.W. of BAZENTIN-LE-PETIT in the line of gt 10 & 14-12. The Bn kept a communication trench & some of its front line with the 8 Rifle Brigade, held the supports known as forward and Lancashire long extending with its comman on the right of Cemetery & the left & change bombs close main of Cemetery on the Fork suffered freely casualty.	
	11-12.16 6pm		The 16th Bn was relieved by the 2nd Suffolks (71st Bngd) moved in to the Reserve line between BOTTOM WOOD & SHELTER WOOD - 16	

WAR DIARY or INTELLIGENCE SUMMARY.

(Erase heading not required.)

Army Form C. 2118.

Date AUGUST 1916
13th BATT RIFLE BRIGADE

Place	Date	Hour	Summary of Events and Information	Remarks and references to Appendices
	17.8.16		Bn remained in the position on 11,12,13 & had 14 also 14th when relieved moves back to billets in BRESLE & found parties who helped them before	
	15.8.16		Bn billets in BRESLE Company Training	
	17"			
	18"		Bn Moved to CITERNE billeted at FRECHECOURT. Bn arr. destrn 6.30pm	
	19		Billets at CITERNE. Officers recce by Motor Lorries to billets at BAYLEUL & Estaires	
	20		Entrained at LAMPRE 3.30 A.M. arrived at BAYLEUL & Estaires	
	21st		12.30 P.M. marched to billets at ESTAIRES Rest at ESTAIRES	
	22nd		Entrained at LA GORGUE 10.45 am CALONNE-RICOURT 2 pm marched to OURTON	
	23rd		Billets OURTON - Series of training	

Army Form C 2118.

WAR DIARY
or
INTELLIGENCE SUMMARY.

(Erase heading not required.)

Instructions regarding War Diaries and Intelligence Summaries are contained in F. S. Regs., Part II. and the Staff Manual respectively. Title pages will be prepared in manuscript.

Date AUGUST 1916
13th BATT. RIFLE BRIGADE.

Place	Date	Hour	Summary of Events and Information	Remarks and references to Appendices
	24th		Billets OURTON - General Training	
	25th			
	26th		Sports	
	27th		Games at Training	
	28th			Church Parade in Morning
	29th			Work keeping any and officers
	30th	9.30am	Marched to Billets at VERDREL (in Reserve) arrived 1.30pm	
	31st		Very wet day	
			Billets VERDREL Some Training	

J. Pickwain Burg?
LT. COLONEL,
COMMANDING 13th Bn. THE RIFLE BRIGADE.

111th Brigade
37th Division.

1/13th RIFLE BRIGADE

SEPTEMBER 1916

Confidential.

War Diary

of

13th Batt. The Rifle Brigade

From   1st September 1916
To   30th September 1916

(Volume 12)

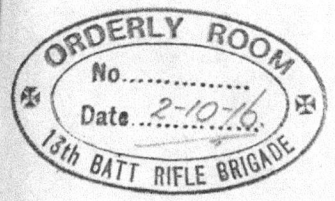

WAR DIARY
or
INTELLIGENCE SUMMARY.

(Erase heading not required.)

Army Form C. 2118.

No. ....
Date SEPTEMBER 1916.
16th BATT RIFLE BRIGADE

Place	Date	Hour	Summary of Events and Information	Remarks and references to Appendices
	September			
VERDREL.	1/10/16.		The Battalion was in Corps Reserve – General Training.	
"	2/10/16 to 3/10/16		do.	
"	9/10/16.		do.	
	10/10/16.	4 am.	The Battalion marched to FOSSE 10 and Billeted for night 9/11 Sept. (Ref. Maps 36cSE. F.9.A.)	
FOSSE. 10.	11/10/16.	8 am.	The Battalion marched to CALONNE and relieved the 4th Batn. Bedfordshire Regt. of the 190th Inf. Bde. 63rd (R.N.) Division, and took over the defences of CITÉ CALONNE. Battn attached to 190th Inf. Bde. 63rd (R.N.) Division (Ref. maps. 36c. S.W. M. 13. B & C, M.15. A & B.)	
CITÉ CALONNE.	12/10/16 to 14/10/16		Battalion remained in CALONNE. Working & Carrying parties supplied to Front Line Battn. (4th Bedford. Regt).	
"	15/10/16.	8 am.	The Battalion relieved the 4th Bed. Regt. in the Front Line in CALONNE Subsector no.2. Relief complete by 10 am. Very quiet in front. Enemy Trench Mortars were fired into our Front Line but caused no damage. Line held :- 2 Coys. infront line, 2 Coys. in Support. Portion of line held :-	

WAR DIARY
or
INTELLIGENCE SUMMARY.
(Erase heading not required.)

Instructions regarding War Diaries and Intelligence Summaries are contained in F.S. Regs., Part II. and the Staff Manual respectively. Title pages will be prepared in manuscript.

SEPTEMBER 1916
13th BATT. RIFLE BRIGADE

Place	Date	Hour	Summary of Events and Information	Remarks and references to Appendices
FRONT LINE.	18/9/16 to 19/9/16		(From M.15. C.2.1. Up to M.9.D.3.3. Ref Maps 36c S.W. Lantoir 78). Battalion in trenches. Extremely quiet on front. Trench mortars fairly active between 8 & 10 p.m. 17/9/16. Also Rifle Grenades. No damage. Mr. Box took over Sector, & Battn. cease to be attached to 190th Supplies.	
"	20/9/16	6 a.m.	The Battalion was relieved by the 13 Bn. Royal Fusiliers and marched back to Billets at BULLY-GRENAY. Ref Maps 36 D S.E. N. 5 & 11. Relief complete by 10 a.m. Enemy shelled C.T.S during relief – one man wounded.	
BULLY-GRENAY.	21/9/16 to 25/9/16	10.	The Battn. remained at BULLY-GRENAY in Reserve. On 24th enemy dropped 4 shells on the village, 3 were duds. No damage.	
do.	26/9/16	6 a.m.	The Battalion relieved the 13th Bn. the Royal Fusiliers on the front line as above. Relief complete by 11 a.m. Very quiet on front. Normal Trench Mortar Activity.	
FRONT LINE.	27/9/16 to 30/9/16	10.	The Bn. on the trenches. Kettle shelling on both sides. Sharets exploded. no enemy movement on nights of 27th & 28th. Trench Mortars fired into our front line causing little damage. 1 Coy. Commander wounded on 28th inst.	

[signature]
LT. COLONEL,
COMMANDING 13th Bn. THE RIFLE BRIGADE.

111th Brigade
37th Division.

1/13th RIFLE BRIGADE

OCTOBER 1916

Confidential.

111/37

War Diary
of
13th Battn. The Rifle Brigade

From   October 1st 1916
To   October 31st 1916.

(Volume 13)

Army Form C.2118.

WAR DIARY
or
INTELLIGENCE SUMMARY

(Erase heading not required.)

Instructions regarding War Diaries and Intelligence Summaries are contained in F. S. Regs., Part II. and the Staff Manual respectively. Title Pages will be prepared in manuscript.

No. OCTOBER.
Date 31-10-16.
18th BATT RIFLE BRIGADE

Place	Date	Hour	Summary of Events and Information	Remarks and references to Appendices
CALONNE	1/10/16		Battalion in the Trenches. Very quiet on front.	
"	2 "	8 am.	The Battalion was relieved by the 13th Bn. The Royal Fusiliers and took up position in CALONNE VILLAGE - holding the CALONNE Defences. Relief complete by 10.30 am.	
CALONNE VILLAGE	3 "		Working Parties supplied to 154th Coy. R.E's - 111th Trench Mortar Battery and Tunnelling Coy. R.E's.	
"	4 "		do.	do.
"	5 "		do.	do.
"	6 "		do.	do.
"	7 "		do	do
"	8 "		do	do
"	9 am.		Very quiet on the front.	
MAROC	10/10/16		The Battalion relieved the 17th Battalion Welsh Regt. 40th Division in the MAROC SECTOR. Relief complete by 11.30 am. Disposition of Battn:- 2 Coys. in Front Line - 2 Coys. in Support. Length of line held:- From M.9.d.3.3. to S. point of DOUBLE CRASSIER (Ref.Map 36c.S.W.Edition 7a). Very quiet on the front.	
"	11/ "		Battalion in trenches. Very quiet on the front.	
			do. Whole front wired during the night and general repairs to to front line trenches.	

WAR DIARY or INTELLIGENCE SUMMARY

Instructions regarding War Diaries and Intelligence Summaries are contained in F. S. Regs., Part II and the Staff Manual respectively. Title Pages will be prepared in manuscript.

(Erase heading not required.)

Place	Date	Hour	Summary of Events and Information	Remarks and references to Appendices
MAROC	12/10/16		Battalion in trenches. A few Rifle Grenades fell in our Trenches during the night killing 2 and wounding 4 Other Ranks. A Patrol examined whole of enemy front opposite and reported all quiet in enemy's lines.	
"	13/ "		Very quiet on front during the day. A great number of Rifle Grenades fell in our trenches during the night but caused no damage.	
"	14/ "		do. Enemy's lines were patrolled during the night but could hear no movement in hostile trenches.	
"	15/ "		Very quiet during the day. One of our Patrols bombed Enemy Sap, but returned to our Lines on being fired on.	
"	16/ "		Very quiet on front during the day. Great Rifle Grenade activity during the night on both sides. No damage was caused to our Trenches.	
"	17/ "		The Battalion was relieved by the 20th Battalion Canadian Regiment in the Trenches, and marched to billets in BARLIN and stayed there for the night.	
BARLIN	18/ "		The Battalion marched to LA THIEULOYE via RANCHICOURT - LA COMTE - BAJUS - and billeted for night.	
LA THIEULOYE	19th		Battalion remained in billets. Battalion Route march in afternoon.	
"	20th		The Battalion marched to HOUVIN-HOUVIGNEUL and billeted for the night. Route via MONCHY-BRETON - BAILLEUL-aux-CORNAILLES - AVERDOINGT - GOUY-en-TERNOIS - MAGNICOURT-sur-CANCHE.	

WAR DIARY or INTELLIGENCE SUMMARY

(Erase heading not required.)

Place	Date	Hour	Summary of Events and Information	Remarks and references to Appendices
HOUVIN-HOUVIGNEUL	21/10/16		The Battalion marched to GEZAINCOURT and billeted for night. Route via REBREUVIETTE - LE SOUICH - GROUCHES - DOULLENS.	
GEZAINCOURT	22/"		The Battalion marched to PUCHEVILLERS and billeted for night. Route via Fme. DU ROSEL - LE VAL DE MAISON.	
PUCHEVILLERS	23/" to 29th		The Battalion remained at PUCHEVILLERS during this period, during which severe weather was experienced.	
"	30th		The Battalion marched to LONGUEVILLETTE and billeted for night. Route via CANDAS.	
LONGUEVILLETTE	31st.		The Battalion remained in Billets.	

J. Pritchard-Brown
Lieut. Colonel.
Commanding 13th Battalion The Rifle Brigade.

111th Brigade
37th Division.

1/13th BATTALION RIFLE BRIGADE

NOVEMBER 1916

Confidential.

War Diary
of
13th Battalion The Rifle Bde.

From November 1st 1916.
To November 30th 1916.
(Volume #)

WAR DIARY
or
INTELLIGENCE SUMMARY

(Erase heading not required.)

Army Form C. 2118.

Place	Date	Hour	Summary of Events and Information	Remarks and references to Appendices
LONGUEVILLETTE	Nov.1st to 10th		The Battalion remained at LONGUEVILLETTE. General Training was carried out during this period. Sports etc. during the afternoons.	
"	11/11/16.		The Battalion marched to PUCHEVILLERS and billeted for the night.	
PUCHEVILLERS.	12/11/16.		The Battalion marched to HEDAUVILLE and bivouaced for the night. Route via TOUTENCOURT - VARENNES.	
HEDAUVILLE.	13/11/16.		The Battalion left bivouacs in HEDAUVILLE and moved to advanced Div.H.Q. (63rd R.N.D) just South of ENGLEBELMER and was placed at the disposal of 63rd (R.N.) Div. At 3.15 pm. the Battalion moved to MESNIL, on through HAMEL to the GREEN LINE West of STATION ROAD. This position was reached about midnight. Hostile barrage was put on the track and the Battalion suffered about 40 Casualties - 2 Officers being wounded.	
	14/11/16.		At 4 am. orders were received to attack at 6. 15 am. The Battalion was to attack BEAUCOURT TRENCH, from RAILWAY ALLEY to a point 400 yards N.W. It was to keep touch with the H.A.C. on Right and with 13th Royal Fusiliers on left who were to take BEAUCOURT TRENCH from the left of this Battalion to LEAVE AVENUE. The Battalion was held up by Rifle and M.Gun fire at 6.10 am. till 7.15 am. The Barrage (first one) of our Artillery had been very high but, the second enabled the advance to be resumed, and by 8 am. BEAUCOURT TRENCH was captured to a point 300 yards N.W. of RAILWAY ALLEY. The men who assaulted BEAUCOURT TRENCH where it cuts the Village of BEAUCOURT, found that the enemy had evacuated it and were forming up to surrender. These were captured, and several of our parties who went into the village captured many more of the enemy after a little opposition. The 13th Royal Fusiliers had come up on the right of the Battalion, and the Left flank of the Battalion was exposed, the enemy sniping heavily from this flank. Hostile Barrage was very slight till 11.30 am. "D" Company started bombing up BEAUCOURT TRENCH towards LEAVE AVENUE and by midnight had advanced 300 yards.	Attached Appendix
	15/11/16.		"D" Company continued to Bomb up BEAUCOURT TRENCH and by 4 pm. reached MUNICH TRENCH. During the 24 hours fighting and Bombing in this Trench, 80 prisoners were captured.	

Army Form C. 2118.

WAR DIARY
or
INTELLIGENCE SUMMARY
(Erase heading not required.)

Instructions regarding War Diaries and Intelligence Summaries are contained in F. S. Regs., Part II. and the Staff Manual respectively. Title Pages will be prepared in manuscript.

Place	Date	Hour	Summary of Events and Information	Remarks and references to Appendices
	15/11/16.		During the night of the 14/15th, Patrols had visited MUCK HUNTER TRENCH and RAILWAY TRENCH and reported that these were untenable owing to Mud and Water and that they were practically non-existent. On the evening of the 15th, the Battalion was relieved by 10th Royal Fusiliers and moved back into the GREEN LINE W. of STATION ROAD N. of STATION ALLEY.	
	16/11/16 to 20/11/16.		The Battalion remained in the above position during this period. At times the enemy heavily shelled the position, and our casualties were nearly 30. On the night 20/21st, the Battalion was relieved and marched to bivouacs at ENGLEBELMER.	
ENGLEBEL-MER.	21/11/16 to 23rd Nov.	"	The Battalion remained in Bivouacs at ENGLEBELMER during which time drafts were received to make up the Battalion.	
"	24th	"	The Battalion marched to LOUVENCOURT and billeted for the night. Route via HEDAUVILLE - FORCEVILLE - ACHEUX.	
LOUVENCOURT.	25th	"	The Battalion remained in billets at LOUVENCOURT.	
"	26th	"	The Battalion marched to PUCHEVILLERS and billeted for the night. Route via ARCQUEUES - RAINCHEVAL.	
PUCHEVILLERS.	27th to 30th Nov.	"	The Battalion remained at PUCHEVILLERS. General training carried out.	

Y B Graham Major.

Commanding 13th Battalion The Rifle Brigade.

WAR DIARY
or
INTELLIGENCE SUMMARY

(Erase heading not required.)

Army Form C. 2118.

Summary of Events and Information

The following were the casualties among the Officers, N.C.O's and men of the Battalion during the fighting mentioned in War Diary attached:-

OFFICERS.

2nd Lieut. W.D.WILKINSON.	5th Essex Regt. attached 13th Rifle Bde.	Killed in Action.
The Rev. E.W. TREVOR C.F.	Attached 13th Rifle Bde.	do.
2nd Lieut. P.J.PITHER.	Wounded in Action.	13th Rifle Bde.
" T.G.Skyrme.	do.	"
Lieut. A.L.Donaldson	do.	"
2nd Lieut. H.J.Fraser	do.	"
" F.A.Kingswell	do.	"
" J.A.V.Duff	do.	"
" B.H.Baker	do.	"
" A.M.Wiseman	do.	"
" R.Colvill-Jones	do.	"
" W.Fowler	do.	"
" C.M.Gilray	do.	"

OTHER RANKS.   312.

111th Brigade.

37th Division.

1/13th BATTALION

RIFLE BRIGADE

DECEMBER 1 9 1 6

Army Form C. 2118.

WAR DIARY
—or—
INTELLIGENCE SUMMARY.
(Erase heading not required.)

Instructions regarding War Diaries and Intelligence Summaries are contained in F. S. Regs., Part II and the Staff Manual respectively. Title pages will be prepared in manuscript.

Place	Date	Hour	Summary of Events and Information	Remarks and references to Appendices
PUCHEVILLERS.	1/12/16.		The Battalion was inspected by Brig.General C.W.Compton C.M.G., Commanding 111th Infantry Bde.	
"	2nd to 5th.		General Training carried out during this period. Sports in afternoons.	
"	6th. to 12th.		Lieut.Col. F.S.M.Savage-Armstrong D.S.O., of 2/7th Essex Regt. joined and assumed command of the Battalion 6/12/16. General Training carried out.	
"	13th.		The Battalion marched to AUTHIEULE and billeted for night. Route via BEAUQUESNE - TERRAMESNIL.	
AUTHIEULE.	14th.		The Battalion marched to NOEUX and billeted for night. Route via DOULLENS - OCCOCHES - MEZEROLES - FROHEN-le-GRAND - WAVANS.	
NOEUX.	15th.		The Battalion marched to OEUF and BEAUVOIS and billeted for night. Route via BEURE -su- BOIS - HARAVESNES - FILLIEVRES - LINZEUX.	
OEUF.	16th.		The Battalion marched to HEUCHIN and billeted for the night. Roite via LIBESSART - FLEURY - ANVIN.	
HEUCHIN.	17th.		The Battalion marched to AUCH-AU-BOIS and billeted for the night. Route via FONTAINE-lez- ROULANS - WESTREHAM.	
AUCHY.	18th.		The Battalion marched to CALONNE-sur-la-LYS and billeted for the night. Route via ST.HILAIRE - BOURECQ - LILLERS - BUSNES - ROBECQ.	
CALONNE.	19th.		The Battalion remained in billets for the day. General Inspection and cleaning up.	
CALONNE.	20th.		The Battalion marched to PARADIS and billeted for the night.	

WAR DIARY
or
INTELLIGENCE SUMMARY.
(Erase heading not required.)

Instructions regarding War Diaries and Intelligence Summaries are contained in F.S. Regs., Part II. and the Staff Manual respectively. Title pages will be prepared in manuscript.

Place	Date	Hour	Summary of Events and Information	Remarks and references to Appendices
PARADIS.	21st.		The Battalion marched to CROIX BARBEE and relieved the 12th Battalion Gloucester Regt. 5th Div. and were in Support to 13th R.Fus. in front Line in NEUVE CHAPELLE Sector.	
CROIX BARBEE.	22nd to 26th.		The Battalion remained in billets during this period. On the night 24th/25th the enemy heavily shelled the village with Lachrymatory Shells, about 60 shells being fired in all. We suffered 4 casualties 1killed and 3 Wounded.	
"	27th.		The Battalion relieved the 13th Royal Fusiliers in the Front Line in the NEUVE CHAPELLE Sector. Distribution of Battalion as follows:- 2 Coys. in Front Line, 2 Coys. in Support Line. Length of Front held:- On the Right HUN STREET (exclusive) to SIGN POST LANE on the Left (inclusive).(Reference Map RICHEBOURG Edition 7. M.35.d.4.8. - S.5.c.3½.05.)	
NEUVE CHAPELLE Trenches.	28th to 31st.		Battalion in the Trenches. First two days considerable bombardment by MINENWERFER of large and Medium Calibre. On commencement of bombardments men were immediately withdrawn to the Flanks and into communication Trenches. Only 4 casualties incurred. The Front Line was considerably damaged on each occasion. Line is now held by Posts and gaps between Posts wired in and covered by Machine,Lewis and 15 pdrs.Guns (in the Support Line). Enemy afford few targets for our sharp shooters. "No man's Land" was patrolled every night by Two Patrols. An enemy patrol of six was dispersed. The ground is very broken and the Dykes impassable. Every difficulty is presented to Patrols by the features of the ground in the NEUVE CHAPELLE LEFT SECTOR. Even the wire entanglements have, in many places, sunk beneath the surface of the ooze.	

F.M. Sharpe-Hurnberry Lieut.Colonel.
Commanding 13th Battalion The Rifle Brigade.

Confidential.

111/37

War Diary

of

13th (S) Batt. The Rifle Bde.

From January 1st 1917.
To   January 31st 1917.

(Volume 16)

ORDERLY ROOM
No.
Date January 31st 1917
13th BATT RIFLE BRIGADE

Vol 17

Army Form C. 2118.

WAR DIARY
or
INTELLIGENCE SUMMARY
(Erase heading not required.)

Place	Date	Hour	Summary of Events and Information	Remarks and references to Appendices
NEUVE CHAPELLE Trenches.	1/7/17		The Battalion in the Trenches in NEUVE CHAPELLE SECTOR. Length of Line held :- From HUN STREET (exclusive) on the Right to SIGN POST LANE (inclusive) on the Left.(Ref.Map RICHEBOURG Edition 7. N.35.d.4.8 - S.5.c.3½.05.) Little Minenwerfer activity on left which was effectively answered by our Trench Mortars.	
"	2/7/17		The Battalion was relieved by the 10th Bn. York & Lancs Regt. (63rd Inf.Bde) and marched to Billets at PARADIS - LA COUTURE - VIELLE CHAPELLE.	
PARADIS.	3/7/17 to 14/7/17.		The Battalion remained in billets during this period during which time general training was carried out by Companies. On the 8th inst. the Corps Commander (Lt.Gen.R.C.B.Haking K.C.B.) presented Medal Ribbons for Honours gained by the Division in connection with the operations on the SOMME and the ANCRE. The Battalion formed a Guard of Honour of 1 Officer and 30 Other Ranks which received the compliments of the Corps Commander, being the best turned out of the whole parade. The undermentioned of the Battalion were recipients of Medal Ribbons :- MILITARY MEDAL. No.S4400 A/CSM Manktelow E. No.S4093 Sgt. Chilcott A. No.6/641 L/Sgt.Davis W. No.23796 Corpl.Grogan J. No.53705 " Lockyer A. No.S4557 L/Cpl.Hughes A. No.S17209 Rfn. Wigg S. No.S4725 " Hedges F. No.S3937 A/CSM.Oliver F. S.4390 CQMS. Fitch L. No.53795 Sergt.Johnson N. No.S3826 Rfn. Stacey R.	

Army Form C. 2118.

WAR DIARY
or
INTELLIGENCE SUMMARY
(Erase heading not required.)

Instructions regarding War Diaries and Intelligence Summaries are contained in F.S. Regs., Part II. and the Staff Manual respectively. Title Pages will be prepared in manuscript.

Place	Date	Hour	Summary of Events and Information	Remarks and references to Appendices
PARADIS	15/1/17		The Battalion relieved the 4th Battn. Middlesex Regt. (63rd Inf. Bde.) in Support Billets at CROIX BARBEE.	
CROIX BARBEE.	16/1/17 to 20/1/17.		The Battalion remained in Billets at CROIX BARBEE. 2 Companies were employed during this period on wiring CHURCH REDOUBT and CHATEAU REDOUBT (in "B" Line) (Map RICHEBOURG) both day and night.	
"	21/1/17		The Battalion relieved the 13th Bn. Royal Fusiliers in Front Line in NEUVE CHAPELLE LEFT SECTOR. A Rifle Grenade fired by the enemy blew up a Stokes Mortar Ammunition Dump at 11 pm. causing 8 Casualties. (7 Killed and 1 Wounded).	
NEUVE CHAPELLE Trenches.	22/1/17 to 26/1/17.		The Battalion in Front Line. 2 Patrols, with a view to Minor enterprise, were sent out every night. Patrolling was very difficult owing to the frozen state of the ground. Considerable Minenwerfer activity during this tour.	
"	27/1/17.		The Battalion was relieved by the 13th Bn. The Royal Fusiliers and marched to Billets at LA FOSSE in Brigade Reserve.	
LA FOSSE	28/1/17 to 31/1/17.		The Battalion remained at LA FOSSE. On the 30th inst. the Army Commander (Gen.Sir H.S.Horne K.C.B.) presented Medal Ribbons at MERVILLE for Honours gained by the Division in connection with the operations on the SOMME and ANCRE. The Battalion formed a Guard of Honour of 2 Officers and 61 Other Ranks, which was again complimented by the Army Commander on its excellent turnout, being the best on parade. The undermentioned of the Battalion were recipients of Medal Ribbons:-	

2nd Lieut. K. ARCHBOLD.
No.S3937 A/CSM. Oliver F. } MILITARY CROSS.

No.S14140 L/Cpl. Phillips J.   Distinguished Conduct Medal.

F.R.Kerr-Smith
Lieut.Col.
Commanding 13th Battalion The Rifle Brigade.

Confidential
Vol 18

War Diary
of
13th (S) Battn. The Rifle Brigade.

From   February 1st 1917
To   February 28th 1917.
        (Volume 17)

ORDERLY ROOM
Date 1-3-17
13th BATT. RIFLE BRIGADE

Army Form C. 2118.

WAR DIARY
INTELLIGENCE SUMMARY.
(Erase heading not required.)

Instructions regarding War Diaries and Intelligence Summaries are contained in F.S. Regs., Part II. and the Staff Manual respectively. Title pages will be prepared in manuscript.

Place	Date	Hour	Summary of Events and Information	Remarks and references to Appendices
LA FOSSE	1/2/17		The Battalion was relieved by the 12th Bn. London Regt. (London Rangers) and marched to Billets at ROBERMETZ. Route via LESTREM - MERVILLE.	
ROBER-METZ.	2nd to 9/2/17.		The Battalion remained at ROBERMETZ during which period General Training was carried out. On the 8th inst. the Battalion was inspected by the Divisional Commander (Maj.Gen.H.B. Williams C.B., D.S.O.)	
"	10/2/17		The Battalion marched to BETHUNE and billeted fr the night. Route via PACAUT - HINGES.	
BETHUNE	11/2/17.		The Battalion marched to PHILOSOPHE and billeted for the night. Route via SAILLY-le-BOURSE.	
PHILO-SOPHE.	12/2/17.		The Battalion relieved the 8th Battn. R.W.Surrey Regt. 72nd Inf. Bde. in the front line HULLUCH LEFT SECTOR. Distribution of Battn:- 3 Coys. in front line - 1 Coy. in Support. Length of Line held:- From G.18.b.8.5 to H.19.a.3½.2½. Ref. Map LOOS.	
HULLUCH LEFT SECTOR.	12/2/17 to 18/2/17)		The Battalion in Front Line. Rather an extraordinary part of Line. Great portion of the Centre front consists of Craters. Trenches at this point are on fairly high commanding ground. The tour was uneventful and only 9 Casualties were caused by the enemy chiefly from "Minnies" and Aerial Darts. The outstanding feature of the tour was a very successful enterprise boldly executed by 2nd Lt. P.M.MEESON and No.S6522 Rfn.GREGG W. who went out in full day-light to Bosche Crater to bring in and obtain identifications from a dead Bosche. Several successful patrols were also made. Enemy were found to be holding line strongly but were not very aggressive. On the morning of the 18th inst. the Battn. was relieved by the 13th Bn. Royal Fusiliers and moved back into Support Lines in 10th Avenue.	*Rfn.Gregg awarded M.M. for this.
"	19/2/17 to 23/2/17.		The Battn. remained in Support. Carrying and working parties supplied to R.E's and T.M.B's the whole time.	
"	24/2/17.		The Battalion relieved the 13th Bn. Royal Fusiliers in the front Line as above.	

Army Form C. 2118.

WAR DIARY
INTELLIGENCE SUMMARY.
(Erase heading not required.)

Place	Date	Hour	Summary of Events and Information	Remarks and references to Appendices
HULLUCH LEFT SECTOR.	24/2/17 to 28/2/17.		Not an altogether uneventful tour. On the night of the 26th an organised "Shoot" by the Corps Artillery and Supporting Batteries took place on German Line. The Bosche appeared to be very excited but retaliated with little artillery and moderate Minny fire and Aerial Darts. On the night of the 27th, a dummy raid was organised preceded by a discharge of Gas accompanied by smoke clouds. This was a most successful operation. Artillery and Trench Mortars and Lewis Guns co-operated. We have every reason to believe that a considerable amount of casualties were inflicted on the enemy. Our casualties NIL. The enemy again showed signs of great nervousness. During this period our "Flying Pigs" with other Light Mortars obtained a clear ascendency over the enemy. At least 3 Minnies were knocked out by direct hits and an appreciable feebleness on the part of the enemy was noticed at the end of the tour. The relief of enemy troops was completed on night of 25th inst. Our snipers were very successful especially in sniping from new posts erected in favourable positions. Several patrols were carried out and it was again determined that enemy were holding line in fair strength.	

A.B. Graham Major.
Commanding 13th Battalion The Rifle Brigade.

Confidential.

War Diary
of
13th (S) Battn. The Rifle Bde.

From 1st March 1917.

To 31st March 1917.

(Volume 78)

Army Form C. 2118.

WAR DIARY
or
INTELLIGENCE SUMMARY.
(Erase heading not required.)

Instructions regarding War Diaries and Intelligence Summaries are contained in F.S. Regs., Part II. and the Staff Manual respectively. Title pages will be prepared in manuscript.

Place	Date	Hour	Summary of Events and Information	Remarks and references to Appendices
HULLUCH LEFT SECTOR	1/3/17	2 am.	The Battalion was relieved by the 2nd Battn. Notts & Derby Regt.(6th Division) and marched to Billets at MAZINGARBE.	
MAZINGARBE	2/3/17		The Battalion marched to CHOCQUES and billeted for the night. Route via PHILOSOPHE - BEUVRY - BETHUNE.	
CHOCQUES	3/3/17		The Battalion remained in Billets. General cleaning up.	
"	4/3/17		The Battalion marched to FONTES and billeted for the night. Route via:- LILERS. Lieut.Col. C.F.Pretor Pinney D.S.O. rejoined the Battalion from England and assumed Command. Lieut.Col. F.S.N.Savage-Armstrong D.S.O. left Battn. to assume Command of the 11th Bn. Royal Warwick Regt.	
FONTES.	5th to 8/3/17.		The Battalion remained at FONTES during which period General Training was carried out.	
"	9/3/17.		The Battalion marched to PERNES and billeted for the night. Route via:- FERFAY - FLORINGHEM.	
PERNES	10/3/17.		The Battalion marched to Billets at MAISNIL-ST-POL and billeted for the night. Route via:- BRYAS - OSTREVILLE - ROELLECOURT - FOUFFLIN-RICAMETZ.	
MAISNIL-ST-POL.	11/3/17 to 31/3/17.		The Battalion remained at MAISNIL-ST-POL during which period General Training was carried out. On the 23rd inst. a presentation of Medal Ribbons by the Army Commander (General Sir E. Allenby K.C.B.) was held. The Battn. found a Guard of Honour consisting of 1 Officer and 25 Other Ranks, and it was complimented by the Army Commander, being the best turned out on parade. The following were recipients of Medal Ribbons:- 2nd Lt. E.R.Wedemeyer. Military Cross. No.S/9477 Sgt. Classen.A. Mer.Ser.Medal. No.S/6522 L/Cpl. Gregg.W. Military Medal.	

C.F.Pretor Pinney
Lieut.Col.
Commanding 13th Bn. The Rifle Brigade.

Confidential.

Vol 20

III/37

War Diary
of
13th (S) Bn. The Rifle Brigade.

From   April 1st 1917.

To   April 30th 1917.

(Volume 19)

Army Form C. 2118.

WAR DIARY
or
INTELLIGENCE SUMMARY

(Erase heading not required.)

Instructions regarding War Diaries and Intelligence Summaries are contained in F.S. Regs., Part II. and the Staff Manual respectively. Title Pages will be prepared in manuscript.

Place	Date	Hour	Summary of Events and Information	Remarks and references to Appendices
MAISNIL ST. POL	1st to 4th.		The Battalion remained at MAISNIL-ST-POL during which period general training was carried out.	
"	5th		The Battalion marched to VILLERS-sir-SIMON and billeted for the night. Route via MAIZIERES PENIN.	
VILLERS-Sir-SIMON.	6th		Remained at Villers-Sir-Simon. A Brigade Tactical Exercise was carried out during the morning.	
"	7th		The Battalion marched to AGNEZ-les-DUISANS via HABARCQ - GOUVES and billeted in Hutments for the night.	
AGNEZ.	8th.		The Battalion marched to Bivouacs at L.16.c.4.0 (Ref.Map 51C) and bivouaced for the night.	
WAGNONLIEU	9th.	5.20 am.	Left Camp near WAGNONLIEU as rear Battalion of Brigade and marched with various halts round North Side of ARRAS to position of assembly beyond BLACK LINE near FRED'S WOOD.	Lt.Col. C.F.Pretor Pinney DSO Commandg.
		4.50 pm.	The Battalion moved in Artillery formation as Reserve Battn. of the Brigade towards BROWN LINE. A considerable amount of hostile shelling. At about 8 pm. I received a message to say that the 10th and 13th Bns. R.Fus. were held up and were digging on line from H.36.a.0.4 to the South along FEUCHY CHAPEL Road. I accordingly took up supporting position in rear of 13th R.Fus. who had asked for my support - 2 Coys.in Front Line and 1 in Support with 4 Lewis Guns in shell holes echeloned on the left to form a defensive flank. I finally established connection with the 63rd Infantry Bde. on the left with the 8th Somersets who had 2 Coy's on ORANGE HILL - 1 Coy., in Support on reverse slope of ORANGE HILL and 1 Coy. in Reserve in BROWN LINE about H.28.	
	10th.	4 am.	We received an order to march at once to a position near BROKEN MILL and to report to GOC 63rd Inf. Bde. We moved there occupying a position at H.28.a.1.3 the 13th KRRC. on our right. About 11 am. we received an order to be ready to form up at 12 noon to move to the attack on MONCHY-LE-PREUX. The Battn. moved in Artillery formation as the Reserve Battn. of the Brigade.	
		5 pm.	The advance was held up at 5 pm. I saw the O.C. 10th Bn. R.Fus. who asked for as much support as we could give. I sent up 2 Coys. to the 10th R.Fus. and 13th R.Fus. and kept 1 Coy. on plateau WEST of MONCHY with 4 Lewis Guns. The situation was now as under:- 10th R.Fus. and 13th R.Fus. had retired about 300 yards from lissure of the village and were	

Army Form C. 2118.

WAR DIARY
or
INTELLIGENCE SUMMARY
(Erase heading not required.)

Instructions regarding War Diaries and Intelligence Summaries are contained in F.S. Regs., Part II. and the Staff Manual respectively. Title Pages will be prepared in manuscript.

Place	Date	Hour	Summary of Events and Information	Remarks and references to Appendices
In front of MONCHY-LE-PREUX.	10th.	5 pm. (Contd)	digging in assisted by 154th Coy. R.E. 2 Coys. of the Battn. were sent up in support or to move into the line if necessary. 2 Coys. 13th KRRC. were also in the line or in Support. 1 Coy. KRRC. was in Reserve about N.5.b.4.7.	
		6 pm.	1 Coy. of the Battn. were digging in 150 yards in rear of this Coy. 4 Lewis Guns of the Battn. were disposed, two on each flank of the 13th KRRC. Coy. in support. 2 Lewis Guns were on each flank of the 13th R.Bde. Coy. in support Reserve. I saw the Commander of the Artillery Group and explained the situation to him. He came into action on Germans to the S. of MONCHY-LE-PREUX. I also saw the Staff Officer of the Yeomanry Brigade in rear and asked him for support if necessary.	
"	11th.	12.30 am.	I saw the Brigade Major and received verbal orders to attack at 5 am. 13th R.Bde on Left - 13th KRRC. on right. 13th R.Fus. supporting us. - 10th R.Fus. supporting 13th KRRC. I only had time to issue verbal orders and get the Coys. into position. Owing to the difficulties of collecting Companies in the assembly trench, the Battalion moved forward to the attack at 5.5 am. I had two Coys. in two waves in front - 1 Coy. in 2 waves in Support - 4 Lewis Guns on the left which I judged to be the exposed flank. As soon as they reached the village I went forward with H.Qrs. to N.6.b.7.8. On moving forward I rallied and collected a good many stragglers of various Battalions and with my H.Qrs. occupied a trench facing N.E. about N.6.b.7.8. Later in the day when the 63rd Inf. Bde. had come up I communicated with the O.C.4th Middlesex Regt. in house No.15 in the village. We were finally relieved about 10.30 pm. when we marched back to the BROWN LINE near which we bivouaced and mo ed on to BATTERY VALLEY in the early morning where we rejoined the Bde.	
	12th.	11 am.	The Battalion marched to ARRAS and billeted in the cellars of the GRAND PLACE for the night.	

Army Form C. 2118.

WAR DIARY
or
INTELLIGENCE SUMMARY

(Erase heading not required.)

Instructions regarding War Diaries and Intelligence Summaries are contained in F. S. Regs., Part II. and the Staff Manual respectively. Title Pages will be prepared in manuscript.

APRIL 1917.

Place	Date	Hour	Summary of Events and Information	Remarks and references to Appendices
ARRAS	13th		The Battalion was conveyed in buses to AGNEZ-les-DUISANS and rested the night in the Hutments.	
AGNEZ.	14th		The Battalion marched to VILLERS-sir-SIMON via HERMAVILLE - IZEL-les-HAMEAU and billeted for the night.	
"	15th to 16th.		Remained in billets. General cleaning up and refitting of Battalion. Specialist Training carried out.	
"	17th. 18th. 19th		The Battalion marched to HABARCQ and billeted for the night. Route via HERMAVILLE. Remained in billets. Specialist Training and training of new drafts. The Battalion marched to AGNEZ-les-DUISANS and billeted for the night in the hutments.	
HABARCQ. " AGNEZ.	20th		The Battalion relieved the 1st Battn. The Rifle Brigade in the Support Trenches N. of the river SCARPE (the BLACK LINE running N. and S. through the village of ST.LAURENT-BLANGY.)	
BLANGY.	21st to 22nd.		Remained in Support Trenches.	
"	23rd.		The 2nd phase of the Battle of ARRAS (Lt.Col.C.F.Pretor-Pinney DSO.Commdg. the Battalion) 1 hour before Zero (4.45 am) the Battalion formed up 2 Coys. in Front Line, 1 Coy. being in Reserve with the 4 L.Guns of "A" Coy. At Zero hour the Battn. moved forward in Artillery formation marching on a compass bering of 104 degrees. Very soon after the Battalion started the enemy put down a heavy barrage of 5.9" H.E.shells. Casualties were very heavy going through this barrage and the men continued to advance without a halt. Just before reaching the enemy's wire we came upon what appeared to be assembly trenches. The first wave had halted in these, the officers leading it having been either killed or wounded. The second wave of the leading Coy. joined the first and together pushed up on through the enemy's wire.into the BLACK LINE which they at once began to consolidate. A few Hermans were found still in the dug-outs. Before we had been there verynlong a bombing attack by the enemy started by the right flank. 2nd Lt. W.M.SMITH got together a party, spreading out on both sides of the trench, and attacked and captured the German Bombing party. Soon after this orders were received by the Capt. The Hon. R.W.Morgan-Grenville to assume command of the Battalion as Lt.Col.C.F.Pretor Pinney had been badly wouned. He went back to find Battn. Hqrs. but was severely wounded. The Adjutant with the remainder of Battn. Hqrs. arrived in the BLACK LINE and Capt. C.N.C.BOYLE assumed command of the Battn.	

Army Form C. 2118.

WAR DIARY
or
INTELLIGENCE SUMMARY

(Erase heading not required.)

Instructions regarding War Diaries and Intelligence Summaries are contained in F.S. Regs., Part II and the Staff Manual respectively. Title Pages will be prepared in manuscript.

Place	Date	Hour	Summary of Events and Information	Remarks and references to Appendices
Nr. village of GAVRELLE.	23rd.	9 am.	Major A.N.S.Jackson assumes command of the Battalion. I left 63rd Inf.Bde.Hqrs. to which I had been attached for the operations and reported to the Hqrs. of the 111th Inf. Bde. at 7.30 am. The Brigade informed Major Jackson that the Battn. was following on in rear of 13th KRRC. He was informed to stop Battalion if he got there in time as the Bde. did not want the Bn. to go in rear of the 13th KRRC. as we might have to support the 10th R.Fus. on the right. Major Jackson joined the Battalion in the BLACK LINE in front of the village of GAVRELLE. The Battn. had become somewhat disorganised and mixed up with the 63rd (R.N.) Division. The 4 Reserve L.Guns of "A" Coy. were missing, and all that could be found of the Battalion was 4 Officers and 120 O.R. The enemy were shelling the BLACK LINE heavily and placing a barrage in front and behind it. At 10 am. orders were received to get into touch with the O.C. 13th KRRC. and to go up and assist them in the consolidation of the final objective. 2nd Lt. W.M.SMITH was sent out with a small patrol to get in touch with O.C.13th KRRC. In the meantime the Battn. was organised for the advance. Owing to "A" Coy. being mixed up in the trench, "D" Coy - the strongest Coy - were ordered to move out into shell holes in front of BLACK LINE to form a first wave. The remainder of the other 2 Coys. to form a second wave. 2nd Lt. W.M.SMITH returned and reported the position of O.C.13th KRRC. The Battalion moved forward the enemy barraging heavily the right flank which had some casualties. The Battalion lined the sunken road, running S.E. from the village, and dug themselves in. The situation not being clear on the final objective and the right flank of the KRRC being in the air, the O.C.KRRC did not wish the Battalion to move forward until further reconnaissance had been made, as it was thought that the Battn. would probably have to form a defensive flank to cover the right of the KRRC. At 12.30 pm. the O.C.KRRC and Major Jackson went up to reconnoitre the position. We found the enemy were holding the high ground in the neighbourhood of the Cross Roads in some strength and more of the enemy were coming in. The 13th KRRC. who were dug in on the road, were completely enfiladed from the Cross Roads and had had casualties from Rifle fire and the situation was certainly unsatisfactory. The O.C.KRRC and Major Jackson made their way back to the BLUE LINE where there was a ½ Coy. of the KRRC. in support. He ordered them to move up at once in skirmishing order and form a defensive flank. At 3.30 pm. a runner came from the KRRC. to say that the enemy were in large numbers on the right flank and were creeping up the road, some being within 60 yards of the position, and the L.Gun which covered the right flank had been knocked out.	

Army Form C.2118.

WAR DIARY
or
INTELLIGENCE SUMMARY

(Erase heading not required.)

Instructions regarding War Diaries and Intelligence Summaries are contained in F. S. Regs., Part II and the Staff Manual respectively. Title Pages will be prepared in manuscript.

APRIL 1917

Place	Date	Hour	Summary of Events and Information	Remarks and references to Appendices
Right of GAVRELLE	23rd		Orders were given to Capt. BOYLE to move up across the open in skirmishing order, and to take up a position so as to cover the right flank of the 13th KRRC. and command the Cross Roads. Capt.BOYLE moved up with "B" Coy. and the remainder of "C" Coy. in skirmishing order joining up with the right of the KRRC and with his right shoulder back so as to command the Cross Roads. 2nd Lt. BOUGHTON-LEIGH was then ordered to move up and support Capt. BOYLE so as to extend the Line to the right. The movement was well carried out with only 1 casualty and our protective flank ran for about 120 yards from the right of 13th KRRC, then running S.W. for 400 yards. This position was consolidated and it covered the right flank of the KRRC. and commanded the Cross Roads. We had 6 Lewis Guns in the Line. Battn. Hqrs. were established in the sunken road.	
"	24th		During the earlyhours of the 24th, three of the Reserve Lewis Guns (prev.missing) returned to the Battn. having got carried on with the 63rd (R.N.) Divn. in the attack of GAVRELLE. These were sent up to secure the safety of the right flank of the 13th KRRC, taking up a position in shell holes between the KRRC right and our left. Later, 2 of the guns were sent up to the KRRC line to help them. At 3 pm. under an intense bombardment on GAVRELLE ending with 40 minutes of Gas Shells the enemy delivered a counter-attack on the DRAKE Battn. of the 63rd (R.N.) Divn. on our left. The Drake Battn. were established 100 yards in front of the village, and as the wind was blowing from N.E. they were not worried, by the Gas, all of it being blown down the sunken road and our Bn. Hqrs. were compelled to wear their Gas Masks. After the bombardment had lifted, O.C.KRRC was sure that he saw enemy moving in the village and moving across the ground due E. of the Cemetary. The position of Bn. Hqrs. would have been rendered untenable had the enemy got through the village, as they could have enfiladed the sunken road. A consultation was held with O.C.KRRC and it was decided that a defensive flank to the left must be formed to meet any attack that came from that direction. It was decided that the 13th KRRC. should man the trench running from the W. of the sunken road and that the Battalion should man trench running E. of sunken road towards the front line. A bombing post was established at junction of BLUE LINE (CANDIA TRENCH). A patrol was sent out to an isolated M.Gun of the Machine Gun Coy. which covered the ground E. of Cemetary and promised support in the event of attack. This M.Gun later did very good work killing about 40 of the enemy retiring on the GAVRELLE-FRESNES Road after counter-attack on village had failed. Our Bn.Hqrs. stood by in this position for 1½ hours	

Army Form C. 2118.

WAR DIARY
or
INTELLIGENCE SUMMARY

(Erase heading not required.)

Instructions regarding War Diaries and Intelligence Summaries are contained in F.S. Regs, Part II. and the Staff Manual respectively. Title Pages will be prepared in manuscript.

APRIL 1917.

Place	Date	Hour	Summary of Events and Information	Remarks and references to Appendices
Right of GAVRELLE	24th.		until patrols reported that the counter-attack had failed and that the village remained entirely in our hands. It was estimated that the 63rd (R.N.)Division killed 200 of the enemy in front of our line and took about 40 prisoners, the last line of the enemy advancing with their hands up.	
"	25th		At 12.30 am. orders were received that as the enemy had lost very heavily on the 23rd, the XVII Corps would renew the attack at 4 pm. in conjunction with the remainder of the Third Army, and that in the first instance the BROWN LINE would be captured throughout, and would be reached by about 4.56 pm. After a halt of 1½ hours in the BROWN LINE the advance to the RED LINE would be continued by the 51st and 37th Divisions. At 3 pm. the order was cancelled. Consequently on the night 24/25th the Battalion continued consolidating the position and sent out patrols up to the high ground in square I.1.d. (BIACHE MAP). They reported the high ground held by the enemy by batches of 3 and 4 at varying intervals. Considerable artillery by the enemy also sniping, which was considerably reduced by our L.Gun fire. Enemy shelled the sunken road all night of 25/26th.

Working and carrying parties laboured under considerable difficulties, many rations and water cans being destroyed by shell fire. During the night 25/26th all our shell holes were consolidated into a continuous line.

On the night 24/25th the Battn. was informed that the BROWN LINE had been taken throughout and was ordered to extend its line from right of KRRC and to join up with 13th R.Fus. The attack by the 63rd and 112th Inf. Bdes. however failed, and the BROWN LINE could not be occupied that night. | |
| | 26th. | | Throughout the day the front systems and back areas were heavily shelled. At 9 pm. orders were received that XVII Corps would attack on the morning of 28th instant with the 37th Divn. on the left of the Corps and the 111th Bde. on left of the Division, with 63rd and 112th Bdes. on right. The objectives were to be the BROWN and RED LINES. The Brigade was to attack on a two Battn. front, 13th R.Fus. on right, ourselves on Left with the 10th R.Fus. in support. Frontage to be from the right of 13th KRRC. on the GAVRELLE-ROEUX Road to 50 yds. N.of the road | |

Army Form C. 2118.

WAR DIARY
or
INTELLIGENCE SUMMARY
(Erase heading not required.)

Instructions regarding War Diaries and Intelligence Summaries are contained in F.S. Regs., Part II. and the Staff Manual respectively. Title Pages will be prepared in manuscript.

Place	Date	Hour	Summary of Events and Information	Remarks and references to Appendices
Right of GAVRELLE.	26th.		junction I.2.c.3.6.(BIACHE MAP). At 9.30 pm. GOC. 111th Inf. Bde. informed Major Jackson that Major W.R.STEWART M.C. (1st Rifle Bde) was on his way to take over the command of the Battalion. Major W.R.Stewart arrived at 10 pm. 26/4/17. On the nights 24/25th, 25/26th, 26/27th the Battalion was engaged in digging communications trenches and strong points.	
"	27th.		Major W.R.Stewart M.C. in command of the Battalion.	
		10 am	The night 26/27th passed without incident except that GAVRELLE was very heavily shelled by the enemy. Major Stewart accompanied by Major Jackson visited the front line and found the men well entrenched in CUBA TRENCH. They appeared very tired but in good spirits. The 13th R.Fus. prolonged the line of CUBA TRENCH to the right. The 13th KRRC. was holding the sunken road running S.E. from GAVRELLE (C.25.c) with their right about I.1.a.90.95. A narrow C.T. had been dug between the left of the Battn. and the right of KRRC. A Fire Trench running N and S. had also been dug to the E. of CUBA TRENCH-about 200 yds. E - this trench was connected with CUBA TRENCH at each end.	
		5.30pm.	Major Stewart proceeded to Bde. Advanced Hqrs. where Brigadier held conference of C.O's. We were told that the Brigade would attack on the morning of the 28th inst. and capture the portion of the original BROWN LINE which had not been captured on the 23rd inst. The attack would take place in conjunction with attacks on right and left.	
		6 pm.	Operation Order was received from Brigade. Capt. BOYLE was sent for from the front line and it was explained to him how the attack was to be carried out.	
		10 pm.	Battn. Operation Orders were issued.	
		11 pm.	Battn. moved from CUBA TRENCH to new trench 200 yds. E. of it.	
	28th.	4.25 am.	Fairly quiet night in Front Line but sunken road in H.6.b. was heavily shelled. ZERO hour.	
		7 am.	As no information had been received from the Front Line and as it was impossible to see anything from Battn.Hqrs. owing to smoke, Major Jackson was sent forward to reconnoitre.	
		7.30 am.	First wounded began to come in and they stated that objective had been gained.	

Army Form C. 2118.

WAR DIARY
or
INTELLIGENCE SUMMARY

(Erase heading not required.)

APRIL 1917.

Place	Date	Hour	Summary of Events and Information	Remarks and references to Appendices
Right of GAVRELLE.	28th.	9 am.	Major Jackson returned and reported that the Battalion had gained its objective and were digging themselves in. We were in touch with the N.Staffs Regt. on the left (this Bn. had relieved the 13th KRRC the previous night). The situation on the right was less clear. Our right rested on the Cross Roads in T.2.c but no sign could be seen of the 13th R.Fus., although there appeared to be some men of different regiments to the S. of the Cross Roads. A Lewis Gun Detachment was ordered to take up a position covering our right flank.	
		11.45 am.	Enemy were seen collecting S. of Railway Copse, evidently with the intention of making a counter-attack. Our Artillery was seen to deal with them very effectively, and they were dispersed with loss.	
		1 pm.	A report was received from the Front Line that GREENLAND HILL was not clear of the enemy and that we were suffering casualties from M.Gun fire from the vicinity of CUTHBERT TRENCH.	
		5 pm.	Major Stewart visited the Front Line and found that a continuous trench had been dug along the whole front of our objective but it was very difficult to move along it owing to hostile fire from our right rear. Several Germans were seen coming from GREENLAND HILL with the intention of surrendering, but most of them were either killed or wounded by their own men who remained behind. Our snipers and Lewis Gunners inflicted casualties on the enemy in front of our position as they were seen moving from one shell hole to another.	
		6 pm.	Information was received from Brigade Hqrs. that the Battn. would not be relieved until the following night.	
		8 pm.	Very heavy Artillery firing in the direction of OPPY and GAVRELLE accompanied by SOS signals.	
"	29th.	2 am.	Considerable artillery activity N. and E. of GAVRELLE. SOS signals also seen.	
		7 am.	Major Stewart and Major Jackson visited Front Line and found the situation quite satisfactory although the enemy were still giving trouble from GREENLAND HILL. By this time the 13th R.Fus. had sent 2 Coys. to prolong the line S. of Cross Roads in I.2.c. The day passed very quietly. Officers from the 26th Inf. Bde. visited Bn. Hqrs. and reconnoitred the line with a view of taking over at night.	
		7 pm.	Enemy put a heavy barrage of Gas Shells on to the road running W. from GAVRELLE. During the night the enemy artillery kept up a heavy fire in the vicinity of Battn.Hqrs. and on the C.T. leading up to the Front Line. This rather hampered the relief.	

Army Form C. 2118.

WAR DIARY
or
INTELLIGENCE SUMMARY
(Erase heading not required.)

Place	Date	Hour	Summary of Events and Information	Remarks and references to Appendices
Right of GAVRELLE	30th.		The Battalion was relieved by about 120 men of the K.O.S.B. and about the same number of 11th Bn.Scottish Rifles. At 1.30 am. the relief was complete. The Battn. on relief proceeded to ST.NICHOLAS reaching there about 5 am. They suffered no casualties on the way back, although the enemy's artillery was very active. On the 28th inst. Lt.Col.C.F.Pretor Pinney DSO. Died of Wounds received on the 23rd inst. The Burial took place on the 30th April 1. at No.30 C.C.S. at AUBIGNY.	

Major.
Commanding 13th Battalion The Rifle Brigade.

Account of "ARRAS 1917".

Action of 13th Rifle Brigade.

by

Lieut. L. S. Chamberlen.

. . . .

7.4.17. Arrive at Talavera Camp (K.6.) (huts) from Villers-sur-Simon (10 Kilos) at 11.30 a.m. Spent day in final preparations, including maps, and gave a last lecture to men. Stay night 7th/8th. Weather cloudy; heavy gunfire - more 9 a.m.

8.4.17. Arrive here (field outside Wagonlieu - L.21.) at 11 a.m. Brigade marched past General Compton (Brigadier) in Duisans (L.7.) and then split up into battalions and marched to allotted positions (see map) L.15. 16. 21. 22. Rest until 12.30 p.m. - lunch - continue minor preparations until 3 p.m. At 3 p.m. Voluntary Holy Communion (150 comts.). 3.45 - 4.15 viewed tomorrows battlefield from L.22.with Archbold and Pidsley. Could see Monchy-le-Preux (app. little damaged). Tea 4.45, followed by rag-rugger match until 6.15, then last instructions from Lt.-Col. C.F. Pretor-Pinney, D.S.O. - "Gentlemen, we will take Monchy "or die." 6.15 - 7.45. Issue of stores followed by thorough inspection of men (my batman, Rfn. Richardson refused to be left behind). Everything ready. Dinner in Wagonlieu - bed 9.30 p.m. - shared tent with Pughe and Pidsley. Weather fine - guns in Dainville (L.29) quietening down - sleep.

9.4.17. Misty. Up 4.15 a.m., equipment ready. breakfast 4.35. Parade 5.15. Move off 5.20. "Jacker" (Major A.N.S.Jackson, D.S.O. - second-in-command at gate, wishes us 'bon chance'. Those left behind clear up bivouacs ready to move into Arras by 1 p.m. Ready here L.16 at Zero (5.30 a.m.) 5.29 all quiet, then crash - 3,000 guns go off accompanied by thousands of bombs - distant cheering - the first wave is over! The Bosch send up numbers of S.O.S. rockets and at 5.45 the enemy barrage falls. The whole landscape before us is now a mass of whirling smoke, flashes and frightful tumult. Suddenly a mile to our right an immense explosion, an enemy shell has hit a dump on the outskirts of Arras in the Fbg. d'Amiens - a huge cloud of black & white (lyddite) smoke like an immense mushroom hangs above it for a time and then disperses. On our left (North) we see the shells bursting over Vimy Ridge. What has happened? We march on awe-struck - its the biggest show in the world's history and we are for it. Eventually we reach L.18 and put gas-helmets at alert. We move on to Fbg. d'Amiens de Baudimont and halt until 12.10. (Zero plus 6 hours 40 minutes) just behind a battery of 6-inch Canadian guns firing rapid on to Vimy. Suddenly - cheers! the first batch of prisoners (91 men) come past - then 10 mins. later 400 all ranks - and others are seen coming from Vimy Ridge. At 11.30 a.m. tea is brought up by transport and at 12.10 we move on.

(2)

As we moved on to our final assembly place in Blangy we met many wounded from the 15th Division, and numerous prisoners. The enemy had retired on his 3rd line (marked green on map). We moved through Arras by platoons at 100 yards intervals, with many halts, as the roads were crowded with troops, wounded, artillery limbers and ambulances. At 1.15 p.m. we reached an assembly position in Blangy and partook of a meat, bully-beef, biscuits, chocolate and tea. Here the enemy first put a few gas shells amongst us, but there were no casualties. At 3.20 p.m. we advanced again and in battle order. 10/R.Fusiliers, 13/R.F., 13/K.R.R.C. and 13/R.Brigade. The C.O. went on with A.Company (Capt. Bowyer). 2nd-Lieut. Balden [? Batten.] with 4 of C.Coy's lewis guns moved just in front of H.Q. company (self) attached to me as a reserve and flank guard. We now split up into artillery formation and went over our old front-line system and on through Blangy chateau grounds (blown to bits) until we reached the Railway △ (19) where we remained an hour. An unlucky shell in B. chateau gardens knocked out 6 men of D.Coy. (2 killed), but no one else. Whilst here (Rly. △) rumour came that the Bosch were on the run and suddenly three bridging trains came past us - covering the trenches as they went. Cavalry and artillery up! It was the 3rd Cavalry Div. 2nd D.G's, 10th Hussars and Essex Yeo. [37?] They formed mass between our lines here and dismounted - next minute we were off. (here we saw an upturned aeroplane (near Fred's Wood)). We moved over 'Observation Ridge' in artillery formation, sections 200 yards apart (all round). Hqrs. in rear. 2nd-Lieut. Pidsley (Int.Officer) took charge of right half and self(Chamberlen) left (signallers, runners and details). We went on for 500 yards across plateau towards Battery Valley and then suddenly came under terrific machine-gun fire from the Bosch 3rd line about Halifax trench system. A few 5.9's and 8-inch. came over also, but the enemy were doing more counter-battery work against our artillery behind us.

Despite enemy's fire we continued to advance in art. formation of sections without heavy casualties, until about 5.30 p.m., when dusk, snow and fire held up the leading battns. 10th and 13th R.F. and we (400 yards in rear) had to halt, and dig in on the line (Squares 27 & 33 in mauve line on map) - railway to Cambrai - Arras road. This mauve line marks position of 15th and 37th Divisions on night of April 9/10th 1917, - the broken line and crosses being the battle outposts.

As soon as we were held up I, as Int. Officer and Signalling officer, went forward and got into touch with A. B. & D. Coys. Hqrs., also the 10th & 13th R.F., 13th K.R.R.C. and 111th Bde. Machine-Gun Company who were following us, and made my report of their dispositions to Col. Pinney and to Bde. Hqrs., and finally took the Colonel round as soon as I had seen to my men. 2nd-Lieut. Pidsley and Lieut. Archbald stayed with our H.Q. company. At 1.30 a.m. orders came to move at once and take up another position ready to support the 15th Division (H.L.Infantry) in an attack at dawn on the Bosch lines about H.28.a. and c. (see map), which had held them up the previous day.

Heavy snow fell all the time until 8 a.m. when we were told that the enemy had retired on our fourth objective, leaving isolated strong points here and there, especially on Orange Hill and Chapel Hill (out of map to south).

At 9 a.m. we moved back again and formed for the advance on Monchy-le-Preux, our final objective,- with the front wave lining the Chapel road and facing Orange Hill. Great excitement was now aroused by the appearance of about 20 batteries of R.F.A. and 6-inch. guns from Battery Valley, who were to co-operate with our 37th Division, now leading the attack. The 3rd Cavalry Division also came up at 10 a.m. and formed up on our left flank. The Bosch hadn't seen us yet................

At 10.30 a.m. the advance began. The 111th Bde. was on our right and the 63rd on our left - 7 tanks also accompanied us but only one reached Monchy. As soon as our heads appeared about the 85 contour line, the enemy opened fire with 5.9's, 4.2's, 3-inch and gas shells, but not very heavily. A few enemy machine guns were put out in Halifax trench by tanks, and the wire crushed/so that we could get on pretty easily - the ground being fairly hard, despite the snow.

The cavalry now moved up, but as soon as they appeared every/sort of weapon opened on us and casualties began to be frequent. The cavalry had to retire back to Battery Valley until the enemy should become less aggressive. Here (see map 34-Halifax trench) I saw an orderly riding, and leading another horse, downed by a 5.9 Woolley Bear bursting almost on his head: he and the lead horse were badly wounded but the other horse escaped. Pidsley shot the wounded horse with his revolver. Our advance was very slow over Orange Hill owing to the terrific tornado of shells and bullets amongst us. It became a matter of leaping from shell hole to shell hole and wondering how you ever escaped that one. One 5.9 actually struck the ground about 15 yards from me and richcheted over me.(It can't have been more than 1 yard above my head).

Nightfall found the 10th and 13th R.F. front line still west of Monchy and 40 % laid out. The K.R.R.C. had lost 200 out of 500 and we, 80 out of 500. The Bosch had us absolutely taped and we had to halt and dig like moles or die. Capt. Bowyer (A) was killed about 7 p.m. and Sergt. Carter (1 Platoon A.Coy., my late platoon) was also killed. Sergt. Champion, L/Cpl. Brooker and Signallers did wonders keeping the line open to Bde. Hqrs. - everyone behaved magnificent. As soon as I got my fellows settled in and established a signal station (1) 3.5.a.) (sic.) in a convenient shell hole, which Brooker dexterously manipulated and increased, I took Sergt. Champion and visited the companies and K.R.R.C., but not the R.F's. We nearly lost ourselves in darkness and snow, but after numerous shaves from bullets etc. we discovered all we wanted, chatted to various fellows: C.S.M.Manktelow (A), C.S.M.Oliver(D), Capt. Wedemeyer (D), Lieut. Hobday (D), Lieut. Reepmaker (A) and Lieut. Carlisle (B) and riflemen here and there. We than returned to our own Hqrs. Company and I left Sergt. Champion with L/Cpl. Brooker and went to see Col. Pinney and report. He, Archbold and Pidsley were in H.Q. (an 8-inch shell hole) close by - and Rfn. Davies, Richardson (my servant), Frankish (P's servant) had made tea for us, -- joy!! I was feeling pretty well chilled to the bone, soaked, and deuced hungry.

So a tin of bully, a few biscuits (our last) were devoured, and so we tried to sleep a bit in turn. <u>Question</u>:- Would C. Coy. (ration carriers) arrive before dawn when we should inevitably advance again?

At 3.30 a.m. orders came to move at 4 a.m. - still no rations - but at 3.40 - joy - up they came plus Rhum!!, and I just had time to issue everything and force the men to have a feed, despite their hatred of bully, before we moved. Rfn. Newman, aged 19, got tight on the Rhum on an empty stomach, so I left him to guard the spare ammunition with Rfn. Keeble and to report to me later.

At 4 a.m. we moved and formed for our last assault as shewn on map (H.35.). 13th R.Bde. and 13/K.R.R.C. in front line, 13th R.F. support and 10/R.F. reserve. We had B. and D. coys. up and A. and Hqrs. in reserve. Col. Rice (10/R.F.) joined forces with our hqrs. until we assaulted, and his signallers luckily left some of their wire behind which Rfn. Warrilow and Whiting picked up and brought on, thus giving us enough to carry the line up to Monchy itself, if need be. L/Cpl. Brooker was left on Orange Hill at an intermediate signal station (1) whilst Champion established another at H.36.c. (2), which spot was battn. hqrs. until we advanced at 5 a.m.

The enemy were quiet whilst we made ready for the assault and I went round the companies with Col. Pinney and Archbold (Adjutant). D. on left and B. on right, and A. in support (see map). At 5 a.m. all were ready and eager to advance. I phoned dispositions to Bde. Hqrs. and answer came to advance. The brigade started in 'Blobs' but extended into waves as soon as they passed the copse (c) and dashed up into the village, splitting up into small parties to deal with houses, cellars, and strong points still held by the huns. Meanwhile the enemy barrage came down on us and numberless machine guns opened on us from in front and on both flanks where the 112th & 63rd Brigades were having a tough time. Hqrs. moved on slowly and finally established itself in a line of hastily-dug trench and shell holes (see map @) at 6.15 a.m. One little story must be told here - Sergt. Champion, myself, and 6 signallers came up with the wire and were looking round for a convenient hole near H.Q. @ when an 8-inch shell pitched almost on us, blowing everyone down but unhurt, and made an immense crater at our feet - sequel - that crater was our signal post (M.3.) for the remainder of the action (until 4 a.m. on the 12th April) - marked "O" on map. This was about 6.20 a.m. on Wednesday, April 11th. Capt. Wedemeyer (D) and 2nd-Lieut. Reepmaker (A) came to report and runners from Carlisle (B) at 7 a.m. The enemy had retired from the village and high ground towards the Bois du Vert and the Bois du Sart and intermediate cover, leaving 40 prisoners in our hands & 200 dead, also some 16 machine guns and 4-5.9 Hows. Their other guns had been evacuated on the previous evening when we were on Orange Hill held up. The coys. were digging in on the E. edge of the village along our last objective (Mauve line) - the enemy shelling gradually increased to absolute drum fire and casualties increased.

Carlisle, Reepmaker, Spooner, Warrilow and Chamberlen were wounded, and Hobday killed. I remained at duty but the others went down. Lt. Rhys took over "A" Coy. and Lieut. Bampfield "B" - the latter doing magnificent work in reorganising the front line and village defences, at the same time taking in/many H.L.I., S.Wales Borderers and others from the 15th Division who had come up.

hand /

C.S.M.Manktelow (A) and Oliver (B) were wounded. Col.Rice,10/R.F. (badly shatered arm), Col.Leyton, 12/R.F. killed and 12 officers of 13/K.R.R.C. killed or wounded. At 9.30 a.m. the Bosch began to return, thinking that their fire had laid us low, but when 300 yards away 16 Lewis guns and 500 rifles told them another tale, and the few who got away didn't return that day; but, by jove, their gunners warmed us up a bit. About 11 a.m. I noticed a few fellows coming back owing to the fire, so at once went out to stop them. I had just got one little H.L.I. man back to his original hole and was standing on the edge talking to him when an 8-inch burst 5 yards away and lifted me a good 15 feet into the air: as I landed another came and blew me flat,but unhurt, and then returned to Col.Pinney.

Story of the Cavalry.

This was a trajedy; a rumour spread that the Bosch had retired to Boiry Notre Dame and beyond and the 3rd Cav. Bde. (General Bulkeley-Johnson) was sent up from Feuchy to go through Monchy and pursue. At 12 noon they appeared, galloping up by squadrons - Cheers! The enemy, however, saw them and shelled them so terribly that in 10 minutes 50% were down. The rest dismounted, left their horses in the village and reinforced our lines, where they behaved magnificently. Only 60 horses out of 400 escaped. Cavalry are not for this warfare! Suffice it to say that during the remainder of the day and until 1 a.m. on the 12th the enemy shelling and machine-gun fire was terrific. Our artillery were prevented from coming up close by the heavy mud, but poured in a tremendous fire nevertheless. Our last tank did excellent work round Monchy and south to Guemappe, operating without stopping for 40 hours-(The "Times" mentioned it afterwards) - unfortunately it got knocked out by a direct hit, about 4 p.m., but the crew escaped. Its commander, whom I met in hospital at Avesnes le Comte on the 14th was kicked by a mule and broke his wrist after reaching Arras, and so came home.

Rfn. Bearton, L/Cpl. Roff and Rfn Thorpe (runners) also Cpl. Caperon did excellently work during the day, but towards evening (5 p.m.) the two latter got wounded and went down. The enemy made no further advance and indeed never showed himself at all. At 6 p.m., having kept our line open to Bde. Hqrs. under intense fire and fearful climatic difficulties, an order came to prepare for an attack half right on Guemappe, which had held up the 112th Brigade. I took the orders verbally from our Staff Captain (a/Bde. Major) and repeated them to Col. Pinney, who was now in command of the 4 battns. in the village and precints, being senior to Col. Chestermaster, 13/K.R.R.C. He,however, rang up again and took them himself from Capt. Paris, and was about to send orders to the companies to move when Paris rang up again to say "wash out" - you will be relieved by the 29th Division as early as possible and they will carry out the attack. We, being down to 40% of our original strength - (2,000 in Bde.) - and about done up said "Thank God!" - made a meal of what bully and biscuits we had left and then went out to see who 'was' and who was 'not'. Altogether we saved some 50 wounded, many half buried in snow, including a few Bosch. The Battn. stretcher bearers, under L/Cpl. Fowler, aided by Rfn. Hamilton and Tucker, also Furniss, who was killed, did splendid work and saved many poor fellows. At 7.30 p.m. it was pitch dark and heavy snow came on again, but we still searched for the wounded. Meanwhile the coys. in the village were fairly sheltered and a dressing station was established in the villa (remains) marked + on map, which had been a Bosch brigade H.Q. and in which a bag of 50 Iron Crosses were found by A.Coy. - ready for distribution after our defeat!!! - instead, they acted as unusually fine souveniers. Sergt. Champion, of course, had gone off to explore and returned with a ripping automatic 1916 Steyn., which he eventually gave to me before I left the battn. on the Saturday at Agnes-les-Douisans.

At 9 p.m. the shelling had died down to a negligable quantity, but the cold was fearful - my hands were absolutely frozen and I had intense frost-bite by midnight. At 2 a.m. the company arose - 'Relief Up'- and with what joy we gathered our remnants and handed over our shell holes to the R.W.Kents can easily be imagined. By 6 a.m. the brigade were once more in Battery Valley, sleeping in the remains of the gun emplacements. 300 guns, chiefly 5.9's and field guns were smashed or taken in that valley, so it well deserves its name. We found a fine dug out (Max Richter's - see map) full of things there too, apparently the M.O's, and I brought back a couple of bayonets, some letters and a helmet and gas-mask from there and a trench near by. About 8 a.m. Rfn. Frankish and Richardson, who had left us on Orange Hill to procure food from Major A.N.S.Jackson, 2nd-i/n at Arras, arrived to our great joy with eggs, cake, butter, and bread ad lib; - we devoured all - I ate 6 eggs.

At 10.30 a.m. L/Cpl. Brooker and 6 signallers who had been on Orange Hill and who had been relieved before us, joined us, and some 30 missing from the battn. came in too. At 11 a.m. Rfn. Whiting brought me a Bosch helmet and a minute later the order came to move to Arras. At 1 p.m., after 3½ days of absolute hell, I saw dear old 'Jacker' and Pughe (T.O.) again, also Capt. Boyne, Capt. Morgan-Grenville and others left behind, and after seeing the men into the cellars in this grand place, their abode that day, we (officers) went off for a clean up and feed to our billet, where all the officers (10) assembled.

We had a splendid evening and dinner at the only good estaminet intact, and so to bed. Unfortunately at 5 a.m. an orderly dashed in to say that we were to move by motor-bus to Agnes-les-Douisans, in half an hour, from this grande place, so we had to up and pack our valises (the servants having disappeared) and trek heavy-laden to the buses ($\frac{1}{2}$ mile). Eventually we reached 'Agnes', put the men into huts with the K.R.R.C. and were again united with those left behind.

After breakfast, wash and sleep, then an immense tea and so, through Dr. Nicholson's hands to hospital at Manin with Archbold. Next day, Sunday, I went to Avesnes-le-Comte for one night, then Frevent (2 nights) and so to Etaples, Calais and London (24 Park Street).

FINIS.

. . . .

LIST OF OFFICERS.   13th Rifle Brigade.
------------------   --------------------

Col.   C.F. Pretor-Pinney, D.S.O.
                    (Ancre)
Lieut. K. Archbold, M.C.   Adjutant.

(A)   Capt. Bowyer.

(B)   Lieut. Carlisle.

(C)   Capt. The Hon. Morgan-Grenville (carrying party)
                         (Ancre)
(D)   Capt. Wedemeyer, M.C.

H.Q. Lieut. L.S. Chamberlen & Lieut. Pidsley.

Padre.   ?

Doctor.   Capt. Nicholson.

Transport. Lieut. Pughe. (to Brigade)

          & Lieut. Walpole.

2nd i/c. Major A.N.S. Jackson, D.S.O.

. . . .

Other Officers.   Lieut. Spanton and those mentioned in
                                         report.

                    (sgd) L.S. CHAMBERLEN.

July, 1932.   Late Lieut. Rifle Brigade.

13th (Service) Battn. The Rifle Brigade.

Winchester District.   Daily Casualty List d/- 16.4.1917.
--------------------   ----------------------------------

Regt.No.   Rank and Name.   C a s u a l t y.   PR.
--------   --------------   ----------------   ---

P. 4159   Rfn. Humberstone A. Died of Wounds, received in   N
                                    action 10.4.17.
                                    Reported by O.C. St.Johns
                                    Ambulance Brigade, Etaples.
                                    10.4.1917.

                                    V e r i f i e d.
                                                     ORs.
                                                              Lieut. for Major.
16.4.1917.   Officer i/c Regular Infantry Section No.2.
----------   ---

13th (Service) Batt., The Rifle Brigade.

WINCHESTER RECORD OFFICE. DAILY CASUALTY LIST D/- 17.4.1917.

Regt.No.	Rank and Name.	C a s u a l t y.	PR.
Z. 2777	L/cpl. Collins R.	Died of Wounds, received in action 11.4.17. Reported by O.C. 41 Casualty Clearing Station on memo dated 12.4.1917.	Nil.

Verified.

ORS.

Lieut. for Major.
Officer i/c Regular Infantry Section No.2.

17.4.17.

13th (Service) Battn. The Rifle Brigade.

WINCHESTER RECORD OFFICE. DAILY CASUALTY LIST D/- 18.4.17.

Regt.No.	Rank and Name.	Casualty.	PR.
S.27076	L/Cpl. Bacon P.W.	Died of Wounds, received in action 13.4.17. Reported by O.C. No. 8 Casualty Clearing Station, 13.4.1917.	Nil.
B.203177	Rfn. Best C.H.	Died of Wounds, received in action 13.4.1917. Reported by O.C. 41 C.C.S. 14.4.1917.	Nil.

Verified.
ORS.

18.4.1917.

Lieut. for Major.
Officer i/c Regular Infantry Section No.2.

13th (Service) Battn. The Rifle Brigade.

WINCHESTER RECORD OFFICE DAILY CASUALTY LIST DATED 20.4.17.

Captain. J.W.Bowyer.	Killed in Action. 10.4.17.	Nil.
2nd Lieut. J.C.Reepmaker.	Wounded in Action. 11.4.17.	Nil.
2nd Lieut. N.N.Wardlaw.	Wounded in Action. 11.4.17.	Nil.
2nd Lieut. P.J.Spooner.	Wounded in Action. 11.4.17.	Nil.
2nd Lieut. W.J.Carlile.	Wounded in Action. 11.4.17.	Nil.
2nd Lieut. W.E.Hobday.	Wounded in Action. 11.4.17.	Nil.

The above Casualties were reported by The Officer Commanding, The 13th Rifle Brigade, on A.F.B.213 dated 13.4.1917.

Verified.

Lieut. for Major.

20.4.1917.   Officer i/c Regular Infantry Section No.2.

13th (Service) Battn. The Rifle Brigade.

WINCHESTER RECORD OFFICE. DAILY CASUALTY LIST D/- 20.4.1917.

Regt.No.	Rank & Name.	Casualty.	PR.
P. 4092	Rfn. Green J.P.	Killed in Action. 9.4.17.	N.
S. 3769	L/C. Allen A.H.	Killed in Action. 11.4.17.	N.
S.23367	Rfn. Berry H.	Killed in Action. 11.4.17.	N.
S. 4494	Rfn. Cosby E.T.	Killed in Action. 11.4.17.	N.
S. 3806	A/S. Carter V.	Killed in Action. 11.4.17.	N.
S. 3458	Rfn. Cox T.	Killed in Action. 11.4.17.	N.
S.15492	Rfn. Cox J.	Killed in Action. 11.4.17.	N.
S.20680	Rfn. Carpenter W.	Killed in Action. 9.4.17.	N.
S. 3856	Rfn. Deer E.	Killed in Action. 11.4.17.	N.
S. 3663	L/S. Harler W.J.	Killed in Action. 11.4.17.	N.
Z. 2805	Sgt. Hewitt A.W.	Killed in Action. 11.4.17.	N.
S. 9445	Rfn. Hales W.	Killed in Action. 11.4.17.	N.
B203253	A/C. Hayes A.	Killed in Action. 11.4.17.	N.
S.15241	L/C. Smart W.	Killed in Action. 11.4.17.	N.
B203309	Rfn. Thompson H.	Killed in Action. 11.4.17.	N.
S. 4720	A/C. Watson J.	Killed in Action. 11.4.17.	N.
S.15614	Rfn. Winter B.	Killed in Action. 11.4.17.	N.

The above Casualties were reported by The Officer Commanding, The 13th (S) Bn. The Rifle Brigade on A.F.B.213 dated 13.4.1917.

Verified ORS.

Lieut. for Major.
20.4.1917.   Officer i/c Regular Infantry Section No.2.

13th (S) Battn The Rifle Brigade.

WINCHESTER RECORD OFFICE. DAILY CASUALTY LIST. D/- 20-4-17.

Regtl No.	Rank & Name.	CASUALTY	P.R.
S/ 27395	Rfn Chinnick. G	DIED FROM WOUNDS. 14.4.17 *	W.

Reported by O.C. 41.C.C.S memo. dated 15-4-17.

VERIFIED.

O.R.S.

G.H.Qrs
3rd Echelon.
20-4-17.

Lieut for Major.
Officer I/C No.2. Regular Infantry Section.

* As phoned 23.4.17

13th (Service) Battn. The Rifle Brigade.

WINCHESTER RECORD OFFICE. DAILY CASUALTY LIST DATED 20.4.17.

Regt.No.	Rank and Name.	Casualty.		PR.
S. 12610	A/C. Archer H.G.	Wounded in Action	11.4.17.	N.
S. 27102	Rfn. Avery E.	ditto	11.4.17.	N.
5903	Rfn. Ansell J.	ditto	11.4.17.	N.
S. 27074	L/C. Ambler W.	ditto	11.4.17.	N.
S. 28588	Rfn. Allen J.	ditto	11.4.17.	N.
S. 5837	A/C. Beeston F.	ditto	11.4.17.	N.
S. 14626	Rfn. Burchell W.	ditto	11.4.17.	N.
S. 15548	Rfn. Boughton J.	ditto	11.4.17.	N.
S. 15965	Rfn. Bawtree C.	ditto	11.4.17.	N.
S. 17261	Rfn. Bradshaw J.	ditto	11.4.17.	N.
B. 203260	Rfn. Brassett H.	ditto	11.4.17.	N.
B. 203262	Rfn. Buxton S.	ditto	11.4.17.	N.
S. 27432	Rfn. Bailey R.	ditto	11.4.17.	N.
S. 27386	Rfn. Banks E.H.	ditto	11.4.17.	N.
S. 27066	Rfn. Brown S.	ditto	11.4.17.	N.
6/466	Rfn. Baker A.	ditto	11.4.17.	N.
S. 25105	Rfn. Bowyer P.	ditto	11.4.17.	N.
S. 4779	A/CSM. Clarke T.	ditto	11.4.17.	N.
S. 4004	A/C. Carpenter H.	ditto	11.4.17.	N.
S. 3748	A/C. Capern F.	ditto	11.4.17.	N.
S. 27395	Rfn. Chinnick G.	ditto	11.4.17.	N.
S. 27397	Rfn. Clark H.	ditto	11.4.17.	N.
S. 27110	Rfn. Cook A.	ditto	11.4.17.	N.
S. 17191	Rfn. Chalkley W.	ditto	11.4.17.	N.
S. 19352	Rfn. Colombo J.	ditto	11.4.17.	N.
S. 23782	Rfn. Clarke C.	ditto	11.4.17.	N.
S. 27081	Rfn. Carter A.	ditto	11.4.17.	N.
S. 23345	Rfn. Claridge G.	ditto	11.4.17.	N.
S. 23253	Rfn. Cumber A.	ditto	11.4.17.	N.
Z. 2793	Rfn. Cowell G.	ditto	11.4.17.	N.
S. 24012	Rfn. Cullen P.	ditto	11.4.17.	N.
S. 3222	Rfn. Davies G.	ditto	11.4.17.	N.
S. 23505	Rfn. Dowler G.	ditto	11.4.17.	N.
S. 1159	Rfn. Doswell H.	ditto	11.4.17.	N.
Z. 1151	L/C. Evans W.	ditto	11.4.17.	N.
S. 21878	Rfn. Edwards F.	ditto	11.4.17.	N.
S. 23591	Rfn. Elwood H.	ditto	11.4.17.	N.
B. 203197	Rfn. Fenn E.	ditto	11.4.17.	N.
B. 203198	Rfn. Foulds V.	ditto	11.4.17.	N.
B. 203330	Rfn. Foster H.	ditto	11.4.17.	N.
Z. 2796	A/C. Grogan J.	ditto	11.4.17.	N.
S. 13051	Rfn. Green E.	ditto	11.4.17.	N.
S. 14165	Rfn. Gurdon R.	ditto	11.4.17.	N.
S. 3761	A/C. Hardy C.	ditto	11.4.17.	N.
S. 4501	Rfn. Hill J.	ditto	11.4.17.	N.
Z. 2817	A/S. Hircock E.	ditto	9.4.17.	N.
S. 2357	Rfn. Hyde E.	ditto	11.4.17.	N.
B. 203208	L.C. Higgins O.	ditto	11.4.17.	N.
B. 203213	Rfn. Hawker W.	ditto	11.4.17.	N.
S. 27416	L/S. Horn W.	ditto	11.4.17.	N.
S. 27424	Rfn. Hart F.	ditto	11.4.17.	N.
S. 15585	L/C. Jones J.	ditto	11.4.17.	N.
B. 203283	Rfn. Jewell F.	ditto	11.4.17.	N.
S. 3785	Rfn. Jordan A.	ditto	11.4.17.	N.
S. 25147	Rfn. Jones H.	ditto	11.4.17.	N.
S. 28622	Rfn. Kite S.	ditto	11.4.17.	N.
S. 3705	A/C. Lockyer A.	ditto	11.4.17.	N.
S. 15557	Rfn. Lack G.	ditto	11.4.17.	N.
S. 17091	Rfn. Lock F.	ditto	11.4.17.	N.
S. 23533	L/C. Lidbury A.	ditto	11.4.17.	N.
S. 11582	Rfn. Lawrence A.	ditto	11.4.17.	N.
S. 28602	Rfn. Law E.	ditto	11.4.17.	N.
S. 15705	L/C. Little W.	ditto	11.4.17.	N.
S. 4094	Rfn. Medhurst W.	ditto	9.4.17.	N.

(1)

(2)   13th Rifle Brigade.

Regt.No.	Rank and Name.	Casualty.		PR.
S. 4400	CSM. Mantelow E.	Wounded in Action	11.4.17.	N.
Z. 2794	A/S. Marshall T.	ditto	11.4.17.	N.
S. 12968	Rfn. Moore E.	ditto	9.4.17.	N.
P. 4178	Rfn. Maskell C.	ditto	11.4.17.	N.
B. 203286	Rfn. Moreton F.	ditto	11.4.17.	N.
S. 27433	Rfn. Matthews W.	ditto	11.4.17.	N.
S. 27430	Rfn. Medlock H.	ditto	11.4.17.	N.
S. 27437	Rfn. Morley W.	ditto	11.4.17.	N.
S. 20609	Rfn. Milan F.	ditto	11.4.17.	N.
S. 28604	Rfn. Mallam G.	ditto	11.4.17.	N.
S. 69	Rfn. Newall A.	ditto	9.4.17.	N.
S. 4202	Rfn. Oram A.	ditto	9.4.17.	N.
S. 25087	Rfn. Oddy G.E.	ditto	11.4.17.	N.
S. 8975	Rfn. O'Connor P.	ditto	9.4.17.	N.
S. 4077	Rfn. Page J.	ditto	11.4.17.	N.
S. 7087	L/S. Phillips R.	ditto	11.4.17.	N.
S. 4257	Rfn. Powell F.	ditto	9.4.17.	N.
S. 3885	Rfn. Price C.	ditto	11.4.17.	N.
S. 23511	L/C. Pettit A.	ditto	11.4.17.	N.
S. 28641	L/C. Pointon B.	ditto	9.4.17.	N.
S. 26551	Rfn. Peffers P.	ditto	11.4.17.	N.
S. 27408	Rfn. Quin P.	ditto	11.4.17.	N.
S. 4270	Rfn. Rodgers E.	ditto	9.4.17.	N.
S. 15477	Rfn. Raven A.	ditto	11.4.17.	N.
S. 15463	Rfn. Rust A.	ditto	11.4.17.	N.
B. 203232	Rfn. Ramsden H.	ditto	11.4.17.	N.
S. 19932	Rfn. Rainbird G.	ditto	11.4.17.	N.
S. 21408	Rfn. Richardson S.	ditto	11.4.17.	N.
6289	Rfn. Ricketts H.	ditto	11.4.17.	N.
S. 15796	Rfn. Ring E.	ditto	9.4.17.	N.
S. 1391	L/C. Staveley S.	ditto	11.4.17.	N.
B. 203234	Rfn. Streakes E.	ditto	11.4.17.	N.
B. 203297	Rfn. Summerley P.	ditto	11.4.17.	N.
S. 27116	Rfn. Baddington D.	ditto	11.4.17.	N.
S. 20840	Rfn. Stewart A.	ditto	11.4.17.	N.
S. 14857	Rfn. Styles F.	ditto	11.4.17.	N.
S. 19678	Rfn. Samuels A.	ditto	11.4.17.	N.
S. 21953	Rfn. Shirley H.	ditto	11.4.17.	N.
S. 21966	Rfn. Smith D.	ditto	11.4.17.	N.
S. 25244	Rfn. Sampson A.	ditto	9.4.17.	N.
S. 6711	Rfn. Smith H.	ditto	11.4.17.	N.
S. 15976	L/C. Timms H.	ditto	11.4.17.	N.
S. 16659	Rfn. Turney R.	ditto	11.4.17.	N.
S. 17208	Rfn. Thorp C.	ditto	11.4.17.	N.
S. 17247	Rfn. Tyler A.	ditto	11.4.17.	N.
S. 20667	Rfn. Tustain J.	ditto	11.4.17.	N.
S. 20676	Rfn. Turner R.	ditto	11.4.17.	N.
S. 27101	A/S. Thorne W.	ditto	11.4.17.	N.
S. 3694	Rfn. White J.	ditto	10.4.17.	N.
B. 203248	Rfn. Whitely S.	ditto	11.4.17.	N.
B. 203312	Rfn. Williams L.	ditto	9.4.17.	N.
S. 26055	Rfn. Woods J.F.	ditto	11.4.17.	N.
S. 27414	Rfn. Ward G.	ditto	11.4.17.	N.
S. 27120	Rfn. Woolley H.C.	ditto	11.4.17.	N.
S. 21895	Rfn. Wines W.	ditto	9.4.17.	N.
B. 234	L/S. Wood R.	ditto	11.4.17.	N.
S. 19711	L/C. Wren F.	ditto	11.4.17.	N.
S. 27366	L/C. Woodhouse F.	ditto	11.4.17.	N.
S. 23515	Rfn. Winter B.	ditto	11.4.17.	N.
S. 14148	Rfn. Wicks H.	ditto	11.4.17.	N.
S. 9645	L/C. Webb E.	ditto	11.4.17.	N.
S. 3753	Rfn. Yare B.	ditto	9.4.17.	N.
B. 203207	Rfn. George H.	ditto	9.4.17.	N.

--------------   Continued.

(3) 13th Rifle Brigade.

Regt.No.	Rank and Name.	Casualty	PR.
S. 14216	Rfn. Collins T.	Wounded at duty 12.4.17.	N.

The above Casualties were reported by The Officer Commanding, The 13th (S) Bn. Rifle Brigade on A.F.B.213 dated 13.4.17.

Verified.
ORS.

20.4.1917. Officer i/c Regular Infantry Section No.2.
Lieut. for Major.

13th (Service) Battn. The Rifle Brigade.

WINCHESTER RECORD OFFICE. DAILY CASUALTY LIST D/- 24.4.17.

Regt.No.	Rank and Name.	Casualty.	PR.
S.27081	Rfn. Carter A.W.	Died of Wounds, received in action 14.4.17. Reported by O.C. 19 CCS on A.F.A.36. E.D.3037 dated 14.4.17.	W.
S.21895	Rfn. Wines W.	Died of Wounds, received in action 10.4.17. Reported by O.C. 19 CCS on A.F.A.36.E.D.3037 dated 14.4.17.	W.
S. 5288	Rfn. Webber L.	Wounded in Action 11.4.17. Reported by O.C.Bn. on A.F.B.213 dated 13.4.17.	N.
S. 69	Rfn. Newall A.	Re-Joined Battalion for duty 15.4.17. Reported by O.C.Bn. 16.4.17.	W.

Verified.

Lieut. for Major.

24.4.17. Officer i/c Regular Infantry Section No.2.

13th (Service) Battn. The Rifle Brigade.

WINCHESTER CASUALTY LIST D/- 24.4.1917.

Regt.No.	Rank and Name.	Casualty.		PR.
S.15644	Rfn. Boyce C.	Wounded in Action 10.4.17. Reported by O.C. 49th F.A. on A.F.A.36.E.D.2737 d/- 10.4.17.		Nil.
S.26551	Rfn. Peffers P.S.	Died of Wounds, received in action 19.4.17. Reported by O.C. No.1. Canadian General Hospital on memo dated 19.4.17.		"W"

Verified.
ORS.

Lieut. for Major.
24.4.17.   Officer i/c Regular Infantry Section No.2.

13th (Service) Battn. The Rifle Brigade.

WINCHESTER RECORD OFFICE. DAILY CASUALTY LIST D/- 21.4.17.

Regt.No.	Rank & Name.	Casualty.	PR.
5903	Rfn. Ansell J.	Died of Wounds, received in action 18.4.17. Reported by O.C. No.11. General Hospital, memo d/- 18.4.17.	"W"
S.18353	Rfn. Arnold H.	Wounded in Action 9.4.17. Reported by O.C. 49th F.A., on A.F.A.36 dated 9.4.17. E.D.2737	N.
S.21976	Rfn. Dean C.	Wounded in Action 13.4.1917. Reported by O.C. 49th F.A. on A.F.A.36 dated 12.4.17. E.D.2903.	N.
S.3994	Rfn. Robertson R.	Wounded in Action 9.4.17. Reported by O.C.Bn. on A.F.B.213 d/- 13.4.17.	N.

Verified.
ORS.

Lieut. for Major.
Officer i/c Regular Infantry Section No.2.

21.4.1917.

13th (Service) Battn. The Rifle Brigade.

WINCHESTER RECORD OFFICE. DAILY CASUALTY LIST D/- 25.4.17.

Regt. No.	Rank and Name.	Casualty.	PR.
6440	Rfn. Swindells A.	Wounded in Action 11.4.17.	N.
S.14811	Rfn. Bromwich N.	Wounded in Action 11.4.17.	N.
S.25284	Rfn. Lewzey T.	Wounded in Action 11.4.17.	N.
S.27411	Rfn. Turnell N.	Wounded in Action 15.4.17.	N.

Reported by O.C.13th Rifle Brigade on memo, dated 17.4.1917.

S. 5512	A/S. Watson L.	Wounded, (acc) 31.3.17.	N.

Reported by O.C.Battn. on memo dated 14.4.1917.

Verified.
ORS.

25.4.1917.   Officer i/c Regular Infantry Section No.2.
Lieut. for Major.

20904.t/w.9-28/4/17.

13th (Service) Battalion The Rifle Brigade.

WINCHESTER RECORD OFFICE. DAILY CASUALTY LIST D/- 26.4.17.

Regt.No.	Rank and Name.	Casualty.	⊕R.
S.23782	Rfn. Clark C.	Died of Wounds, received in action 23.4.1917. Reported by O.C. 13 Staty Hospital 23.4.1917.	"W"
	2nd Lieutenant RHYS. W.L.T.	Died of Wounds, received in action 24.4.1917. Reported by O.C. No. 8 Casualty Clearing Station 24.4.1917.	Nil.

Verified
ORS.

26.4.17.
Lieut. for Major.
Officer i/c Regular Infantry Section No.2.

13th (Service) Battalion The Rifle Brigade.

WINCHESTER RECORD OFFICE. DAILY CASUALTY LIST D/- 28.4.1917.

Regt.No.	Rank and Name.	Casualty.	PR.
	LIEUT.COLONEL. C.F.PRETOR-PINNEY.(DSO)	WOUNDED IN ACTION 23.4.1917.	Nil.
	LIEUT.(A/CAPT) HON. R.W.MORGAN-GRENVILLE.	DITTO.	Nil.
	The above Casualties were reported by The Officer Commanding, 13th (S) Bn. The Rifle Brigade 24.4.1917.		
S.30816	Rfn. Challis A.	Died of Wounds, received in action 23.4.1917. Reported by O.C. 48 Field ambulance 25.4.1917.	Nil.
S.25290	Rfn. Mills H.E.	Died of Wounds, received in action 24.4.1917. Reported by O.C. 1 Can.C.C.S. 25.4.1917.	Nil.

verified.
ORS.

Lieut. for Major.
28.4.1917. Officer i/c Regular Infantry Section No.2.

*Amended in accordance with telephone message of to-day's date. (30/4/17.)

13th (Service) Battn. The Rifle Brigade.

WINCHESTER RECORD OFFICE. DAILY CASUALTY LIST D/- 28.4.1917.

Regt.No.	Rank & Name.	Casualty.	PR.
S. 4613	Rfn. Donavan J.	Died of Wounds, received in action 24.4.1917. Reported by O.C. No. 30 C.C.S. 25.4.1917.	Nil.

Verified.
ORS.

28.4.1917.

Lieut. for Major.
Officer i/c Regular Infantry Section No.2.

13th (Service) Battalion The Rifle Brigade.

WINCHESTER RECORD OFFCIE. DAILY CASUALTY LIST D/- 30.4.1917.

2ND. LIEUT. F.C.HALL.	WOUNDED (ACC) 21.4.1917. Reported on A.G's List No.965 dated 24.4.1917.	Nil.
2ND. LIEUT. F.S.LEE.	WOUNDED IN ACTION 23.4.1917. Reported on A.G's.List No.967 dated 26.4.1917.	Nil.
LIEUT-COLONEL. C.F.PRETOR-PINNEY.DSO.	DIED OF WOUNDS,RECEIVED IN ACTION 28.4.1917. Reported by O.C. No. 30 Casualty Clearing Station dated 28.4.17.	"W"

Verified.

30.4.1917.

Lieut. for Major.
Officer i/c. Regular Infantry Section No.2.

13th (Service) Battalion The Rifle Brigade.

WINCHESTER RECORD OFFICE. DAILY CASUALTY LIST D/- 30.4.17.

P. 4060   L/Cpl. Mason. W.   Died of Wounds, received in action
                                 23.4.17. Reported by O.C. 3rd   Nil.
                                 Field Ambulance R.N.D. d/- 24.4.17.

                     Verified.
                        ORS.

                                                              Lieut. for Major.
30.4.17.   Officer i/c Regular Infantry Section No.2.

13th Rifle Brigade
January to December
1917

Index..............

SUBJECT.

No.	Contents.	Date.

(41,365). Wt.9392—94. 2000. 6/19. **Gp.164**. A.&E.W.
(44,173).   „   21,613—105. 500. 10/19.   „   „

II/39 a 21

Confidential

War Diary
-of-
15th Australian Rifle Brigade
from May 1st to May 31st 1917

(Volume I)

Army Form C. 2118.

WAR DIARY
or
INTELLIGENCE SUMMARY.

(Erase heading not required.)

MAY 1917.

Place	Date	Hour	Summary of Events and Information	Remarks and references to Appendices
VILLERS-SIR-SIMON.	1st to 17th.		During this period the Battalion was billeted at VILLERS-SIR-SIMON, where General Training was carried out - including Specialist Training, Route Marching, and Brigade and Battalion Tactical Exercises. Battalion Concerts were held on various dates, and on the 10th, the Divisional Concert Party, ("The Barn Owls"), gave a performance. The Battalion Football Competition was won by a team from 'D' Company.	
"	18th		The Battalion marched to BERNEVILLE, and billeted for the night.	
BERNEVILLE.	19th.		The Battalion marched to ARRAS, and billeted for the night in SCHRAMM Barracks.	
ARRAS.	20th.		The Battalion remained in ARRAS for the day. The same evening the Battalion relieved the 6th Bedfords. Regt. in the Reserve Trenches just East of the village of TILLOY, relief being completed by 11.30 p.m.	
TILLOY.	21st.		The Battalion remained in Reserve Trenches East of TILLOY for 8 days. During this time Specialist Training was carried out, working parties were sent up to the front line, and general work towards improvement of Reserve Trenches proceeded with. Fine weather prevailed, and all ranks enjoyed the best of health.	

Army Form C. 2118.

WAR DIARY
or
INTELLIGENCE SUMMARY.
(Erase heading not required.)

Place	Date	Hour	Summary of Events and Information	Remarks and references to Appendices
MONCHY-LE-PREUX.	28th. & 29th.		The Battalion relieved the 6th Bedfords. Regt., on the night 28/29th, taking over from them the left sub-sector of the MONCHY-GUEMAPPE front. An interesting condition of warfare was found to exist there, the enemy having no definite line or system of trenches, seeming to favour a system of organised shell-holes, making him difficult to detect, and presenting an ill-defined target for artillery. Our own trenches were poor, but have been much improved since taking over. The enemy snipers were discovered to be in the ascendant. Our sniper posts were organised in shell-holes in advance of our lines — the first day's bag yielded 7 of the enemy, and a considerable decrease of the enemy snipers activity was at once noticeable.	
"	30th.		On the night of the 30th/31st, the two Companies in the front line, carried out a demonstration in conjunction with, and in support of, the Division on our left. At 11-30 a.m. on this date the C.O. visited Brigade Headquarters, and was asked by the Brigadier whether he was willing to undertake a minor operation in conjunction with the attack by the 29th Division on the left. The Commanding Officer agreed to carry it out. The plan for attack was discussed by the Brigadier, G.S.O.1, 2 Artillery Group Commanders, and the Commanding Officer. 12-20 p.m. The Commanding Officer returned to Battn. Headquarters, and saw Company	

Army Form C. 2118.

WAR DIARY
or
INTELLIGENCE SUMMARY.
(Erase heading not required.)

Instructions regarding War Diaries and Intelligence Summaries are contained in F. S. Regs., Part II and the Staff Manual respectively. Title pages will be prepared in manuscript.

- 3 -

Place	Date	Hour	Summary of Events and Information	Remarks and references to Appendices
MONCHY-LE-PREUX.	30th.		Commanders and discussed plan with them. Operation entrusted to 'C' Coy. (2/Lt. W.M.SMITH), 2/Lt. F.B.JOHNSON of 'A' Coy., being lent to 'C' Company.	
		4 p.m.	Orders for the attack issued.	
		11.30 p.m.	Zero hour. For description of action see Commanding Officer's report attached, copy of which was forwarded to Brigade.	
	31st.		Quiet day. Our snipers claimed several hits. 2nd Lieut. R.O.BASSHAM was killed just before leaving trenches, on patrol. Reconnoitring parties from 184th Brigade visited line.	
			During the month the following Honours and Awards (for acts of gallantry in the field) were notified :-	
			Military Cross. 2nd Lieut. L.S.CHAMBERLEN.	
			do. " W.M.SMITH.	
			Military Medal. B. 234. L/Sgt. Woods R. 'B' Coy.	
			do. S. 7196 A/Sgt. Crane T. 'A' "	
			do. B.203313 L/Sgt. Warner H. 'C' Coy.	
			do. S. 8955 A/Cpl. Roff S. 'H.Q.' Coy.	

Army Form C. 2118.

WAR DIARY
or
INTELLIGENCE SUMMARY.
(Erase heading not required.)

Place	Date	Hour	Summary of Events and Information	Remarks and references to Appendices
			- 4 -	
			Military Medal. S. 3716. A/Cpl. O'Connor M.J. 'D' Coy. ✓	
			do. S. 4004. " Carpenter H. 'A' " ✓	
			do. S. 3749. L/Cpl. Sherwin A. 'B' " ✓	
			do. Z. 2737. " Brooker F. 'H.Q.' Coy. ✓	
			do. S. 3804 Rfn. Davies W.D. 'H.Q.' " ✓	
			do. S. 4229 " Whiting S. " ✓	
			do. S. 4772 " Eastment C. 'A' Coy. ✓	
			do. B.203251 " Warrilow S. 'H.Q.' Coy. ✓	
			do. S. 3996 L/Cpl. Jackson H. 'A' Coy. ✓	
			do. S. 5 Rfn. Schofield T. 'A' " ✓	
			do. S. 27090 A/Cpl. Goodman W.H. 'D' " ✓	
			do. S. 1161 Sgt. Curtis J. 'A' " ✓	
			do. S. 4600 A/Cpl. Louden A.D. 'C' " ✓	

Lieut. Col.
Commanding 13th Battalion The Rifle Brigade.

Sheet 3.   Casualties.   13th (S) Rifle Brigade.

S. 16633   Rfn. Teeling   C.   Wounded in Action 24.4.1917.   N

The above Casualties were reported by The Officer Commanding,
The 13th (S) Battn. The Rifle Brigade on memo dated 24.4.17.

S. 29989   Rfn. Payne   E.   Died of Wounds, received in action   N.
                              27.4.1917. Reported by O.C. 42 CCS
                              dated 27.4.1917.

                        Verified.
                            ORS.

1.5.1917.   Officer i/c Regular Infantry Section No.2.

13th (Ser) Battn. The Rifle Brigade.

WINCHESTER RECORD OFFICE. DAILY CASUALTY LIST D/- 1.5.17.

CAPT. (T/MAJOR) JACKSON. A.N.S.   WOUNDED, AT DUTY 24.4.17.   Nil.
)L.N.Lanc. Rgt.Att:--------   Reported on A.G's.List No.
                                 968 dated 27.4.1917.

                    Verified.
                              ORS.

                                    Lieut. for Major.
1.5.17.   Officer i/c Regular Infantry Section No.2.

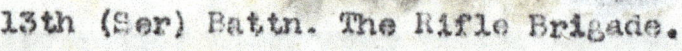

13th (Service) Battalion The Rifle Brigade.

WINCHESTER RECORD OFFICE. DAILY CASUALTY LIST D/- 1.5.1917.

Regt.No.	Rank and Name.	Casualty.	PR.
B. 203258	Rfn. Andrews P.	Wounded in Action 23.4.1917.	N.
374164	Rfn. Aylott A.	ditto	N.
S. 24100	Rfn. Adams J.	ditto	N.
S. 27383	Rfn. Austen E.H.	ditto	N.
P. 628	Rfn. Aglinton G.	ditto	N.
S. 4367	L/C. Ames A.	ditto	N.
B. 203322	Rfn. Brett E.A.	ditto	N.
S. 30513	Rfn. Backhouse G.	ditto	N.
S. 25683	Rfn. Bagnall A.	ditto	N.
S. 27520	Rfn. Bullard G.	ditto	N.
S. 28591	Rfn. Barnett L.	ditto	N.
S. 20654	Rfn. Besgrove H.	ditto	N.
S. 27391	Rfn. Bush R.	ditto	N.
S. 27444	Rfn. Brown A.L.	ditto	N.
S. 10830	Rfn. Ball C.J.	ditto	N.
S. 17220	Rfn. Brennan W.	ditto	N.
S. 15452	Rfn. Bearton F.	ditto	N.
S. 16010	Rfn. Brown W.	ditto	N.
S. 3608	Rfn. Brownson C.H.	ditto	N.
S. 2034	Rfn. Brackenbury A.	ditto	N.
Z. 1625	Rfn. Birch S.	ditto	N.
B. 203264	L/C. Caulton S.G.	ditto	N.
S. 3439	Rfn. Colbourn H.	ditto	N.
3533	L/C. Crocker A.	ditto	N.
S. 30969	Rfn. Clarke J.	ditto	N.
S. 30750	Rfn. Clark F.	ditto	N.
S. 14934	Rfn. Charrington S.	ditto	N.
S. 27382	Rfn. Clayden G.T.	ditto	N.
B. 706	Rfn. Callis J.E.	ditto	N.
S. 10436	Rfn. Cross J.	ditto	N.
S. 29699	Rfn. Denny J.	ditto	N.
S. 27458	Rfn. Dell W.F.	ditto	N.
S. 19710	Rfn. Dulien H.	ditto	N.
S. 8529	Rfn. Davies E.D.	ditto	N.
P. 4236	L/C. Drew H.S.	ditto	N.
B. 203272	Rfn. Esplin A.C.	ditto	N.
B. 203192	Rfn. Evans F.F.	ditto	N.
S. 28619	L/S. Falconer D.A.	ditto	N.
S. 7956	L/C. Foley T.	ditto	N.
S. 19915	Rfn. Freeman G.	ditto	N.
S. 4041	L/C. Finnegan J.	ditto	N.
S. 27065	Cpl. Gurney E.W.	ditto	N.
S. 30961	Rfn. Grass A.	ditto	N.
S. 10891	Rfn. Greenfield S.	ditto	N.
S. 22315	Rfn. Hewitt W.	ditto	N.
S. 30972	Rfn. Hartley H.	ditto	N.
373742	Rfn. Hill T.A.	ditto	N.
B. 203214	Rfn. Hunt J.J.	ditto	N.
S. 27378	Rfn. Heathcote J.	ditto	N.
S. 16650	Rfn. Hemmings S.G.	ditto	N.
5310	Rfn. Hawthorne G.	ditto	N.
S. 3958	L/C. Jennings C.F.	ditto	N.
S. 3614	Rfn. Jackson T.	ditto	N.
P. 4016	Rfn. Jago H.A.	ditto	N.
5316	Rfn. Jay H.	ditto	N.
S. 6882	Rfn. Knight F.J.	ditto	N.
S. 10190	Rfn. King T.	ditto	N.
B. 203317	L/C. Lane A.	ditto	N.
S. 18379	Rfn. Lilley F.	ditto	N.
S. 4812	A/C. Loader A.E.	ditto	N.
6050	Rfn. Llewellyn A.	ditto	N.
S. 19709	Rfn. Mortlock E.	ditto	N.

Continued.

Sheet 2. Casualties. 13th (S) Rifle Brigade.

S. 4512	Rfn.	Millbank	J.	Wounded in Action 23.4.17.	N.
P. 1054	Rfn.	Murphy	J.	ditto	N.
P. 137	Rfn.	Mallett	W.	ditto	N.
P. 4008	Rfn.	Mitchell	W.	ditto	N.
S. 4820	Rfn.	Neal	A.G.	ditto	N.
374112	Rfn.	Newman	R.H.	ditto	N.
S. 28639	Rfn.	Olive	G.H.	ditto	N.
S. 15934	A/C.	O'Donnell	J.	ditto	N.
S. 4087	A/S.	Oakes	T.	ditto	N.
374200	Rfn.	Pollicutt	I.J.	ditto	N.
S. 30979	Rfn.	Pearce	H.	ditto	N.
S. 30981	Rfn.	Plaice	W.	ditto	N.
373771	Rfn.	Palloster	J.	ditto	N.
B. 203226	Rfn.	Phillips	G.	ditto	N.
S. 3730	L/C.	Phillips	J.	ditto	N.
S. 20956	Rfn.	Price	A.	ditto	N.
S. 19865	Rfn.	Pyner	E.	ditto	N.
S. 22445	Rfn.	Richards	S.	ditto	N.
373505	Rfn.	Reid	W.	ditto	N.
S. 30882	Rfn.	Rayment	G.	ditto	N.
S. 30983	Rfn.	Roberts	G.	ditto	N.
S. 19694	Rfn.	Ridley	G.	ditto	N.
S. 21861	Rfn.	Spooner	G.	ditto	N.
S. 30842	Rfn.	Shears	A.	ditto	N.
S. 30802	Rfn.	Sawkins	A.	ditto	N.
S. 30787	Rfn.	Stocker	A.	ditto	N.
B. 203303	L/C.	Stott	J.	ditto	N.
B. 203301	Rfn.	Sprowell	W.	ditto	N.
B. 203300	Rfn.	Sanders	P.	ditto	N.
B. 203238	Rfn.	Sykes	B.	ditto	N.
B. 203236	Rfn.	Scott	W.	ditto	N.
S. 20612	Rfn.	Smith	W.	ditto	N.
S. 21915	Rfn.	Scott	F.	ditto	N.
S. 28650	Rfn.	Simcock	F.	ditto	N.
S. 24298	Rfn.	Smith	T.E.	ditto	N.
S. 17212	Rfn.	Sargent	G.E.	ditto	N.
S. 3749	L/C.	Sherwin	A.H.	ditto	N.
S. 4425	Rfn.	Styles	A.	ditto	N.
Z. 2719	CSM.	Tarlton	F.	ditto	N.
S. 20678	Rfn.	Tibbles	E.	ditto	N.
S. 15552	Rfn.	Thompson	W.	ditto	N.
S. 15936	Rfn.	Tucker	E.	ditto	N.
S. 27118	Rfn.	Veitch	J.	ditto	N.
374252	Rfn.	West	L.	ditto	N.
S. 30777	Rfn.	Watts	E.	ditto	N.
S. 30752	Rfn.	Walpole	B.	ditto	N.
B. 203255	Rfn.	Walker	C.	ditto	N.
S. 28872	Rfn.	Whelan	J.	ditto	N.
S. 21531	Rfn.	Willis	W.	ditto	N.
S. 22426	Rfn.	Walke	J.	ditto	N.
S. 6743	A/C.	Wisdom	H.	ditto	N.
P. 605	Rfn.	Winter	R.C.	ditto	N.
S. 4303	L/C.	Wyatt	W.	ditto	N.
P. 648	Rfn.	Whitbread	C.	ditto	N.
S. 15940	Rfn.	Algar	S.	Wounded in Action 24.4.1917.	N.
6284	Rfn.	Bennett	J.W.	ditto	N.
P. 4180	Rfn.	Cody	P.	ditto	N.
B. 203191	Rfn.	Draper	A.	ditto	N.
S. 30033	Rfn.	Farmer	T.	ditto	N.
S. 4024	Rfn.	Hamilton	J.W.	ditto	N.
S. 27095	Rfn.	Hislop	F.W.	ditto	N.
S. 15543	Rfn.	Kinsey	W.	ditto	N.
S. 6739	Rfn.	Jennings	J.R.	ditto	N.
S. 15606	Rfn.	Leu	J.	ditto	N.
S. 29746	Rfn.	Munton	H.	ditto	N.
S. 24040	Rfn.	Nicholls	J.H.	ditto	N.
S. 16181	Rfn.	Pilgrim	A.L.	ditto	N.
S. 21221	Rfn.	Shelter	A.	ditto	N.
S. 19083	Rfn.	Taylor	T.	ditto	N.
Z. 2743	Rfn.	Travis	A.	ditto	N.

Continued.

13th (Service) Battalion The Rifle Brigade.

WINCHESTER RECORD OFFICE. DAILY CASUALTY LIST D/- 2.5.1917.

Regt.No.	Rank and Name.	Casualty.		PR.
P. 4058	Rfn. Boddy E.	MISSING. 11.4.1917.	"D" Coy.	N.
S. 21978	Rfn. Coventry G.	ditto	"B"	N.
S. 3416	Rfn. Duffy B.	ditto	"B"	N.
S. 24975	Rfn. Earler G.	ditto	"A"	N.
S. 23451	Rfn. Edwards E.	ditto	"A"	N.
S. 28614	Rfn. Fletcher W.	ditto	"C"	N.
6460	L/C. Forster G.R.	ditto	"A"	N.
B. 203218	Rfn. Jackson F.J.	ditto	"A"	N.
S. 16206	Rfn. Langrish T.	ditto	"D"	N.
S. 21920	Rfn. Methven W.	ditto	"B"	N.
P. 558	Rfn. McAuliffe M.	ditto	"A"	N.
S. 27114	Rfn. Still H.J.	ditto	"A"	N.
S. 15074	Rfn. Shapley C.	ditto	"C"	N.
S. 16672	Rfn. Stacey W.	ditto	"B"	N.
Z. 1489	Rfn. Stevens R.	ditto	"C"	N.
S. 27469	Rfn. Turnbull W.	ditto	"B"	N.
S. 3227	Rfn. Thomas D.	ditto	"B"	N.
S. 7354	Rfn. Thornley J.	ditto	"B"	N.
S. 21734	Rfn. Wick H.	ditto	"D"	N.
S. 20679	Rfn. Winnett W.	ditto	"A"	N.
S. 15422	Rfn. Wall J.	ditto	"C"	N.
S. 15837	Rfn. Webster S.T.	ditto		N.

The above Casualties were reported by The Officer Commanding 13th (S) Bn. The Rifle Brigade, on A.F.B.213 dated 13.4.1917.

| S. 27518 | Rfn. Coles W. | Wounded in Action 23.4.1917. Reported by O.C.Bn. 24.4.17. | N. |
| S. 4235 | A/CSM. Humphrey E. | Died of Wounds, received in action 28.4.17. Reported by O.C. 48th Field Ambulance, on memo dated 29.4.1917. | N. |

Verified.
ORS.

Capt
Lieut. for Major.
2.5.1917. Officer i/c Regular Infantry Section No.2.

13th (Service) Battn. The Rifle Brigade.

WINCHESTER RECORD OFFICE. DAILY CASUALTY LIST D/- 3.5.1917.

2ND. LIEUT. BAGNALL, G.B.   KILLED IN ACTION 23.4.1917.   N.
2ND. LIEUT. RAE, A.I.   KILLED IN ACTION 24.4.1917.   N.
2ND. LIEUT. SPANTON, J.W.   WOUNDED IN ACTION 25.4.1917. N.

The above casualties were reported by The Officer Commanding 13th (S) Bn. The Rifle Brigade on memo dated 28.4.17.

Verified.
ORS.

Capt. for Major.
Officer i/c Regular Infantry Section No.2.

3.5.17.

13th (Service) Battn. The Rifle Brigade.

WINCHESTER RECORD OFFICE. DAILY CASUALTY LIST D/- 3.5.17.

Regt.No.	Rank & Name.	Casualty.		PR.
Z. 2800	L/C. Huxley S.	Wounded in Action	27.4.1917.	N.
B.2033D2	Rfn. Smith H.	do	27.4.1917.	N.
4588	L/C. Steward H.	do	25.4.1917.	N.
S. 29831	Rfn. Ind J.	do	25.4.1917.	N.
S. 3751	Sgt. Wheeler J.	do	26.4.1917.	N.
S. 4795	L/S. Bennett J.	do	26.4.1917.	N.
7286	A/Cpl. Stickley H.	do	26.4.1917.	N.
B.203290	Rfn. McCormack T.	do	25.4.1917.	N.
S. 4837	Rfn. Collins J.	do	25.41917.	N.
S.21977	Rfn. Drayton N.	do	26.4.1917.	N.
Z. 515	Rfn. Dandy R.	do	26.4.1917.	N.
374254	Rfn. Elsey W.	do	25.4.1917.	N.

The above Casualties were reported by The Officer Commanding 13th (S) Bn. The Rifle Brigade on memo dated 28.4.1917.

Verified.
ORS.

Capt. for Major.
3.5.1917.   Officer i/c Regular Infantry Section No.2.

13th (Service) Battn. The Ri[fle Brigade]

WINCHESTER RECORD OFFICE. DAILY CASUALTY LIST D/- 4.5.17.

Regt.No.	Rank & Name.	Casualty.	PR.
S. 23591	Rfn. Elwood H.	*Amended* / *Now reptd* Killed in Action 11.4.1917. Reported by O.C.Bn. on A.F.B.213 dated 28.4.1917.	Cancel PR of "W" to W.O. 22/4/17
S. 3213	Rfn. Cutts W.	Died of Wounds, received in action 26.4.1917. Reported by O.C. 19 C.C.S. "N" on A.F.A.36 dated 30.4.17. E.D.3680.	
S. 25574	L/C. Cozens A.	Died of Wounds, received in action 28.4.1917. Reported by O.C. 19 C.C.S. "N" on A.F.A.36 dated 30.4.17. E.D. 3680.	
S. 27453	Rfn. Taylor A.	Died of Wounds, received in action 29.4.1917. Reported by O.C. 41 C.C.S. "N" 30.4.1917.	
P. 1645	L/C. Meekings H.F.	Died of Wounds, received in action 30.4.1917. Reported by O.C. 41 C.C.S. "N" 30.4.1917.	

Verified.
ORS.

Capt. for. Major.
4.5.17.   Officer i/c Regular Infantry Section No.2.

13th (Service) Battn. The Rifle Brigade.

WINCHESTER RECORD OFFICE. DAILY CASUALTY LIST D/- 5.5.1917.

Regt.No.	Rank and Name.	Casualty.	BR
P. 648	Rfn. Whitbread C.	Died of Wounds, received in action 2.5.17. Reported by O.C. No. 13 Stationary Hospital on A.F.W.3034 dated 2.5.17.	"W"

Verified.
ORS.

Lieut. for Major.
Officer i/c Regular Infantry Section No.2.

5.5.17.

13th (Service) Battalion The Rifle Brigade.

WINCHESTER RECORD OFFICE. DAILY CASUALTY LIST D/- 6.5.1917.

2ND. LIEUT. L.S.CHAMBERLEN.   WOUNDED IN ACTION 13.4.1917.   N.
                                Reported by O.C.Battalion
                                2.5.1917.

                    Verified.
                              ORS.

                                        Capt. for Major.
6.5.17.   Officer i/c Regular Infantry Section No.2.

13th (Service) Battn. The Rifle Brigade.

WINCHESTER RECORD OFFICE. DAILY CASUALTY LIST D/- 6.5.17.

Regt.No.	Rank and Name.	Casualty.	PR.
S.10891	Rfn. Greenfield S.B.	Died of Wounds, received in action 2.5.1917. Reported by O.C. 13 Gen.Hspl. 3.5.17.	"W"

Verified.
ORS.

6.5.17.

Capt. for Major.
Officer i/c Regular Infantry Section No.2.

13th (Service) Battalion The Rifle Brigade.

WINCHESTER RECORD OFFICE. DAILY CASUALTY LIST D/- 6.5.17.

Regt.No.	Rank and Name.	Casualty.	PR.
S. 27390	Rfn. Bennett J.	Wounded in Action 28.4.1917.	N.
S. 30776	Rfn. Braybrook A.	Wounded in Action 27.4.1917.	N.
Z. 2969	A/C. Brill J.L.	Wounded in Action 28.4.1917.	N.
S. 30800	Rfn. Chaplin J.	Wounded in Action 28.4.1917.	N.
B. 203252	Cpl. Champion N.	Wounded in Action 28.4.1917.	N.
S. 19587	L/C. Cox C.	Wounded in Action 28.4.1917.	N.
S. 4378	Rfn. Dawson G.F.	Wounded in Action 28.4.1917.	N.
S. 30846	Rfn. Field C.	Wounded in Action 27.4.1917.	N.
S. 30512	Rfn. Foot J.	Wounded in Action 28.4.1917.	N.
D. 30774	Rfn. Harris E.	Wounded in Action 28.4.1917.	N.
B. 203625	Rfn. Harris W.J.A.	Wounded in Action 28.4.1917.	N.
Z. 2447	Rfn. Hill J.	Wounded in Action 23.4.1917.	N.
S. 30866	Rfn. Jane A.	Wounded in Action 28.4.1917.	N.
S. 3996	L/C. Jackson H.	Wounded in Action 28.4.1917.	N.
S. 30792	Rfn. Kenefick H.	Wounded in Action 27.4.1917.	N.
370119	Rfn. Lawrence G.F.	Wounded in Action 28.4.1917.	N.
S. 27466	Rfn. Lougher D.T.	Wounded in Action 28.4.1917.	N.
P. 1559	L/C. Marshall J.H.	Wounded in Action 28.4.1917.	N.
S. 3937	CSM. Oliver F.J.	Wounded in Action 28.4.1917.	N.
S. 28642	Rfn. Read J.	Wounded in Action 28.4.1917.	N.
S. 30494	Rfn. Ruffles G.	Wounded in Action 28.4.1917.	N.
S. 14529	L/S. Robbins F.	Wounded in Action 28.4.1917.	N.
S. 3851	Rfn. West D.	Wounded in Action 28.4.1917.	N.
S. 6224	L/C. White L.A.	Wounded in Action 27.4.1917.	N.

The above Casualties were reported by Officer Commanding, 13th (S) Bn. Rifle Brigade on memo dated 29.4.1917.

| P. 704 | Rfn. Carnell E. | Killed in Action 23.4.1917. | N. |
| S. 16766 | Rfn. Gibbs E.W. | Wounded in Action 30.4.17. | N. |

The above Casualties were reported by Officer Commanding, 13th (S) Bn. Rifle Brigade on memo dated 2.5.1917.

| S. 2851 | Rfn. Thomas T. | Died of Wounds, received in action 1.5.17. Reported by O.C. 8 Casualty Clearing Station, 2.5.1917. | N. |

Verified.
ORS.

Lieut. for Major.
6.5.17. Officer i/c Regular Infantry Section No.2.

13th (Service) Battalion The Rifle Brigade.

WINCHESTER RECORD OFFICE. DAILY CASUALTY LIST D/- 7.5.1917.

Regt.No.	Rank and Name.	Casualty.		PR.
P. 4148	Rfn. Allison A.	Killed in Action	28.4.1917.	N.
S. 4452	Rfn. Bell F.H.	-do-	23.4.1917.	N.
S. 20501	Rfn. Booker E.	-do-	28.4.1917.	N.
S. 30860	Rfn. Battersby G.	-do-	27.4.1917.	N.
S. 13413	Rfn. Brown C.	-do-	28.4.1917.	N.
S. 27447	Rfn. Craske L.D.	-do-	28.4.1917.	N.
S. 17205	Rfn. Dix A.J.	-do-	23.4.1917.	N.
S. 28613	Rfn. Evans W.H.	-do-	27.4.1917.	N.
S. 3247	Rfn. Edwards W.	-do-	23.4.1917.	N.
S. 30863	Rfn. Gascoyne R.	-do-	28.4.1917.	N.
S. 3671	A/S. Hunt G.	-do-	23.4.1917.	N.
B. 203217	Rfn. Ingram P.	-do-	23.4.1917.	N.
S. 14901	Rfn. Jackson H.	-do-	28.4.1917.	N.
S. 4278	A/C. Knowles G.E.	-do-	28.4.1917.	N.
S. 15568	L/C. Lockwood H.	-do-	28.4.1917.	N.
B. 203256	A/C. Lee S.	-do-	28.4.1917.	N.
S. 3792	Rfn. Merrin T.S.	-do-	28.4.1917.	N.
S. 22294	Rfn. Musselwhite W.	-do-	29.4.1917.	N.
S. 30781	Rfn. Mayston W.	-do-	28.4.1917.	N.
S. 4336	Rfn. Springett W.	-do-	23.4.1917.	N.
S. 2349	Rfn. Smith W.J.C.	-do-	28.4.1917.	N.
S. 17254	Rfn. Sanders A.E.	-do-	23.4.1917.	N.
S. 18110	Rfn. Shillingford W.	-do-	23.4.1917.	N.
B. 203341	Rfn. Tucker F.	-do-	23.4.1917.	N.
P. 306	Rfn. Trustam W.	-do-	29.4.1917.	N.
S. 15584	Rfn. Webberley P.	-do-	23.4.1917.	N.
S. 30753	Rfn. Winter W.	-do-	23.4.1917.	N.
P. 1385	Rf. Walker H.	-do-	23.4.1917.	N.
B. 203171	Rfn. Arnold W.	Wounded in Action	29.4.1917.	N.
P. 828	Rfn. Baldock A.	-do-	23.4.1917.	N.
S. 22290	L/C. Brown E.	-do-	29.4.1917.	N.
P. 4250	Rfn. Couzens P.A.	-do-	23.4.1917.	N.
S. 3767	Rfn. Croxford J.	-do-	23.4.1917.	N.
B. 203188	Rfn. Carne T.	-do-	23.4.1917.	N.
S. 2165	Rfn. Callaghan W.	-do-	23.4.1917.	N.
S. 28629	Rfn. Driver J.W.	-do-	23.4.1917.	N.
S. 21669	Rfn. Ford W.C.	-do-	28.4.1917.	N.
B. 203201	Rfn. Gray J.	-do-	23.4.1917.	N.
S. 13877	Rfn. Gordon J.M.	-do-	28.4.1917.	N.
S. 29986	Rfn. Godfrey J.	-do-	29.4.1917.	N.
S. 3971	A/S. Hills W.	-do-	23.4.1917.	N.
S. 18749	Rfn. Handford J.	-do-	23.4.1917.	N.
B. 203101	Rfn. Jenden E.	-do-	29.4.1917.	N.
Z. 2782	A/C. Long F.E.	-do-	29.4.1917.	N.
6445	Rfn. Lovelock W.S.	-do-	23.4.1917.	N.
S. 3249	Rfn. Morgan A.	-do-	23.4.1917.	N.
S. 9296	Rfn. Murkin F.E.	-do-	29.4.1917.	N.
B. 203629	Rfn. Macfarlane J.H.	-do-	23.4.1917.	N.
S. 30978	Rfn. Oliver W.	-do-	28.4.1917.	N.
9888	Rfn. Potter W.	-do-	23.4.1917.	N.
S. 21779	Rfn. Rouse A.	-do-	28.4.1917.	N.
S. 29949	Rfn. Richards G.	-do-	23.4.1917.	N.
S. 19920	Rfn. Simmons H.	-do-	28.4.1917.	N.
B. 203623	Rfn. Tollett G.A.	-do-	23.4.1917.	N.
S. 19936	Rfn. Underwood F.	-do-	23.4.1917.	N.
S. 30139	Rfn. Webb C.	-do-	23.4.1917.	N.

The above Casualties were reported by O.C.Battn. 1.5.1917.

Capt. for Major.
Officer i/c Reg.Infantry Sect.No.2.

13th (Servi.B)., The Rifle Brigade. Brigade.

WINCHESTER RECORD OFFICE. DAILY CASUALTY LIST D/- 8.5.17.

Regt.No.	Rank & Name.	Casualty	PR.
Z. 2781	Rfn. Cox C.J.	Died of Wounds, received in action 30.4.1917. Reported on A.F.A.36, E.D.3680, by O.C. 19 C.C.S. dated 30.5.1917.	N.
S. 4812	A/C. Loader A.E.	Died of Wounds, received in action 2.5.17. Reported by O.C. No.3 Can.G.H. on memo dated 3.5.17.	"W"
P. 4236	L/C. Drew H.S.	Died of Wounds, received in action 3.5.1917. Reported by O.C. 20.G.H. on memo dated 3.5.1917.	"W"
S.24302	Rfn. Stephens C.J.	Wounded in Action 24.4.1917. Reported by O.C. 48th F.A. on A.F.A.36 E.D.3639 dated 25.4.1917.	"W"

Verified.
ORS.

Capt. for Major.
8.5.17.   Officer i/c Regular Infantry Section No.2.

13th Battalion　　　　　Brigade.

WINCHESTER RECORD OFFICE DAILY CASUALTY LIST D/ 9-5-17.

Regtl No.	Rank & Name.	CASUALTY.	P.R.
S/ 21878	Rfn. Edwards, F.J.	DIED OF WOUNDS. 29-4-17.	W.

Reported by O.C. 26th General Hospital.
W 3034 dated 29-4-17.

V E R I F I E D.

O.R.S.

Capt for Major.
Officer I/C Regular Infantry Section No. 2.

G.H.Qrs
3rd Echelon.
9-5-17

13th. (S)   The Rifle B

WINCHESTER RECORD OFFICE DAILY CASUALTY LIST D/- 13-5-17.

2nd. Lieut. W.E.HOBDAY.   Wounded & Missing 11-4-17.   W in A.
                       Reported by O.C.Battn. on memo
                       dated 8-5-17.

                Verified.
                   ORS.

                                       Capt. for Major.
13-5-17.   Officer i/c Regular Infantry Section No.2.

13th. (S) Bn. The Rifle Brigade.

WINCHESTER RECORD OFFICE. DAILY CASUALTY LIST D/- 13-5-17.

Regt.No.	Rank and Name.	Casualty.		PR.	Coy
S.16672	Rfn. Stacey W.	~~Amended~~ Now reptd Rejoined for duty 11-4-17.		Prevly reptd Missing.	15 W.O. 4/5/17
S.23345	Rfn. Claridge G.	Wounded & Missing 11-4-17.		W in Act.	B
B203283	Rfn. Jewell F.W.	ditto		" "	A
S.27430	Rfn. Medlock H.	ditto		" "	A
B203286	Rfn. Moreton F.N.	ditto		" "	B
S. 3885	Rfn. Price C.H.	ditto		" "	D
S.21408	Rfn. Richardson S.	ditto		" "	B
S.21953	Rfn. Shirley H.	ditto		" "	D
B203312	Rfn. Williams J.	ditto	9-4-17	" "	D
B203248	Rfn. Whiteley S.	ditto	11-4-17	" "	B

The above Casualties were reported by The Officer Commanding 13th. Bn. Rifle Brigade on memo dated 8-5-17.

Verified.
ORS

13-5-17.

Capt. for Major.
Officer i/c Regular Infantry Section No.2.

13th. (S) Bn. The Rifle Brigade.

WINCHESTER RECORD OFFICE DAILY CASUALTY LIST D/- 13.5.17.

374112 Rfn. Newman R.H.   Died of Wounds, received in action
                            25-4-17. Reported by O.C. No.1
                            Casualty Clearing Station 25-4-17.

                    Verified.
                            ORS.

                                    Capt. for Major.
13-5-17.   Officer I/C Regular Infantry Section No2.

X. As phoned 15/5/17

13th (Service) Battalion The Rifle Brigade.

WINCHESTER RECORD OFFICE. DAILY CASUALTY LIST D/- 16.5.17.

CAPTAIN (T/MAJOR) JACKSON. A.N.S.   Reported Wounded (At Duty) 24.4.17. Admitted to Hospital 3.5.17.

P.R.

Reported on A.G's. List No. 979 dated 8.5.1917.

Wounded, at duty 24.4.17.

to W.O. 3/5/17.

Verified.

ORS.

Lieut. for Major.

16.5.17.   Officer i/c Regular Infantry Section No.2.

13th (Service) Battalion The Rifle Brigade.

WINCHESTER RECORD OFFICE. DAILY CASUALTY LIST D/- 17.5.1917.

2ND LIEUT. F.C.HALL.   WOUNDED IN ACTION 21.4.1917.   Wounded PR. (Acc)
Reported by O.C.Battalion on   to W.I. 2/5/17.
A.F.B.213 dated 11.5.1917.

Cancel report of "accidental"

Verified.
ORS.

Lieut. for Major.
Officer i/c Regular Infantry Section No.2.

17.5.17.

13th (Service) Battalion The Rifle Brigade.

WINCHESTER RECORD OFFICE. DAILY CASUALTY LIST D/- 17.5.1917.

Regt.No.	Rank and Name.	Casualty.	PR.
P. 558	Rfn. McAuliffe M.	Killed in Action 11.4.1917.	"Missing"
S. 21734	Rfn. Wick H.	Killed in Action 11.4.1917.	"Missing"
S. 30978	Rfn. Oliver W.	Amended report. Admitted Hospital (Sick) 28.4.1917.	Cancel "W in A" IBW.O. 9/5/17

The above Casualties were reported by The Officer Commanding, 13th (S) Bn. Rifle Brigade on A.F.B.213 dated 11.5.1917.

Verified.
ORS.

Lieut. for Major.
Officer i/c Regular Infantry Section No.2.

17.5.1917.

13th (Service) Battn. The Rifle Brigade.

WINCHESTER RECORD OFFICE. DAILY CASUALTY LIST 17.5.17.

Regt.No.	Rank and Name.	Casualty.	PR.
S. 28613	*Amended* Rfn. Evans W.H.	Reported Killed in Action 27.4.17. in Cas List to W.O. d/- 9.5.17. please read Wounded in Action 27.4.17. Reported by O.C.Bn. 13.5.1917.	K in A.
	Amended		
S. 21669	Rfn. Ford W.	Killed in Action. 28.4.1917.	Cancel "W" "W"
B. 203629	Rfn. Macfarlane J.	Killed in Action. 23.4.1917.	" "W"
S. 30870	Rfn. Bailey H.	Killed in Action. 27.4.1917.	"N"
S. 27123	Rfn. Dove H.	Killed in Action. 23.4.1917.	"N"

Above Casualties were reported by The Officer Commanding 13th (S) Bn. Rifle Brigade on memo dated 13.5.1917.

Verified.
ORS.

17.5.17. Officer i/c Regular Infantry Section No.2.
Lieut. for Major.

13th (Service) Battalion The Rifle Brigade.

WINCHESTER RECORD OFFICE. DAILY CASUALTY LIST D/- 23.5.1917.

Regt.No.	Rank and Name.	Casualty.	PR.
S. 433	Rfn. Powers G.	Killed in Action. 23.4.1917.	Nil.
S. 1159	Rfn. Doswell H.	Wounded & Missing 11.4.1917.	"W"

"C" Coy.

Reported by O.C.Battn. 18.5.17.

S. 7768	L/C. Bennett W.	MISSING. 28.4.1917. "C" Coy.	Nil.
S. 16194	Rfn. Bear E.G.	MISSING. 23.4.1917. "A" Coy.	Nil.
S. 4435	L/S. Crees F.A.	MISSING. 28.4.1917. "C" Coy.	Nil.
S. 3229	A/C. Griffith J.	MISSING. 28.4.1917. "C" Coy.	Nil.
S. 27345	Sgt. Moss J.	MISSING. 28.4.1917. "C" Coy.	Nil.
S. 17226	Rfn. Pearce E.W.	MISSING. 28.4.1917. "C" Coy.	Nil.
S. 25145	Rfn. Robbins W.J.	MISSING. 23.4.1917. "A" Coy.	Nil.
S. 30834	Rfn. Scott D.	MISSING. 28.4.1917. "C" Coy.	Nil.
S. 4483	Rfn. Smith H.	MISSING. 28.4.1917. "C" Coy.	Nil.
S. 9140	L/C. Scothern H.	MISSING. 28.4.1917. "C" Coy.	Nil.
S. 15537	Rfn. Smith J.	MISSING. 28.4.1917. "B" Coy.	Nil.
S. 2407	Rfn. Squires A.	MISSING. 28.4.1917. "C" Coy.	Nil.
S. 30988	Rfn. Tesseyman J.	MISSING. 28.4.1917. "B" Coy.	Nil.
S. 30839	Rfn. Verlander H.	MISSING. 28.4.1917. "B" Coy.	Nil.

Reported by O.C.Battalion on A.F.B.213 dated 4.5.1917.

Verified. ORS.

Capt. for Major.

23.5.17. Officer i/c Regular Infantry Section No.2.

13th (Service) Battalion The Rifle Brigade.

WINCHESTER RECORD OFFICE. DAILY CASUALTY LIST D/- 24.5.1917.

Regt. No.	Rank and Name.	Coy.	Casualty.		pH.
S. 2165	Rfn. Callaghan W.	"A"	Wounded & Missing	23.4.17.	"W"
S. 3767	Rfn. Croxford J.	"A"	-ditto-	23.4.17.	"W"
S. 28629	Rfn. Driver J.W.	"B"	-ditto-	23.4.17.	"W"
S. 28613	Rfn. Evans W.H.	"A"	-ditto-	27.4.17.	"W"
B. 203201	Rfn. Gray J.	"B"	-ditto-	23.4.17.	"W"
S. 3971	A/S. Hills W.	"B"	-ditto-	23.4.17.	"W"
6445	Rfn. Lovelock W.S.	"A"	-ditto-	23.4.17.	"W"
S. 3249	Rfn. Morgan A.	"B"	-ditto-	23.4.17.	"W"
B. 203623	Rfn. Tollett G.A.	"A"	-ditto-	23.4.17.	"W"
S. 30139	Rfn. Webb C.	"B"	-ditto-	23.4.17.	"W"

The above casualties were reported by O.C. Battalion on memo dated 21.5.17.

Verified.
ORS.

Lieut. for Major.
24.5.17. Officer i/c Regular Infantry Section No. 2.

13th (Service) Battalion The Rifle Brigade.

WINCHESTER RECORD OFFICE. DAILY CASUALTY LIST D/- 26.5.17.

Regt.No.	Rank and Name.	Casualty.	PR.
S. 25145	Rfn. Robbins W.J.	Killed in Action 23.4.1917. Reported by O.C. 189 Machine Gun Company. 19.5.1917.	"Missing"

Verified.
ORS.

Lieut. for Major.
Officer i/c Reg. Infantry Section No.2.

26.5.1917.

13th (Ser) Battn. The Rifle Brigade.

Winchester Record office daily casualty dated 31.5.17.

Amended Report.

Reference Daily Casualty List to War Office dated 25.5.1917.

For S.3229 A/C. Griffith J. MISSING 28.4.17. "C" Coy
please read S.3229 A/C. JONES. G. MISSING 28.4.17. "C" Coy.

G.H.Q.
3rd Ech.
31.5.17.   Officer i/c Regular Infantry Section No.2.   Lieut. for Major.

11th Inf Brigade.

Secret
R.W.B/97/13.

With regard to last night's operations I beg to report as follows:-

1. From dusk to about 11-15pm the enemy's artillery activity was about the same as usual, from 11-15pm onwards, his rate of fire increased and it was directed on to our front and support trenches.

2. At 11-20pm the party which was to form the 1st line left the sap at OBC80.25 and lay down in front of the trench with their left on SADDLE LANE.

3. At ZERO the 1st line under 2nd Lt F.B. JOHNSON advanced, followed 50 yds in rear by the 2nd line consisting of 2 Lewis gun teams, which was followed in its turn by the 3rd line under 2nd Lt H.D. JACKSON 100 yds in rear. The strength of the 1st and 3rd lines was about 20 O.R.

4. The first line had not gone more than about 50 yds, when they were fired on by machine guns, and the enemy's artillery put up a heavy barrage on to TOOL TRENCH.

The first line reached a point about
50 yards from the objective, there, owing to
casualties, it was held up.
Both Lewis gun detachments were knocked
out, one gun is missing, the other was
brought back damaged.
The 3rd line also suffered rather severely.
2nd Lt. JOHNSON was either killed or wounded
and is missing.
2nd Lt. JACKSON was wounded.

5. I attribute the failure of the attack to
reasons.
(1) It was apparently anticipated by the enemy
(2) M.G. which escaped our artillery
barrage.
(3) Loss of both officers, and too heavy
casualties in O.R. to push the attack
home.

6. M.G.s were said to be firing from south
corner of B. du VERT, and from some pt
west of LANYARD TRENCH and south of
SADDLE LANE
                                            which
about 25% of the casualties that have
been seen so far, were caused by bullets.

7. Up to the time of writing them report
the total number of casualties has not

as yet been ascertained. Estimated
casualties [illegible]
1 Officer killed 1/Lt. F.B. JOHNSON
1 " wounded 2/Lt. H.M. JACKSON
53 O.R. killed and wounded.

8. I visited the front line at 4AM
this morning, it had been much knocked
about during the night, but the men were
at work digging out places which had
been blown in. It was possible to
walk along the whole front line.

I have the honor to be
Sir
Your obedient servant
W R Stewart
Lt Col
Comnd 13th Batt R Irish Rif

31/5/17

WAR DIARY
or
INTELLIGENCE SUMMARY.

(Erase heading not required.)

Army Form C. 2118.

Place	Date	Hour	Summary of Events and Information	Remarks and references to Appendices

Confidential

War Diary

of

13th Bn. The Rifle Brigade.

From June 1st 1917
To June 30th 1917.

(Volume 21)

WAR DIARY
or
INTELLIGENCE SUMMARY.
(Erase heading not required.)

Army Form C. 2118.

Instructions regarding War Diaries and Intelligence Summaries are contained in F.S. Regs., Part II. and the Staff Manual respectively. Title pages will be prepared in manuscript.

ORDERLY ROOM
Date JUNE 1917
13th BATT. RIFLE BRIGADE

Place	Date	Hour	Summary of Events and Information	Remarks and references to Appendices
MONCHY-LE-PREUX	1/6/17		The Battalion in the trenches 2000 yds. S. of MONCHY-LE-PREUX. Enemy artillery very active on our front line causing 6 casualties.	
"	2/6/17		The Battalion was relieved by the 1/4th Berkshire Regt. of the 51st Division and proceeded to billets at SCHRAMM BARRACKS in ARRAS. At 5 pm. the Battn. were conveyed in busses to BERLENCOURT.	
BERLEN-COURT.	3-5/6/17.		The Battalion remained in billets. General inspection of all clothing - stores - and refitting was carried out.	
"	6/6/17		The Battalion was conveyed in buses to SACHIN and billeted for the night.	
SACHIN	7/6/17		The Battalion marched to ERNY-ST-JULIEN and billeted for the night. Route via FLECHIN.	
ERNY-ST-JULIEN.	8-22/6/17.		The Battalion remained at ERNY-ST-JULIEN. Division was un-attached at this time. General Training and Specialist training carried out. Battn. held its sports on the afternoon of the 20th and some very excellent running was seen. On the afternoon of the 22nd a presentation of medal ribbons by the First Army Commander, Gen.Sir H.S.Horne, K.C.B. was held at FRUGES. The following were recipients of ribbons:- Major A.N.S.Jackson. D.S.O. & Bar. " O.B.Graham D.S.O. 2nd Lt. M.Smith. M.C. S/4075 Sgt. Bailey H. D.C.M. S/1161 " Curtis J. M.M. S/4600 L/Sgt.Louden A. " S/27090 Cpl. Goodman W. " S/8955 " Roff S. " S/3716 " O'Connor M. " Z/2737 L/Cpl. Brooker F. " S/3996 " Jackson H. " B/203251 Rfn.Worrilow S. M.M. S/3804 " Davies W. " S/4772 " Eastment C. " Z/2742 Sgt.Streeton H. "	
"	23/6/17		The Battn. marched to GUARBECQUE via LAMBRES - MOLINGHEM and billeted for the night.	

Army Form C. 2118.

WAR DIARY
or
INTELLIGENCE SUMMARY.
(Erase heading not required.)

Instructions regarding War Diaries and Intelligence Summaries are contained in F. S. Regs., Part II. and the Staff Manual respectively. Title pages will be prepared in manuscript.

Place	Date	Hour	Summary of Events and Information	Remarks and references to Appendices
GUARBECQUE	24th.		The Battalion marched to Camp near LA KREULE, 2 Kilos. N. of HAZEBROUCK. Route via METERIN - HAZEBROUCK. The Division had now been transferred to the Second Army.	
LA KREULE	25th.		The Battalion marched to Camp near LOCRE via METERIN - BAILLEUL. Division is now transferred to IX Corps, Second Army.	
LOCRE.	26th.–27th.		The Battalion remained in Camp. Inspection of Arms etc. under Coy. arrangements.	
"	28th.	6 pm.	The Battalion moved up to Support Trenches in LEFT SUB SECTOR on the forward slope of the WYTSCHAETE – MESSINES RIDGE.	
WYTSCHAETE	29th. 30th		Reconnaissances were made in view of pending minor operations. Work on the improvement of trenches and position.	

A.W. Shode Jackson
Major.
Commanding 13th Bn. The Rifle Bde.

13th (Service) Battalion The Rifle Brigade.

WINCHESTER RECORD OFFICE. DAILY CASUALTY LIST D/- 1.6.17.

Regt.No.	Rank and Name.	Casualty	PR.
S. 3249	Rfn. Morgan A.	Died of Wounds 23.4.1917.	"W & M"
S.16685	Rfn. Hooker C.T.	Wounded in Action 20.5.17.	Nil.

Reported by The Officer Commanding,
13th (S) Bn. The Rifle Brigade, on A.F.B.213
dated 25.5.1917.

Verified.
ORS.

Lieut. for Major.
Officer i/c Regular Infantry Section No.2.

1.6.17.

13th (Service) Battalion The Rifle Brigade.

WINCHESTER RECORD OFFICE. DAILY CASUALTY LIST D/- 6.6.17.

Rank and Name.	Casualty.	PR.
2ND. LIEUT. R.O. BASSHAM.	KILLED IN ACTION 31.5.1917.	Nil.
2ND. LIEUT. H.M. JACKSON.	WOUNDED IN ACTION 31.5.1917.	Nil.
2ND. LIEUT. F.B. JOHNSON.	MISSING. 31.5.1917.	Nil.

The above Casualties were reported by The Officer Commanding 13th (S) Bn. Rifle Brigade on memo dated 1.6.1917.

Verified.
ORS.

Lieut. for Major.
Officer i/c Regular Infantry Section No.2.

6.6.17.

13th (Service) Battalion The Rifle Brigade.

WINCHESTER RECORD OFFICE. DAILY CASUALTY LIST DATED 6.6.17.

Regt.No.	Rank and Name.	Casualty		PR.
B. 200790	Rfn. Geleit G.F.	Killed in Action	29.5.1917.	N.
574518	Rfn. Barchou B.J.	Killed in Action	31.5.1917.	N.
5534	L/S. Le Cras R.C.	Killed in Action	31.5.1917.	N.
P. 1062	Rfn. Page J.	Killed in Action	31.5.1917.	N.
S. 30965	Rfn. Ashford A.	Killed in Action	31.5.1917.	N.
S. 3405	Rfn. Jones C.E.	Killed in Action	1.6.1917.	N.
6050	Rfn. Llewellyn A.	Killed in Action	1.6.1917.	N.
304527	Rfn. Darvell H.S.	Wounded in Action	29.5.1917.	N.
S. 30001	Rfn. Powell S.	-ditto-	29.5.1917.	N.
574422	Rfn. Hubball W.	-ditto-	30.5.1917.	N.
B. 203174	Rfn. Beasley W.	-ditto-	30.5.1917.	N.
B. 200825	Rfn. Jane E.E.	-ditto-	31.5.1917.	N.
423708	Rfn. Hussey A.	-ditto-	31.5.1917.	N.
423704	Rfn. Job H.G.	-ditto-	31.5.1917.	N.
S. 30857	Rfn. Smallman C.	-ditto-	31.5.1917.	N.
S. 30833	Rfn. Richards H.	-ditto-	31.5.1917.	N.
S. 30852	Rfn. Swain H.	-ditto-	31.5.1917.	N.
S. 30787	Rfn. Stocker A.	-ditto-	31.5.1917.	N.
B. 203337	Rfn. Rose W.	-ditto-	31.5.1917.	N.
B. 200822	Rfn. Holtby E.W.	-ditto-	31.5.1917.	N.
374381	Rfn. Taylor G.J.A.	-ditto-	31.5.1917.	N.
B. 203277	Rfn. Gatehouse E.	-ditto-	31.5.1917.	N.
574719	Rfn. Harris F.W.J.	-ditto-	31.5.1917.	N.
574474	Rfn. Weston W.	-ditto-	31.5.1917.	N.
S. 5	Rfn. Schofield T.	-ditto-	30.5.1917.	N.
Z. 1812	Rfn. Griffin A.	-ditto-	31.5.1917.	N.
P. 1422	Rfn. Salter A.E.	-ditto-	31.5.1917.	N.
S. 3895	Rfn. Davey E.G.	-ditto-	31.5.1917.	N.
S. 4359	Rfn. Day G.T.	-ditto-	31.5.1917.	N.
P. 4093	Rfn. Moore J.D.	-ditto-	31.5.1917.	N.
P. 657	Rfn. Welch J.C.	-ditto-	31.5.1917.	N.
S. 16174	Rfn. Saltoun A.	-ditto-	30.5.1917.	N.
S. 9686	L/C. Fuller W.	-ditto-	31.5.1917.	N.
S. 15982	Rfn. Smith J.	-ditto-	31.5.1917.	N.
S. 19306	Rfn. Tilling C.G.	-ditto-	31.5.1917.	N.
S. 17212	Rfn. Sargent G.E.	-ditto-	31.5.1917.	N.
S. 19696	Rfn. Daniels A.	-ditto-	31.5.1917.	N.
S. 8990	Rfn. Foggerty J.	-ditto-	31.5.1917.	N.
S. 18038	Rfn. Simpson A.J.	-ditto-	31.5.1917.	N.
S. 14051	Rfn. Baker G.S.	-ditto-	31.5.1917.	N.
S. 18359	Rfn. Grimster J.	-ditto-	1.6.1917.	N.
S. 28612	Rfn. Ellis E.J.	-ditto-	31.5.1917.	N.
S. 20674	Rfn. Wiles A.	-ditto-	31.5.1917.	N.

Reported by O.6. Battn. 1.6.17

Verified.
ORS.

6.6.17.

Lieut. for Major.
Officer i/c Regular Infantry Section No.2.

) Battalion The Rifle B.
13th (Service) Battalion The Rifle Brigade.

Winchester Record Office. Daily Casualty List dated 9.6.17.

Regt.No.	Rank and Name.	Casualty.	PR.
S. 23468	Rfn. Dent R.	Wounded in Action 1.6.17.	Nil.
P. 4169	Rfn. White F.	ditto	Nil.

Reported by O.C. Battalion. 3.6.1917.

Verified.
ORS.

Lieut. for Major.
9.6.17.   Officer i/c Regular Infantry Section No.2.

13th (Service) Battalion The Rifle Brigade.

...ESTER RECORD OFFICE. DAILY CASUALTY LIST D/- 11.6.17.

Regt.No.	Rank & Name.	Casualty.	PR.
S. 15422	Rfn. Wall J.	Killed in Action 11.4.1917. Reported by O.C. 1st Bn. R.Dub. Fus. on Effects List No.2. dated 5.6.1917.	Missing.

Verified. ORS.

Capt. for Major.
Officer i/c Regular Infantry Section No.2.

11.6.17.

...th (Service) ...igade.

WINCHESTER RECORD OFFICE. DAILY CASUALTY LIST D/- 13.6.17.

Regt.No.	Rank and Name.	Casualty.	PR.
B.203248	Rfn. Whiteley S.	Killed in Action 11.4.17. Reported by O.C. 79th Brigade R.F.A. on memo dated 3.6.1917.	Missing.

Verified. ORS.

[signature] Capt. for Major.
Officer i/c Regular Infantry Section No.2.

13.6.17.

13th (Service) Battalion The Rifle Brigade.

WINCHESTER RECORD OFFICE. DAILY CASUALTY LIST DATED 19.6.1917.

Regt.No.	Rank and Name.		Coy.	Casualty.		PR.
S. 19696	Rfn. Daniels	A.	"C"	Wounded & Missing	31.5.17.	"W"
423708	Rfn. Hussey	A.	"C"	-ditto-	31.5.17.	"W"
423704	Rfn. Job	H.G.	"C"	-ditto-	31.5.17.	"W"
B.200825	Rfn. Jane	E.E.	"C"	-ditto-	31.5.17.	"W"
S. 30833	Rfn. Richards	H.	"C"	-ditto-	31.5.17.	"W"
S. 15982	Rfn. Smith	J.	"C"	-ditto-	31.5.17.	"W"
P. 1422	Rfn. Salter	A.E.	"C"	-ditto-	31.5.17.	"W"
S. 30852	Rfn. Swain	H.	"C"	-ditto-	31.5.17.	"W"
S. 17212	Rfn. Sargent	G.E.	"C"	-ditto-	31.5.17.	"W"
S. 30857	Rfn. Smallman	C.	"C"	-ditto-	31.5.17.	"W"
S. 20654	Rfn. Wiles	A.	"C"	-ditto-	31.5.17.	"W"

The above Casualties were reported by
The Officer Commanding 13th Rifle Brigade
on memo dated 16.6.1917.

Verified.
ORS.

Capt. for Major.
Officer i/c Regular Infantry Section No.2.

19.6.1917.

13th (Service) Battn. The Rifle Brigade.

WINCHESTER RECORD OFFICE. DAILY CASUALTY LIST DATED 20.6.1917.

Regt.No.	Rank and Name.	Coy.	Casualty.	PR.
Z. 2205	Rfn. Birch G.	"C"	MISSING 31.5.1917.	Nil.
B.200796	L/C. Butzbach A.S.	"C"	MISSING 30.5.1917.	Nil.
423686	Rfn. Crake S.G.	"C"	MISSING 1.6.1917.	Nil.
S. 24294	A/S. Crane P.	"C"	MISSING 31.5.1917.	Nil.
S. 6868	Rfn. Clarke H.	"C"	MISSING 31.5.1917.	Nil.
S. 6735	L/C. Field W.	"C"	MISSING 31.5.1917.	Nil.
S. 871	A/C. White S.	"C"	MISSING 31.5.1917.	Nil.
B.203313	L/S. Warner H.	"D"	MISSING 31.5.1917.	Nil.

The above Casualties were reported by O.C.Battalion 1.6.1917.

Verified.
ORS.

Capt. for Major.
Officer i/c Reg. Infantry Section No.2.

20.6.17.

13th. (Ser,   The RIFLE BRIGADE. Brig.

WINCHESTER RECORD OFFICE DAILY CASUALTY LIST DATED 21-6-1917.

Regt.No.	Rank and Name.	Casualty.	PR.
S. 9140	R/n. Soothern H.	Killed in Action 28-4-17. Reported by O.C. 16th Battn. West Yorks Regiment on memo dated 16-6-17.	"MISSING"

Verified. ORS.

Capt. for Major.

21-6-17. Officer i/c Regular Infantry Section No. 2.

...th (Service) Battal... ...ifle Brigade.

WINCHESTER RECORD OFFICE. DAILY CASUALTY LIST DATED 29.6.1...

Regt. No.	Rank and Name.	Casualty	PR.
S. 30139	Rfn. Webb C.	Killed in Action 23.4.17.	Wounded & Missing.
S. 3229	A/C. Jones G.	Killed in Action 28.4.1917.	Missing.

The above Casualties were reported by O.C. 13th Rifle Brigade on A.F.B.213 dated 22.6.1917.

Verified.

G.H.Q. 3rd Ech.
29.6.1917.

Capt. for Major.
i/c Regular Infantry Section No.2.

Confidential

War Diary

of

13th (S) Batn. The Rifle Brigade

From 1st July 1917
To 31st July 1917

(Volume 22)

Army Form C. 2118.

bn.23

WAR DIARY
or
INTELLIGENCE SUMMARY.
(Erase heading not required.)

Instructions regarding War Diaries and Intelligence Summaries are contained in F. S. Regs., Part II. and the Staff Manual respectively. Title pages will be prepared in manuscript.

Place	Date	Hour	Summary of Events and Information	Remarks and references to Appendices
TORREKEN FARM (O.20.d.2.3.)	1/7/17 to 7/7/17.		The Battalion remained in support in LEFT SECTOR with Headquarters at TORREKEN FARM. Digging and carrying parties were supplied to 153rd Field Coy. R.E. and to 13th Bn. K.R.R.C. who were holding the line.	
	7/7/17.		The Battalion relieved the 13th Bn. K.R.R.C. in the Front LEFT SECTOR. Relief complete by 2.30 am. 8/7/17. The Line was held as follows:- 2 Coys. in Front line as under:- 2 Platoons in line of Outposts running approximately from O.23.a.5.4. to O.29.a.2.7. - 2 Platoons in Support about 500 yards in rear - 2 Platoons in Reserve in "Z" Line about 500 yards in rear of Supports in "R" Line. 2 Coys. in Battalion Reserve. 19th Division connected up on Left at O.23.a.5.4. (exclusive) and 10th R.Fus. on right.	
FRONT LEFT SECTOR.	8/7/17 to 11/7/17.		The Battalion remained in Front Line as above. On the evening of the 9th thu 56th Infantry Bde. (19th Div) on our left attacked and captured the line O.23.a.5.4. thence North to include buildings at O.23.a.5.5. and O.23.a.4.7. We withdrew our posts at O.23.a.5.4. and as far SOUTH as the WAMBEKE RIVER for this operation. The enemy artillery retaliated strongly on our "R" and "Z" Lines but we only suffered 2 Casualties. On the night 10/11th we extended our left by taking over Posts from the 8th Gloucester Regt. (19th Div) at O.23.a.38.10 and O.23.a.45.35. On the night of 11/12th we were relieved by the 8th Lincolnshire Regt. and marched back to Hutments at DRANOUTRE.	
DRANOUTRE.	12/7/17 to 25/7/17.		The Battalion remained at the Hutments. Working parties of 400 were supplied daily to 153rd and 154th Coys. R.E. for salvaging material from Old British and German Trenches. On nights of 23rd and 24th a party of 300 were supplied to Div. Signal Coy. R.E. for burying cables.	
"	25/7/17.		The Battalion relieved the 4th Middlesex Regt. in Front Line. One Coy. in Front Line running approximately from O.23.a.55.45 to O.23.c.3.4. 1 Coy. in immediate Support (in Trenches about JOY FARM (O.23.d.3.6.) and ODOUR TRENCH. 1 Coy. in Trenches about GUY FARM (O.26.a.3.8.) and 1 Coy. at TORREKEN FARM (O.20.d.2.5.) 19th Div. on our Left, 13th KRRC. on our Right.	

Army Form C. 2118.

WAR DIARY
or
INTELLIGENCE SUMMARY.
(Erase heading not required.)

Instructions regarding War Diaries and Intelligence Summaries are contained in F.S. Regs., Part II. and the Staff Manual respectively. Title pages will be prepared in manuscript.

Place	Date	Hour	Summary of Events and Information	Remarks and references to Appendices
OOSTAVERNE LEFT SECTOR.	27/7/17.		A patrol left our Front Line on night of 27/28th and reconnoitred ground in front of our positions. Axxxx They reported MAY FARM (O.23.c.65.85) as held by the enemy and an M.G. emplacement there.	
"	28/7/17		On the night of 28/29th a special patrol went out to take MAY FARM and any of the enemy garrisoning it. This raid was made in view of a possible raid on RIFLE FARM. No enemy were encountered and MAY FARM and trenches in vicinity were found unoccupied.	
"	29/7/17.		The Battalion was relieved by the 4th Middlesex Regiment and marched to Camp at LIGHTNING FARM and BEAVER HALL on KEMMEL HILL.	
KEMMEL HILL.	30/7/17.		The Battalion remained in Camp.	
"	31/7/17.		The Battalion marched to, and bivouaced in, field near STORE FARM at N.29.a.5.4. Party of 240 Other Ranks was supplied to Div. M.G.Coy. and 111th M.G.Coy. (120 each) for carrying ammunition to the FRONT LINE.	

J B Taylor Capt
for Lieut.Col.
Commanding 13th Battalion The Rifle Brigade.

13th. (S) Bn. The Rifle Brigade.

WINCHESTER RECORD OFFICE. DAILY CASUALTY LIST D/- 3-7-17.

Regt.No.	Rank and Name.	Casualty.		PR.
S. 28629	Rfn. Driver J.W.	Killed in Action	23-4-17.	Wounded & Missing.
S. 17226	Rfn. Pearce E.W.	Killed in Action	28-4-17.	Missing.
2407	Rfn. Squires A.	Killed in Action	28-4-17.	Missing.

The above Casualties were reported by The Burial Officer XIII Corps dated 20-6-1917.

Verified.

ORS.

Capt. for Major.

3-7-17.   Officer i/c Regular Infantry Section No.2.

13th (Service) Battn. The Rifle Brigade.

WINCHESTER RECORD OFFICE. DAILY CASUALTY LIST D/- 6.7.17.

Regt. No.	Rank & Name.	Casualty.	PR.
S.23451	Rfn. Edwards E.	Killed in Action 11.4.17. "MISSING" Reported by VI/C.B.O.(D?G.R. & E) List No. 17527 B. undated.	

Verified.
ORS.

Capt. for Major.
6.7.17.   Officer i/c Regular Infantry Section No.2.

...rigade.

WINCHESTER RECORD OFFICE. DAILY CASUALTY LIST D/- 10.7.17.

| Regt.N. | Rank and Name. | Casualty. | PR. |

S. 3227   Rfn. Thomas D.   Killed in Action 11.4.1917.   "Missing"
                             Reported by T.H.Cleworth C.F.
                             attd., 12th Manchester R.
                             (D.G.R.&.E. List No.17527 B. undated.

Verified.
ORS.
Capt. for Major.
10.7.17.   i/c Regular Infantry Section No.2.

13th (Service) Battn. The Rifle Brigade.

Winchester Record office. Daily Casualty List d/- 11.7.17.

Regt.No.	Rank and Name.	Casualty	PR.
S. 23520	L/C. Gardiner R.	Wounded at Duty 2.7.1917.	NIL.
S. 24341	Rfn. Donaghy J.	Wounded in Action 2.7.17. To Duty 5.7.17.	NIL.
S. 16711	Rfn. Curson H.	Wounded in Action 2.7.17.	NIL.
S. 19929	Rfn. Karby A.	Wounded in Action 4.7.17.	NIL.

The above casualties were reported by The Officer Commanding, 13th (S) Battn. The Rifle Brigade on A.F.B.213 dated 6.7.1917.

Verified.
ORS.

Capt. for Major.
11.7.17.
i/c Regular Infantry Section No.2.

13th. (S) Bn. The Rifle Brigade.

WINCHESTER RECORD OFFICE DAILY CASUALTY LIST DATED 14-7-17.

Regt.No.	Rank and Name.	Casualty.	PR.
S. 27394	Rfn. Cudmore S.	Died of Wounds, received in action 11-7-17. Reported by O.C. No. 2 Casualty Clearing Station 11-7-17.	Nil.

Verified. ORS.

Capt. for Major.
Officer i/c Regular Infantry Section No. 2.

14-7-17.

13th (S) Battn. The Rifle Brigade.

WINCHESTER RECORD OFFICE. DAILY CASUALTY LIST D/- 16.7.17.

2nd Lieut. H.W.O.SMITH.   Wounded in Action 11.7.1917.   Nil.
                           Reported by Officer Commanding
                           13th Rifle Brigade 12.7.17.
                Verified.
                           ORS.

                                Capt. for Major.
16.7.17.   Officer i/c Regular Infantry Section No.2.

13th (Service) Battn. The Rifle Brigade.

WINCHESTER RECORD. OFFICE. DAILY CASUALTY LIST D/- 16.7.17.

Regt.No.	Rank and Name	Casualty		PR.
S. 17177	Rfn. Dark P.J.	KILLED IN ACTION	5.7.17.	Nil.
S. 30979	Rfn. Pearce H.	KILLED IN ACTION	5.7.17.	Nil.
S. 17189	Rfn. Mullins W.	KILLED IN ACTION	5.7.17.	Nil.
S. 13064	Rfn. Perry W.	KILLED IN ACTION	5.7.17.	Nil.
B. 371	Rfn. Turner T.	KILLED IN ACTION	5.7.17.	Nil.
S. 19865	Rfn. Pyner E.	KILLED IN ACTION	5.7.17.	Nil.
S. 10436	Rfn. Cross J.	KILLED IN ACTION	9.7.17.	Nil.
421480	Cpl. Titmarsh J.	KILLED IN ACTION	9.7.17.	Nil.
B.200795	Rfn. Hall S.	WOUNDED IN ACTION	5.7.17.	Nil.
422948	Rfn. Gargrave E.	-ditto-	5.7.17.	Nil.
574734	Rfn. Palmer J.W.	-ditto-	5.7.17.	Nil.
423879	Rfn. Ferryman A.S.	-ditto-	8.7.17.	Nil.
S. 27444	Rfn. Brown A.L.	-ditto-	5.7.17.	Nil.
S. 15705	L/C. Little W.J.	-ditto-	9.7.17.	Nil.
S. 17083	Rfn. Ashley B.H.	-ditto-	6.7.17.	Nil.

The above Casualties were reported by Officer Commanding 13th Bn. Rifle Brigade 12.7.1917.

Verified.

ORS.

Capt. for Major.

16.7.17. Officer i/c Regular Infantry Section No.2.

13th (S) Bn. The Rifle Brigade.

Winchester Record Office Daily Casualty List dated 18-7-17.

Regtl No.	Rank and Name.	Casualty		PR.
S. 25465	Rfn. EVANS C.F.W.F.	Wounded in Action 9-7-17.		
		Returned to Duty 12-7-17.		Nil.
423676	Rfn. PLOTZKER J.	Wounded in Action 9-7-17.		
		Returned to duty 11-7-17.		Nil.
S. 4291 ⁴²⁹¹	A/C. Branson J.	Wounded at Duty 11-7-17.		Nil.
S. 19929	Rfn. Karby A.W.	Returned to Duty 11-7-17.		Wounded in Act. To W.O. 14-7-17.

The above Casualties were reported by The Officer Commanding 13th (S) Bn. Rifle Brigade on A.F.B.213 dated 13-7-17.

Verified.
ORS.

18-7-1917.

Capt. for Major.
i/c Regular Infantry Section No.2.

Date A&11th July 1917.

Serial Number	Corps	No	Rank and Name	Date of Admission	Wound or Disease	Date of Death
T 524	13th Rifle Brigade.	S/27394	Rfn S. CUDMORE.	10-7-17.	G.S.Wd. Neck. Fracture Spine.	2-40am. 11-7-17.

To be buried in the Military Cemetery BAILLEUL.

J McLean
Lieut Colonel R.A.M.C.
O.C., No 2 Casualty Clearing Station.

D.A.G.,
3rd Echelon.

13th (S) Bn. The Rifle Brigade.

WINCHESTER RECORD OFFICE DAILY CASUALTY LIST DATED 19-7-17.

S. 7354 Rfn. Thornley J.   Killed in Action 11-4-17.   "Missing" W.O. 4-5-17.

Reported by 12th Divl. B.O. 6-7-17 on
List No. G.4085.
Burial report No. 1168.

Verified.
ORS.

Capt. for Major.
i/c Regular Infantry Section No.2.

19-7-17.

13th (Service) Battn. The Rifle Brigade.

Winchester Record Office Daily Casualty List dated 21-7-17.

Regt.No.	Rank and Name.	Casualty.	PR.
B.203286	Rfn. Moreton F.N.	Killed in Action 11-4-17. Reported by H.Q. XII D.B.O. (D.G.R.&E. List 18828 B. undated.	"Wounded & "Missing" to W.O.15-5-17.

Verified. ORS.

Capt. for Major.
i/c Regular Infantry Section No.2.

21-7-17.

13th (Service) Battn. The Rifle Brigade.

WINCHESTER RECORD OFFICE. DAILY CASUALTY LIST DATED 20-7-17.

2nd Lieut. F.B. JOHNSON. Killed in Action 31-5-1917.   PR.
                              Reported by O.C. 13th (S)   "MISSING" to W.O.
                              Bn. The Rifle Brigade, on   8-6-17.
                              memo dated 16-7-1917.

                       Verified.
                           ORS.

20-7-17.   Capt. for Major.
          Officer i/c Regular Infantry Section No.2.

(Service) Battn. The Rifle Brigade.

Winchester Record Office Daily Casualty List dated 24-7-17.

Regt.No.	Rank and Name.	Casualty.	PR.
6440	Rfn. Swindells A.	Wounded & Missing 11-4-17. "D" Coy. Reported by O.C.Battn, 20-7-17.	W.i.A. To W.O. 28-4-17.
423686	Rfn. Crake S.G.	Killed in Action 1-6-1917. Reported By H.Q. 29th Div.on D.G.R.&.E. List No.19064 B. undated.	"MISSING" To W.O. 22-6-17.

Verified.
ORS.

Capt. for Major.
24-7-17.   Officer i/c Regular Infantry Section No.2.

13th (Ser) Bn. The Rifle Brigade.

Winchester Record Office. Daily Casualty List d/- 24.7.17.

Captain (T/Major) JACKSON. A.N.S.　　TO DUTY 5.6.17. Reported　　　PR.
　　　　　　　　　　　　　　　　　　by O.C. 37 C.C.S. on memo
　　　　　　　　　　　　　　　　　　No. 7467 dated 8.6.17.　　　To Hos.
　　　　　　　　　　　　　　　　　　　　　　　　　　　　　　　Wounded
　　　　　　　　　　　　　　　　　　　　　　　　　　　　　　　To W.O.
　　　　　　　　　　　　　　　　　　　　　　　　　　　　　　　19.5.17.

　　　　　　　　　　　　　　　Verified.
　　　　　　　　　　　　　　　　　　　ORS.

　　　　　　　　　　　　　　　　　　　　　　Capt. for Major,
24.7.17.　　　　　　　　　　i/c Regular Infantry Section No.2.

13th (Service) Battalion, The Rifle Brigade.

WINCHESTER RECORD OFFICE. DAILY CASUALTY LIST DATED 27.7.17.

Regt. No.	Rank and Name.	Casualty.	PR.
S. 16711	Rfn. Curson H.	RETURNED TO DUTY. 13.7.17. Reported by O.C. 37 DRS. 20.7.17.	W in A.
574474	Rfn. Weston W.	RETURNED TO DUTY. 12.6.17.	W in A.
P. 657	Rfn. Welch J.C.	RETURNED TO DUTY. 15.6.17. Reported by O.C. 36th F.A. 24.7.17.	W in A.
S. 28612	Rfn. Ellis J.E.	RETURNED TO DUTY. 17.6.17. Reported by O.C. 36th F.A. 22.7.17.	W in A.

Verified.
ORS.

Capt. for Major.
27.7.17.   i/c Regular Infantry Section No.2.

SECRET

13th (Service) Battalion The Rifle Brigade

WAR DIARY

From   1st August 1917

To   31st August 1917

Volume No 23.

Army Form C. 2118.

WAR DIARY
or
INTELLIGENCE SUMMARY.

(Erase heading not required.)

Instructions regarding War Diaries and Intelligence Summaries are contained in F. S. Regs., Part II. and the Staff Manual respectively. Title pages will be prepared in manuscript.

Place	Date	Hour	Summary of Events and Information	Remarks and references to Appendices

Army Form C. 2118.

WAR DIARY
of
INTELLIGENCE SUMMARY.
(Erase heading not required.)

Instructions regarding War Diaries and Intelligence Summaries are contained in F. S. Regs., Part II. and the Staff Manual respectively. Title pages will be prepared in manuscript.

Place	Date	Hour	Summary of Events and Information	Remarks and references to Appendices
WYTSCHAETE	1917 August 1st		On the night of the 1st/2nd August the Battalion moved up from the Reserve position behind WYTSCHAETE to the Front Line - TORREKEN FARM being Battalion Headquarters. The weather was exceptionally bad, heavy rains making the roads and trenches most difficult.	
	3rd		The Battalion moved into the RIDGE DEFENCE LINE on the night of the 3rd/4th on relief by the 13th K.R.R.C., Battalion Headquarters being transferred to LUMM FARM.	
	6th		On the night of the 6th/7th the Battalion succeeded in establishing Posts at and North of RIFLE FARM - the patrols of occupation passing through the 13th K.R.R.C., and by peaceful penetration gaining their objectives with few casualties. Observation over this Ridge - an important object - was thus attained.	
KEMMEL	7th		The Battalion was relieved on the night 7th/8th by the 45th and 46th Battalions of the AUSTRALIAN INFANTRY, marching back to billets on the KEMMEL HILL (LIGHTNING FARM and BEAVER HALL).	
LOCRE	8th		On the afternoon of the 8th the Battalion marched to BIRR BARRACKS at LOCRE, the officers' Mess being established in the Convent School of ST. ANTHONY.	
"	25th		From the 8th to 25th (inclusive) the Battalion remained in BIRR BARRACKS. Working parties were found for the Line and behind it; training and organisation were proceeded with as far as possible, and a certain amount of recreational training was carried out.	
			On the 15th the funeral of Brigadier-General R.C.MACLACHLAN, D.S.O. (Rifle Brigade), Commanding 112th Infantry Brigade, took place in the grounds of the HOSPICE at LOCRE. The Battalion provided the 'following' party and also the firing party.	
			On the 23rd the Battalion was inspected by Brigadier-General C.W.COMPTON, C.M.G., Commanding 111th Infantry Brigade, who expressed his satisfaction with the general turn-out of the men and their steadiness on parade.	

Army Form C. 2118.

WAR DIARY
INTELLIGENCE SUMMARY
(Erase heading not required.)

Instructions regarding War Diaries and Intelligence Summaries are contained in F. S. Regs., Part II. and the Staff Manual respectively. Title pages will be prepared in manuscript.

Place	Date 1917 AUGUST	Hour	Summary of Events and Information	Remarks and references to Appendices
LOCRE.	25th		On the 25th the Battalion celebrated the Regimental Birthday. Football matches (Rugby and Association) were played. Tea, under Battalion arrangements, was followed by an excellent Concert. The Divisional Band and the 8th SOMERSETS Band contributed to the success of the celebrations.	
ROSSIGNOL WOOD.	26th		On the morning of the 26th the Battalion moved into the Reserve Area, ROSSIGNOL WOOD.	
DENYS WOOD.	27th		On the night of the 27th/28th the Battalion relieved the 8th East Lancs. Regiment in the Front Line - DENYS WOOD. Relief was carried out without any casualties. The weather was extremely bad. Battalion Headquarters were situated at DENYS WOOD.	
	29th		At about 12-30 p.m., the Acting Adjutant (2nd Lieut. H.N.RIES) was wounded in the thigh. 2nd Lieut. (A/Capt.) R.COLVILL-JONES took over the duties of Adjutant. The weather was still bad.	
	30th) 31st)		During these two days nothing of importance occurred. The weather continued unfavourable.	

1/9/17.

[signature]
Lt. Colonel,
Commanding 13th Battalion The Rifle Brigade.

13th (Service) Battn. The Rifle Brigade.

Winchester Record Office Daily Casualty List dated 1-8-17.

Regt.No.	Rank and Name.	Casualty.	PR.
B. 200823	Rfn. Ion W.	Killed in Action 28-7-17.	Nil.
S. 8029	Sgt. Carney R.	Killed in Action 28-7-17.	Nil.
S. 4376	Rfn. Laws H.T.	Killed in Action 28-7-17.	Nil.
P. 1617	Rfn. Pegg S.	Killed in Action 28-7-17.	Nil.
S. 19797	Rfn. Bromwell C.	Killed in Action 28-7-17.	Nil.

The above Casualties were reported by The Officer Commanding 13th Rifle Brigade 28-7-17.

| B. 203626 | Rfn. Money C.G. | Wounded in Action 26-7-17. | Nil. |

Reported by O.C.Bn. 27-7-17.

****

Capt. for Major.

1-8-1917.   Officer i/c Regular Infantry Section No.2.

13th (Service) Battn. The Rifle Brigade.

WINCHESTER RECORD OFFICE. DAILY CASUALTY LIST DATED 1.8.17.

2ND. LIEUT. BUNT. N.B.   WOUNDED IN ACTION 28.7.1917.   Nil.
Reported by A.G&ms.List No. 1061
dated 29.7.1917.

Verified. ORS.

Capt. for Major.
Officer i/c Regular Infantry Section No.2.

1.8.1917.

13th (Service) Battn. The Rifle Brigade.

WINCHESTER RECORD OFFICE. DAILY CASUALTY LIST D/- 1-8-17.

Regt.No.	Rank and Name.	Casualty.	PR.
S. 20662	Rfn. Day R.	Wounded in Action 23-7-17. Reported by O.C.Battalion 26-7-1917.	Nil.

Verified. ORS.

Capt. for Major.
Officer i/c Regular Infantry Section No.2.

1-8-17.

13th (Service) Battalion The Rifle Brigade.

Winchester Record Office. Casualty List d/- 3.8.17.

2nd Lieut. P.F.DAVY.   WOUNDED 29.7.17. (AT DUTY)   Nil.
                         Reported on A.G's.List 1062
                         dated 30.7.17.

Verified.
ORS.

3.8.17.   Capt. for Major.
                         i/c Reg.Infantry Section No.2.

13th (Service) Battn. The Rifle Brigade.

Winchester Record Office Daily Casualty List dated 3.8.17.

Regt.No.	Rank and Name	Casualty	Pr.
S. 14811	Rfn. Bromwich H.E.	Died of Wounds 30.7.1917. Reported by O.C. 53 C.C.S. 31.7.17.	Wounded.

Verified.
ORS.

Capt. for Major.
i/c Regular Infantry Section No.2.

3.8.17.

13th (Service) Ba[ttalion] The [Ri]fle Brigade.

Winchester Record Office Daily Casualty List dated 7.8.17.

Regt.No.	Rank and Name.	Casualty.	PR.
S. 23345	Rfn. Claridge G.	Killed in Action 11.4.1917. Reported by O.C.Battalion 26.7.1917.	"Missing" To W.O. 15.5.17.

Verified.
ORS.

Capt. for Major.
i/c Regular Infantry Section No.2.

7.8.17.

Brigade.

Winchester Record Office daily casualty list dated 9-8-17.

	Regt.No.	Rank and Name.		Casualty.		PR.
	5439	Rfn. Goldthorpe	S.	Wounded in Action	30-7-17.	N.
S.	2283	Rfn. Anderson	D.	Wounded at duty.	30-7-17.	N.
S.	27371	Rfn. Groome	E.	Wounded in Action	30-7-17.	N.
S.	13186	L/C. Heywood	H.	Wounded in Action	31-7-17.	N.
P.	4365	L/C. Martin	C.	Wounded at duty.	31-7-17.	N.
B.	203182	Rfn. Chadaway	W.	Wounded in Action	2-8-17.	N.
*B.	203026	Rfn. Money	C.	Returned to duty.	28-7-17.	N.
S.	20636	L/C. Acourt	W.	Wounded (Gas) at Duty.	30-7-17.	N.
	374252	Rfn. West	L.	--ditto--		N.
S.	9767	Rfn. Laws	F.	--ditto--		N.
S.	8006	L/C. Bumstead	W.	--ditto--		N.
	5984	Rfn. Kelman	R.	--ditto--		N.
S.	14454	Rfn. Barton	R.	--ditto--		N.
S.	30790	Rfn. Babbs	J.	--ditto--		N.
S.	30977	Rfn. Morris	T.	--ditto--		N.
	574108	Rfn. Cooper	W.	--ditto--		N.
B.	203182	Rfn. Chadaway	W.	--ditto--		N.
S.	28935	Rfn. Ely	F.	--ditto--		N.
S.	2035	Rfn. Hancock	J.	--ditto--		N.
P.	366	Rfn. Langmead	G.	--ditto--		N.
	304564	Rfn. Edwards	R.	--ditto--		N.
S.	6700	L/C. Staunton	P.	--ditto--		N.
S.	25421	Rfn. Cook	W.	--ditto--		N.
S.	4003	L/C. Bassett	J.	--ditto--		N.
S.	27118	Rfn. Veitch	J.	--ditto--		N.
S.	23512	Rfn. Cross	E.	--ditto--		N.
B.	203274	Rfn. Fielding	M.	--ditto--		N.
	423911	Rfn. Parfitt	G.	--ditto--		N.
S.	16047	Rfn. Cole	W.J.	--ditto--		N.

The above Casualties were reported by O.C. Battalion 3-8-1917.

Verified.
ORS.

Capt. for Major.
9-8-1917.
Officer i/c Regular Infantry Section No.2.

* Deleted in accordance with telephonic communication 11.8.17.

13th (Service) Battalion The Rifle Brigade.

Winchester Record Office. Daily Casualty List dated 10.8.17.

Regt.No.	Rank and Name.	Casualty	PR.
S. 21408	Rfn. Richardson S.	Killed in Action 11.4.17. Reported by VI. C.B.O. on List D.G.R.&.E. List No.20983 undated.	Wounded & Missing. To W.O. 15.5.17.
S. 9272	Rfn. Smith W.	Wounded at Duty. 28.7.1917. Reported by O.C.Battalion. 3.8.1917.	Nil.
S. 21082	Rfn. Lancaster R.	Wounded (Acc) 29.7.1917. Reported by O.C. 111th T.M.Battery 28.1917.	Nil.
B. 200794	Rfn. Gasson E.H.	Died of Wounds 7.8.1917. Reported by O.C. 53 C.C.S. 7.8.1917.	Nil.

Verified.
ORS.

Capt. for Major.
10.81917.   Officer i/c Regular Infantry Section No.2.

13th (S........ion the ....gade.

Winchester Record Office Daily Casualty List dated 11.8.17.

| Regt.No. | Rank and Name. | Casualty. | PR. |

2nd LIEUT. A.G.LAWSON.   WOUNDED IN ACTION 6.8.1917.   Nil.
2nd LIEUT. E.WALPOLE.   WOUNDED IN ACTION.7.8.1917.   Nil.

The above Casualties were reported by O.C. Battalion. 8.8.1917.

Verified.
ORS.

11.8.17.

Capt for,
O.i/c, Reg Inf Sect. №2

13th (Service) Battalion The Rifle Brigade.

Winchester Record Office Daily Casualty List dated 11.8.1917.

Regt. No.		Rank and Name.		Casualty.	PR.
	303587	Rfn. Boult	A.H.	Killed in Action 5.8.1917.	Nil.
S.	24012	Rfn. Cullen	P.	Killed in Action 5.8.1917.	Nil.
S.	24060	Rfn. Chaplin	H.	Killed in Action 5.8.1917.	Nil.
S.	27090	Cpl. Goodman	W.H.	Killed in Action 2.8.1917.	Nil.
S.	30850	Rfn. Hills	W.	Killed in Action 2.8.1917.	Nil.
P.	4304	Rfn. Olah	G.E.	Killed in Action 3.8.1917.	Nil.
	423911	Rfn. Parfitt	G.J.	Killed in Action 3.8.1917.	Nil.
S.	3956	Rfn. Robinson	O.	Killed in Action 5.8.1917.	Nil.
	740961	A/S. Siriett	G.M.	Killed in Action 5.8.1917.	Nil.
Z.	2742	Sgt. Streeton	H.C.	Killed in Action 2.8.1917.	Nil.
Z.	2112	Rfn. Williams	J.	Killed in Action 7.8.1917.	Nil.
	3531	Rfn. Dark	H.	Wounded in Action 6.8.1917.	Nil.
P.	1652	Rfn. Powell	J.	" " 6.8.1917.	Nil.
S.	3716	L/S. O'Connor	M.J.	" " 7.8.1917.	Nil.
Z.	1799	Cpl. Hopley	G.	" " 7.8.1917.	Nil.
	3034	L/C. Bunn	W.	" " 7.8.1917.	Nil.
P.	1628	Rfn. Pettitt	J.	" " 7.8.1917.	Nil.
P.	1623	Rfn. Sibley	T.	" " 7.8.1917.	Nil.
S.	19798	Rfn. Vincent	J.	" " 2.8.1917.	Nil.
S.	19214	Rfn. Bayne	G.	" " 2.8.1917.	Nil.
S.	16280	Rfn. Stewart	S.	" " 6.8.1917.	Nil.
S.	19098	Rfn. Lee	T.	" " 6.8.1917.	Nil.
S.	15135	Rfn. Linney	W.	" " 7.8.1917.	Nil.
S.	11283	Rfn. Dingley	J.	" " 6.8.1917.	Nil.
S.	8631	Sgt. Pearson	J.B.	" " 7.8.1917.	Nil.
S.	7276	Rfn. Robinson	A.	" " 7.8.1917.	Nil.
S.	25156	Rfn. Wright	G.H.J.	" " 2.8.1917.	Nil.
S.	27392	Rfn. Budd	A.	" " 7.8.1917.	Nil.
S.	27411	Rfn. Turnell	N.E.	" " 7.8.1917.	Nil.
S.	28508	Rfn. Hibbert	R.B.	" " 6.8.1917.	Nil.
S.	29061	Rfn. Haines	W.	" " 7.8.1917.	Nil.
S.	21966	Rfn. Smith	D.	" " 7.8.1917.	Nil.
S.	23474	Rfn. Tribe	F.	" " 7.8.1917.	Nil.
S.	30497	Rfn. Carter	E.	" " 7.8.1917.	Nil.
	422766	L/C. Webberley	P.T.	" " 2.8.1917.	Nil.
	424109	Rfn. Joseph	J.	" " 2.8.1917.	Nil.
	304476	Rfn. Levy	G.L.	" " 3.8.1917.	Nil.
S.	27756	Rfn. Bosher	C.	" " 7.8.1917.	Nil.
B.	200803	Rfn. Aitchison	J.	" " 4.8.1917.	Nil.
B.	200811	Rfn. Brown	R.	" " 5.8.1917.	Nil.
B.	203212	L/C. Haunton	R.E.	" " 6.8.1917.	Nil.
B.	203222	Rfn. Marshall	F.R.	" " 7.8.1917.	Nil.
B.	200749	Rfn. Smith	A.	" " 6.8.1917.	Nil.
	423691	Rfn. Curtis	F.	" " 6.8.1917.	Nil.
	422172	Rfn. Stephens	D.	" " 7.8.1917.	Nil.
B.	200842	L/C. Selby	W.H.	" " 7.8.1917.	Nil.
B.	200806	Rfn. Bamford	G.H.	" " 7.8.1917.	Nil.
B.	200809	Rfn. Bryson	R.	" " 7.8.1917.	Nil.
	423565	Rfn. Burgess	W.	" " 7.8.1917.	Nil.
B.	200826	Rfn. Jones	I.	" " 7.8.1917.	Nil.
	304484	Rfn. Stevens	H.	" " 7.8.1917.	Nil.
B.	200820	Rfn. Hammond	H.	" " 7.8.1917.	Nil.
	374686	Rfn. Upchurch	F.	Returned to duty. 4.8.1917.	"W"
S.	9751	L/S. Woods	S.	Returned to duty. 6.8.1917.	"W"

The above Casualties were reported by
The Officer Commanding 13th Bn. Rifle Brigade
dated 8.8.1917.

Verified.

ORS.

11.8.17.

Capt. for Major
O i/c Reg. Infantry Section No 2

13th (Service) Battn. The Rifle Brigade.

Winchester Record Office. Daily Casualty List Dated 13.8.17.

Regt.No.	Rank and Name.	Casualty.	PR.
B. 203626	Rfn. Money C.	Returned to duty 28.7.17. Reported by O.C.Battalion 3.8.1917.	"W"
423691	Rfn. Carter F.	Died of Wounds 8.8.17. Reported by O.C. 53 CCS dated 9.8.17.	"W"

Verified. ORS.

Capt. for.
O.i/c Regular Infantry Section No.2.

13.8.17.

(Service) Battn. The Rifle Brigade.

Winchester Record Office Daily Casualty List dated 14.8.17.

Regt.No.	Rank and Name.	Casualty.	PR.
P. 1623	Rfn SIBLEY. T.	Died of Wounds, 8.8.1917. Reported by O.C. No.2 Cas Clearing Station 9.8.17.	"W".

Verified.
ORS.

Capt. for Major.

14.8.17.   O.i/c Regular Infantry Section No.2.

✗ As phoned 16.8.17.

13th (Service) Battn. The Rifle Brigade.

WINCHESTER RECORD OFFICE. DAILY CASUALTY LIST da/- 16.8.17.

2nd. LIEUT.	A.G.LAWSON.	WOUNDED(GAS) 6.8.17. Reported by O.C.Battalion 10.8.1917.	W in A. to W.I. 14/8/17.

Verified.

ORS.

Capt. for Major.

16.8.17. Officer i/c Regular Infantry Section No.2.

...) Battn. The Rifle Brigade.

Record Office Daily Casualty List dated 16-8-17.

Regt.No.	Rank and Name.	Casualty.		PR.
Z. 1799	Cpl. Hopley G.	Wounded (Gas)	7-8-17.	W in A.
3034	L/C. Bunn W.	Wounded (Gas)	7-8-17.	" "
P. 1628	Rfn. Pettitt J.	" "	7-8-17.	" "
S. 16280	Rfn. Stewart S.	" "	6-8-17.	" "
S. 19098	Rfn. Lee T.	" "	6-8-17.	" "
S. 11283	Rfn. Dingley J.	" "	6-8-17.	" "
S. 8631	Sgt. Pearson J.B.	" "	7-8-17.	" "
S. 7276	Rfn. Robinson A.	" "	7-8-17.	" "
S. 28598	Rfn. Hibbett R.B.	" "	6-8-17.	" "
S. 29061	Rfn. Haines W.	" "	7-8-17.	" "
S. 21966	Rfn. Smith D.	" "	7-8-17.	" "
B. 200811	Rfn. Brown R.	" "	6-8-17.	" "
B. 203222	Rfn. Marshall F.	" "	6-8-17.	" "
B. 200749	Rfn. Smith A.	" "	6-8-17.	" "
B. 200842	L/C. Selby W.H.	" "	6-8-17.	" "
B. 200806	Rfn. Bamford G.H.	" "	7-8-17.	" "
B. 200809	Rfn. Bryson R.	" "	7-8-17.	" "
423565	Rfn. Burgess W.	" "	7-8-17.	" "
B. 200826	Rfn. Jones I.	" "	7-8-17.	" "
304484	Rfn. Stevens H.	" "	7-8-17.	" "
B. 200820	Rfn. Hammond H.	" "	7-8-17.	" "
423691	Rfn. Curtis F.	Reported Wounded in Action 7-8-17. read 423691 Carter F.		----
S. 30856	Rfn. Brooks J.	Wounded in Action 2-8-17.		Nil.
B. 203277	Rfn. Gatehouse E.	Wounded (At duty) 7-8-17.		Nil.

The above Casualties were reported by O.C. Battalion on A.F.B.213 dated 10-8-17.

| S. 27392 | Rfn. Budd A. | Returned to duty 11-8-17. | W in A. |
| 5439 | Rfn. Goldthorpe S. | Returned to duty 12-8-17. | W in A. |

Reported by O.C. Battalion on memo dated 12-8-17.

Verified..
.... ORS.

Capt. for Major.
16-8-17.   Officer i/c Regular Infantry Section No.2.

...ice) Battn. The Rifle Brigade.

...rd Office Casualty List dated 17.8.17.

Regt.No.	Rank and Name.	Casualty.	FR.
374686	Rfn. Upchurch F.W.	Returned to duty 4.8.1917. Reported by O.C. 48th F.A. 4.8.17.	W in A.
S.21082.	Rfn. Lancaster R.W.	Returned to duty 10.8.17. Reported by O.C. 111th T.M.B. 10.8.17.	"W"(Acc)

Verified.
ORS.

Capt. for Major.

17.8.17. Officer i/c Regular Infantry Section No.2.

13th (Service) Bn. The Rifle Brigade.

...ester Record Office. Daily Casualty List dated 18-8-17.

Regt.No.	Rank and Name.	Casualty.	PR.
S. 1159.	Rfn. Doswell H.	Killed in Action 11-4-1917. Reported by G.O.C. XVIII. Corps 13-7-1917.	W & M.
6098	Rfn. Steel E. (Att. 1/1st Camb. Regiment)	Wounded in Action 31-7-17. Reported by O.C. 1/1st Camb. Regt. 11-8-1917.	Nil.

Verified.
ORS.

Capt. for Major..
Officer i/c Regular Infantry Section No.2.

18-8-17.

13th (Ser) Battn. The Rifle Brigade.

...ester Record Office. Daily Casualty List dated 23.8.17.

Regt.No.	Rank and Name.		Casualty.	PR.
S. 17192	Rfn. Davies A.	"C" Coy.	MISSING. 2.8.1917.	Nil.
S. 14820	Rfn. Barnes G.	"B" Coy.	MISSING. 4.8.1917.	Nil.
S. 27108	Rfn. Chandler A.	"A" Coy.	MISSING. 5.8.1917.	Nil.

The above Casualties were reported by O.C.Battalion. 10.8.1917.

Verified.

ORS.

Capt. for Major.

23.8.17.   O.i/c Regular Infantry Section No.2.

13th (S) Bn. The Rifle Brigade

Infantry Record Office. Daily Casualty List of 24.8.17

Regt No	Rank Name	Casualty	
422172	Rfn. Stephens D.	Died F/wounds 20.8.17 "W" Reported by O.C. 1/Can. G.H. 21.8.1917	

Verified OPS

Capt. for Major
O i/c Reg. Infantry Section No 2

24 AUG

24.8.17

13th Battn. The Rifle Brigade.

WINCHESTER RECORD OFFICE. DAILY CASUALTY LIST DATED 25.8.17.

Regt. No.	Rank and Name.	Casualty		PR.
Z. 205	Rfn. Vickery E.	Killed in Action.	21.8.1917.	Nil.
B.200750	Rfn. Fisher H.	Died of Wounds.	21.8.1917.	Nil.

Reported by Officer Commanding
13th (S) Bn. Rifle Brigade 22.8.17.

Verified.
ORS.

25.8.17.

Capt, for Major.
O.i/c Reg. Infantry Section No.2.

13th (S) Bn. The Rifle Brigade.

Winchester Record Office Daily Casualty List dated 25-8-17.

P.R.

2nd Lieut A.G.LAWSON.   WOUNDED(GAS) 6-8-1917.   W in A.
                                                        To W.O.14-8-17.

           Reported by Officer Commanding.
           13th Rifle Brigade on corrected list
           dated 10-8-17.

               Verified.
                 ORS.
                          Capt. for Major..
25-8-17.   O.i/c Reg.Infantry Section No.2.

Army Form C. 2118.

WAR DIARY
or
INTELLIGENCE SUMMARY.

(Erase heading not required.)

Instructions regarding War Diaries and Intelligence Summaries are contained in F. S. Regs., Part II. and the Staff Manual respectively. Title pages will be prepared in manuscript.

Place	Date	Hour	Summary of Events and Information	Remarks and references to Appendices

Army Form C. 2118.

WAR DIARY
or
INTELLIGENCE SUMMARY.
(Erase heading not required.)

Place	Date	Hour	Summary of Events and Information	Remarks and references to Appendices
DENYS WOOD.	1/9/17.		The Battalion continued to hold the line before DENYS WOOD until the night of the 2nd, when they were relieved by the 19th King's Liverpool Regt.	
IRISH HOUSE. SPOIL BANK.	2/9/17. 7/9/17.		The Battalion on relief came back to IRISH HOUSE, remaining there until the night of the 7/8th, when trenches at SPOIL BANK were taken over.	
BEAVER CORNER.	11/9/17.		The Brigade was relieved on the afternoon of the 11th, and the Battalion went back to Camp at BEAVER CORNER.	
YPRES-COMINES CANAL.	14/9/17.		On night of 14/15th the Battalion moved up to trenches in YPRES-COMINES CANAL area. Good work in patrolling was done by the Companies, this being especially valuable, and preceding an attack, on the eve of which the Battalion was withdrawn, and returned to WAKEFIELD HUTS encampment--night 18th/19th.	
WAKEFIELD HUTS.	19/9/17.		The Battalion remained at WAKEFIELD HUTS until the 27th. Training was carried out, all specialist Classes being put into full swing; a Musketry week was planned, and competitions at end of week were arranged; signs of revived interest in the rifle were visible in all ranks. Owing to the return of the Battalion to the trenches, this meeting was postponed.	
MENIN ROAD.	27/9/17.		On night of 27/28th, the Battalion returned to the trenches near MENIN ROAD, and were there on night of 30th.	

(signature)
Lieut. Col.
Commanding 13th Battalion The Rifle Brigade.

1st (...ice) Battalion The Rifle Brigade.

WINCHESTER RECORD OFFICE. DAILY CASUALTY LIST DATED 3.9.1917.

2ND. LIEUT.	H.N. RIES.	Wounded in Action 29.8.1917. Reported on A.G's. List No.1093 dated 30.8.1917.	PR. N11.

Verified.
ORS.
Capt. for Major.
3.9.1917.   Officer i/c Regular Infantry Section No.2.

13th (S) Bn Rifle Bde

16th (S) Bn. The Rifle Brigade.

WINCHESTER RECORD OFFICE. DAILY CASUALTY LIST DATED 5.9.17.

2ND. LIEUT. THOMPSON. R.H.   WOUNDED IN ACTION 31.8.1917.   Nil.
                              Reported on A.G&s List No. 1096
                              dated 2.9.1917.

                              Verified.
                                        ORS.

                                        Capt. for Major.
5.9.17.   Officer i/c Regular Infantry Section No.2.

13th (S) Battn. The Rifle Brigade.

Winchester Record Office Daily Casualty List dated 6-9-17.

Regt.No.	Rank and Name.	Casualty.	PR.
S. 2283	Rfn. Anderson D.	Wounded in Action 1-9-1917.	Nil.
Z. 284	Cpl. Craig R.	Wounded in Action 2-9-1917.	Nil.
P. 449	Rfn. Newman A.	Wounded in Action 2-9-1917.	Nil.
S. 21903	Rfn. Dunnett J.	Wounded in Action 2-9-1917.	Nil.
S. 13890	Rfn. Marsh W.	Wounded in Action 2-9-1917.	Nil.
S. 13755	Rfn. Middleton J.	Wounded in Action 2-9-1917.	Nil.
S. 9817	Rfn. Heath V.	Wounded in Action 2-9-1917.	Nil.
B. 200833	Rfn. Laflin E.	Wounded in Action 2-9-1917.	Nil.
B. 200839	Rfn. Roome A.	Wounded in Action 31-8-17.	Nil.

The above Casualties were reported by O.C. Battalion 3-9-1917.

| S. 27067 | Rfn. Davies F.H. | Died of Wounds 3-9-1917. Reported by O.C. 53 C.C.S. 3-9-1917. | Nil. |

Verified.
ORS.

6-9-1917.

Capt. for Major,
Officer i/c Regular Infantry Section No. 2.

3th (S) Bn. The Rifle Brigade.

Winchester Record Office Daily Casualty List dated 12-9-17.

Reference Casualty List to War Office dated 26-8-1917.
S. 14820 Rfn. Barnes G. Missing 4-8-1917 please read S. 14820
Rfn. Barnes G. Wounded in Action. A.F.W.3083 has now been
received fro this man. H.S. Pilter de Counch ex 7 Can. G. Hkl. 15-8-17.✳

C. Bramwell

G.H.Q.
3rd Ech.   Lieut. for Major.
12-9-17.   Officer i/c Regular Infantry Section No.2.

✳ As phoned 15.9.17.

Winchester Record Office Daily Casualty List Dated 14.9.17

Regt.No.	Rank and Name.	Casualty.	PR.
S. 27756	Rfn. Bosher C.	Reported Wounded in Action 4.8.17. on Cas List to W.O. d/- 15.8.17. Please cancel. Reported by O.C.Bn. 10.9.1917.	"W"
S. 967	Rfn. Gibbetts F.	Wounded in Action 9.9.1917. Reported by O.C.Bn. 10.9.17.	Nil.

Verified. ORS.

14.9.17.

Lieut. for Major.
Officer i/c Regular Infantry Section No.2.

"Winchester Record Office daily casualty list dated 15.9.17.

Regt. No.	Rank and Name.	Casualty.	PR.
S. 30509	Rfn. Davis A.	Died of Wounds, received in action 10.9.1917. Reported by O.C. No. 3 Can.General Hospital. 11.9.1917.	"W in A"

Verified.

ORS. G.W. Lieut. for Major.
Officer i/c Regular Infantry Section No.2.

15.9.1917.

13th (Service) Battalion The Rifle Brigade.

Winchester Record Office Daily Casualty List dated 17.9.17.

2ND LIEUT. W.E.HOBDAY.	KILLED IN ACTION. 11.4.1917. Reported by Officer Commanding 13th Rifle Brigade on memo dated 13.9.1917.	PR. Wounded & Missing. To W.O.8.5.17.

Verified.
ORS.

Lieut. for Major.

17.9.17.   Officer i/c Regular Infantry Section No.2.

13TH (S) BATTALION THE RIFLE BRIGADE

District, Rifle Records, Winchester.　　　　Daily Casualty Report.

　　　　　　　　　　　　　　　　　　　　　　　　　　　　　　　　P. R.
2nd/Lieut. FREEDMAN A.H.D.　Wounded in Action 16. 9. 1917.　　NIL.

　　Reported by Officer Commanding 13th (S) Battalion
　　　　The Rifle Brigade on memo. dated 17. 9. 1917.

　　　　　　　　　　　　Verified.
　　　　　　　　　　　　　　　　O.R.S.

G. H. Q.　　　　　　　　　　　　　　　　　　　　　　　　　　Major for,
3rd Echelon.　　　　　　Officer i/c Regular Infantry Section No.2.
20. 9. 1917.

13th (S) BATTALION THE RIFLE BRIGADE

District, Rifle Records, Winchester.   Daily Casualty Report.

Reg. No.	Rank and Name	Casualty				P. R.
6444	Rfn. Hutty A.V.	Wounded in Action	15.	9.	1917.	Nil.
B. 203348	L/C. Davey H.	do.	15.	9.	1917.	do.
374659	Rfn. Cameron R.	do.	15.	9.	1917.	do.
B. 1917	Rfn. Walker J.	do.	16.	9.	1917.	do.
3531	Rfn. Dark H.	do.	16.	9.	1917.	do.
S. 19576	Rfn. Nurse F.	do.	16.	9.	1917.	do.
S. 18853	Rfn. Chillingworth F.	do.	16.	9.	1917.	do.
S. 8184	Sgt. Leach R.	do.	16.	9.	1917.	do.
574512	Rfn. Prager J.A.	do.	16.	9.	1917.	do.
304446	Rfn. Westbury W.	do.	16.	9.	1917.	do.

Reported by O.C. 13th (S) Battalion The Rifle Brigade
17. 9. 1917.

+ + + + + + + + + + + + + +

Verified.
O.R.S.

G. H. Q.
3rd Echelon.
20. 9. 1917.

Major for
Officer i/c Regular Infantry Section No. 2.

District, Rifle Records, Winchester.   Daily Casualty R

Reg. No.	Rank and Name.	Casualty.	P. R.
S. 8085	Rfn. Hancock G.	Wounded in action 17. 9. 1917.	Nil.
S.28634	Rfn. Illingworth H.	do. 18. 9. 1917.	Nil.

Reported by O.C., 13th (S) Battn. The Rifle Brigade,
19. 9. 1917.

✢ ✢

Verified.
O.R.S.

G. H. Q.
3rd Echelon.
22. 9. 1917.

Officer i/c Regular Infantry Section No. 2.
Major for

BATTALION THE RIFLE BRIGADE

District. Rifle Records, Winchester.   Daily Casualty Report.

Reg. No.	Rank and Name.	Casualty.		P. R.
S. 8184	Sgt. Leach R. *Amended*	Wounded (At Duty).	16. 9. 1917.	W. in Ac. 16. 9. 17
3531	Rfn. Dark H.	Do.	Do.	Do.
S. 19576	Rfn. Nurse F.	Do.	Do.	Do.
S. 16633	Rfn. Teeling D.	Do.	18. 9. 1917.	Nil.
S. 8085	Rfn. Hancock G.	Died of Wounds	17. 9. 1917.	W. in Ac. 17. 9. 17

Reported by O.C. 13th (S) Battn. The Rifle Brigade in
B.213 dated 22. 9. 1917.

✢ ✢ ✢ ✢ ✢ ✢ ✢ ✢ ✢ ✢ ✢ ✢ ✢ ✢ ✢ ✢

Verified.
O.R.S.

G. H. Q.
3rd Echelon.
26. 9. 1917.

Major for
Officer i/c Regular Infantry Section No. 2.

13TH (S)

District. Rifle Records, Winchester.   Daily Casualty Report.

P.R.

B. 1917 Rfn. Walker J.   To Duty   22. 9. 1917.   W. in Ac.
16. 9. 17.

     Reported by O.C. 13th (S) Battalion The Rifle Brigade
           in B.213 dated 22. 9. 1917.

+ + + + + + + + + + + + + + +

Verified.
J. Hobson
O.R.S.

                                           Major for

G.H.Q.
3rd Echelon.   Officer i/c Regular Infantry Section No. 2.
27. 9. 1917.

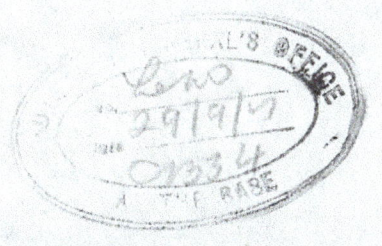

13th Bn. The Rifle Brigade

War Diary

From .. 1st Oct., 1917

To .. 31st Oct., 1917.

(Volume 25)

Army Form C. 2118.

WAR DIARY
or
INTELLIGENCE SUMMARY

(*Erase heading not required.*)

Place	Date	Hour	Summary of Events and Information	Remarks and references to Appendices

Instructions regarding War Diaries and Intelligence Summaries are contained in F. S. Regs., Part II. and the Staff Manual respectively. Title Pages will be prepared in manuscript.

Army Form C. 2118.

WAR DIARY
or
INTELLIGENCE SUMMARY.
(Erase heading not required.)

Instructions regarding War Diaries and Intelligence Summaries are contained in F. S. Regs., Part II. and the Staff Manual respectively. Title pages will be prepared in manuscript.

Place	Date	Hour	Summary of Events and Information	Remarks and references to Appendices
MENIN ROAD.	1/10/17.		The Battalion continued to hold the line on and South of the MENIN ROAD, from the 1st of October to the 5th Oct. 1917, one deliberate counter-attack being made on the Battalion Front on the morning of the 3rd. This counter-attack was repulsed. Capt. (A/Major) S.S.JENKYNS, proceeded to take over Temporary Command of 9th Battn. North Staffs. Regt., on the 1st.	
WILLIBEKE CAMP.	5th.		The Battalion was relieved on the night 5/6th Oct., by the 11th Warwicks, and returned to Rest Camp at WILLIBEKE CAMP, remaining there for 36 hours.	
MONT SORREL.	7th.		On the night 7/8th, the Battalion returned to trenches, and occupied the Support Line in the MONT SORREL Sector, and was relieved by the 13th Battn. Royal Fusiliers on the night of 11/12th. Maj. A.N.S.JACKSON, D.S.O., left to take over Temporary Command of 13th Battn. King's Royal Rifle Corps.	
DEAD DOG FARM.	11th.		The Battalion remained in Camp at DEAD DOG FARM for 4 days, being relieved there by the 16th Battn. Notts & Derby Regt., on the 15th. The Battn., proceeded to LOCREHOF FARM. Capt. J.B.G.TAYLOR, M.C., rejoined the Battalion on the 11th Oct., 1917, from Staff duties, and assumed the position of Second in Command.	
LOCREHOF FARM.	15th.		At LOCREHOF FARM training was again resumed. A draft of 141 other ranks joined the Battalion on 19th Oct. 1917.	
ST. JEAN.	22nd.		On the morning of the 22nd the Battalion proceeded by bus to ST. JEAN, and relieved the 11th Warwicks. Working parties were found by the Battalion at WIELTJE and neighbourhood. The Battn., was relieved by the 9th Battn. Somerset L.I., and returned by bus to billets in the STRAZEELE Area, on the afternoon of the 29th.	

Army Form C. 2118.

WAR DIARY
of
INTELLIGENCE SUMMARY.
(Erase heading not required.)

Sheet No. 2.

Place	Date	Hour	Summary of Events and Information	Remarks and references to Appendices
STRAZEELE.	29th.		Here a number of new Officers joined the Battalion, and training was at once resumed, sports organised, and re-fitting proceeded with.	
			During the month the following Honours and Rewards for Gallantry and Good Work at the places and on the dates shewn, were notified:-	
			T/2nd Lt. (A/Capt.) N.W.NOTHARD. Bar to M.C. GHELUVELT. 3/4th Oct. 1917.	
			T/2nd Lt. A.L.COOPER. M.C. do. 1/5th Oct. 1917.	
			No. Z. 1890 Sgt. H. Draper. Bar to D.C.M. E. of YPRES. 4/5th " "	
			" S. 3214 " E.G.Thompson. D.C.M. do. 3/4th " "	
			" S. 6522 " W. Gregg. D.C.M. GHELUVELT. 30th Sept. "	
			" 304530 L/Cpl. E.R.Tyler. D.C.M. do. 3rd Oct. "	
			" S. 27446 " L. Hartley. M.M. do. " " "	
			" S. 17302 Rfn. J. Wilmot. M.M. Near YPRES. 4th Oct. "	
			" S. 15220 " J. Tindell. M.M. Nr ZILLEBEKE. 3/7th Oct. "	
			" S. 4527 " J. Arnold. M.M. E. of YPRES. 3/4th Oct. "	
			" 304509 " E. Travis. M.M. GHELUVELT. 3rd Oct. "	
			" S. 27375 " A. Nash. M.M. do. " " "	

Army Form C. 2118.

WAR DIARY
or
INTELLIGENCE SUMMARY.

(Erase heading not required.)

Sheet No. 5.

Place	Date	Hour	Summary of Events and Information	Remarks and references to Appendices
	1/11/17		Strength on 1st Oct. 1917.......... O. 38. OR. 752.	
			Deduct Casualties during month..... 9. 159.	
			27. 593.	
			Add reinforcements during month.... 8. 206.	
			35. 799.	
			Strength on 31st Oct. 1917.........	
			J.M. Stewart	
			Lieut. Colonel.	
			Commanding 13th Battalion The Rifle Brigade.	

Instructions regarding War Diaries and Intelligence Summaries are contained in F. S. Regs., Part II. and the Staff Manual respectively. Title pages will be prepared in manuscript.

District, Rifle Records, Winchester.   Daily Casualty Report.

Reg. No.	Rank and Name.	Casualty.	P.R.
S.28613	Rfn. Evans W.H.	Killed in Action 27. 4. 1917.	W. and M. 27. 4. 1917.
S.21920	" Methven W.J.	do. 11. 4. 1917.	Missing. 11. 4. 1917.

Reported by O.C. 13th (S) Battn. The Rifle Brigade in Memo. dated 24. 9. 1917.

✠ ✠ ✠ ✠ ✠ ✠ ✠ ✠ ✠ ✠ ✠ ✠ ✠ ✠ ✠ ✠

Verified.
O.R.S.

G.H.Q.
3rd Echelon.
2. 10. 1917.

Major for
Officer i/c Regular Infantry Section No. 2.

...th (Service) Bt.tn The RIFLE BRI...

WINCHESTER RECORD OFFICE DAILY CASUALTY LIST DATED 5-10-1917.
****

Regt.No.	Rank and Name.	Casualty.	PR.
B. 200827	Rfn. Judd G.	Killed in Action 28-9-1917.	Nil.
S. 19837	Rfn. Vassie R.	Wounded in Action 28-9-1917.	Nil.
B. 203297	Rfn. Summerley P.	Wounded in Action 28-9-1917.	Nil.
P. 522	L/C. Mann E.	Wounded in Action 29-9-1917.	Nil.
304564	L/C. Edwards R.	Wounded in Action 29-9-1917.	Nil.
S. 3223	A/S. Driscoll W.	Wounded in Action 1-10-17.	Nil.
S. 3730	Cpl. Phillips J.	Wounded in Action 1-10-17.	Nil.
S. 4057	L/C. Bracey J.	Wounded in Action 1-10-17.	Nil.
6/454	Rfn. Coley C.	Wounded in Action 1-10-17.	Nil.
B. 200799	Rfn. Gardwell P.	Wounded in Action 1-10-17.	Nil.
B. 200782	Rfn. Statham E.	Wounded in Action 1-10-17.	Nil.

The above casualties were reported by The
Officer Commanding 13th Rifle Brigade 1-10-17.

Verified. ORS.

5-10-17.

Major for,
Officer i/c. Regular Infantry Section No.2.

13th RIFLE BRIGADE.

LIST No. 1130 6.10.17.

2/LIEUT	McDONALD-CAMPBELL	E.	Killed 5.10.17.
LIEUT	OBALDESTON	G.	Wounded 5.10.17.

...] Bn. [...]ield's Brigade

WINCHESTER RECORD OFFICE DAILY CASUALTY LIST D/- 7.10.1917.

A/CAPTAIN. BOUGHTON - LEIGH E. WOUNDED 2.10.1917. (GAS)   NIL.
2/LIEUT.   SPENCE   J.F.   ditto.   Nil.
2/LIEUT.   PIPER   C.D.   ditto.   NIL.

Reported on A.G's.List No. 1128 dated 4.10.1917.

Verified.
ORS.

Major for,
Officer i/c Regular Infantry Section No.2.

7.10.1917.

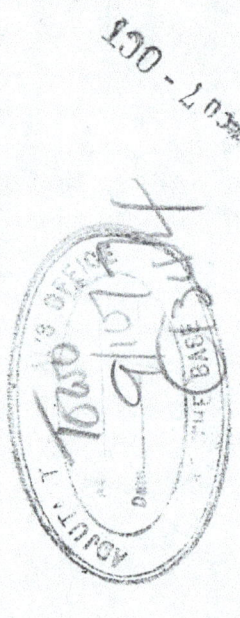

13th (S) Battn. The Rifle Brigade.

WINCHESTER RECORD OFFICE. DAILY CASUALTY LIST DATED

Regt.No.	Rank and Name.	Casualty	PR.
B.200791	Rfn. Gough F.	Wounded in Action 30.9.1917.	Nil.
S. 12650	Rfn. Killick A.	Wounded in Action 30.9.1917.	Nil.
S. 30967	Rfn. Brogden A.	Wounded in Action 29.9.1917.	Nil.
S. 4057	L/C. Bracey J.	Wounded at duty 1.10.1917.	W in A.

Reported by O.C. 13th Rifle Brigade 2.10.1917.

Verified. ORS.

Major for,

7.10.1917.   Officer i/c Regular Infantry Section No.2.

...th ... Batt...

Winchester Record Office Daily Casualty List dated 10.10.17.

2nd Lieut. G. OSBALDESTON.   Wounded in Action 5.10.17.   Nil.
Reported on A.G's. List No. 1130 dated 6.10.17.

Verified.
ORS.

10.10.17.   Major for O.i/c Reg. Infantry Section No.

13th (Service) Battalion The Rifle Brigade.

Winchester Record Office Daily Casualty List dated 10.10.17.

Regt.No.	Rank and Name.	Casualty.	PR.
S. 15585	Cpl. Jones J.	Killed in Action 2.10.1917.	Nil.
S. 3825	L/C. Watson R.	Wounded in Action 2.10.17.	Nil.
S. 8664	Rfn. Bampton F.	ditto	Nil.
S. 28633	Rfn. Hughes T.	ditto	Nil.
B. 203265	L/C. Curtlin H.	ditto	Nil.
S. 25023	Rfn. Follett S.	ditto	Nil.
S. 29710	Rfn. Champion L.	ditto	Nil.
S. 15919	Rfn. Blythe H.	ditto	Nil.
S. 27375	Rfn. Nash A.	ditto	Nil.
574474	Rfn. Weston W.	ditto	Nil.
S. 30977	Rfn. Morris T.	ditto	Nil.
S. 16766	Rfn. Gibbs E.	ditto	Nil.
S. 15936	Rfn. Tucker E.	ditto	Nil.
S. 10416	L/C. Binks H.	ditto	Nil.
S. 3977	Sgt. Sowter V.	ditto	Nil.
S. 27446	L/C. Hartley L.	ditto	Nil.
B. 203288	L/C. Moore J.	Wounded at Duty. 2.10.17.	Nil.
374252	Rfn. West L.	ditto	Nil.
S. 21913	Rfn. Strange S.	ditto	Nil.
S. 30790	Rfn. Babbs J.	Wounded in Action. 2.10.17.	Nil.
B. 200388	L/C. Legge A.	ditto	Nil.
5/472	Rfn. Lardlaw J.	Wounded(Gas) 2.10.17.	Nil.
S. 28628	Rfn. Higgins J.	ditto	Nil.
6447	Rfn. Suggers J.	ditto	Nil.
S. 17639	L/C. Land T.	ditto	Nil.
S. 27408	Rfn. Quin P.	ditto	Nil.
S. 24068	L/C. Lansdown S.	ditto	Nil.
S. 27370	L/C. Bradford A.	ditto	Nil.
373303	L/S. Tizzard R.	ditto	Nil.
S. 30573	Rfn. Smith T.	ditto	Nil.
S. 3686	Sgt. Goddard F.	ditto	Nil.
S. 16273	L/C. Sowden H.	ditto	Nil.
S. 27401	Rfn. Giles S.	ditto	Nil.
S. 4029	L/C. Berry L.	ditto	Nil.
S. 25272	Rfn. Duncan W.	ditto	Nil.
S. 27402	Rfn. Goodman N.	ditto	Nil.
S. 11636	L/C. Burtenshaw H.	ditto	Nil.
423677	Rfn. Delieu S.	ditto	Nil.
S. 4154	Rfn. Fox C.	ditto	Nil.
S. 25172	Rfn. Court A.	ditto	Nil.
574754	Rfn. Walker F.	ditto	Nil.

Reported by Officer Commanding 13th Rifle Brigade 4.10.1917.

Verified.
ORS.

Major for,
O.i/c Reg.Infantry Section No.2.

10.10.17.

A.O. 13.10.17 C1748

13TH (S) BATTALION THE RIFLE BRIGADE.

District, Rifle Records, Winchester.   Daily Casualty Report.

P.R.

2ND/LIEUT. CAMPBELL E. McDONALD   Killed in Action 5. 10. 1917.   Nil.

Reported by O.C. 13th (S) Battn. The Rifle Brigade
6. 10. 1917.

† † † † † † † † † † †
† † † † † † † † † † †
† † † † † † † † † † †
† † † † † † † † † † †

Verified.

G.R.S.

G.H.Q.
3rd Echelon.
11. 10. 1917.

Major for
Officer i/c Regular Infantry Section No. 2

13th (S) BATTALION RIFLE BRIGADE.

District, Rifle Records, Winchester.   Daily Casualty Report.

Reg. No.	Rank and Name.	Casualty.		P.R.
304454	Rfn. Gurney C.W.	Died of Wounds	4. 10. 1917.	Nil.
	Reported by O.C. 57th Field Ambulance dated 6. 10. 1917.			
S. 30502	L/C. Elliott A.	Killed in Action	2. 10. 1917.	"
S. 7536	Rfn. Potts H.	do.	4. 10. 1917.	"
423133	" Cavalier G.C.	do.	do.	"
S. 1585	L/S. Austin E.	do.	5. 10. 1917.	"
S. 4100	Cpl. Crust A.E.	do.	5. 10. 1917.	"
5115	Sgt. Gaunt A.	do.	5. 10. 1917.	"
S. 19716	Rfn. Carpenter W.	Wounded in Action	2. 10. 1917.	"
B. 200819	Cpl. Goulding M.	do.	3. 10. 1917.	"
B. 203171	Rfn. Arnold W.	do.	do.	"
B. 200783	" Alford F.	do.	do.	"
304493	" Banks J.F.	do.	do.	"
S. 29739	" Bennett C.	do.	do.	"
S. 20601	" Tillott G.	do.	do.	"
B. 203485	" Oldham J.	do.	do.	"
423478	" Bannon G.	do.	4. 10. 1917.	"
304458	" Everest F.A.C.	do.	do.	"
304476	" Levy G.L.	do.	do.	"
304512	" Conyer T.G.	do.	do.	"
373768	" Wood J.D.	do.	do.	"
B. 200803	" Aitchison J.	do.	do.	"
S. 28935	" Ely F.	do.	do.	"
S. 27467	" Schofield T.	do.	do.	"
S. 28635	" Johnson W.	do.	do.	"
S. 20625	L/C. Smith J.	do.	do.	"
S. 4392	Cpl. Henderson	do.	do.	"
S. 2357	Rfn. Hyde E.	do.	do.	"
S. 3230	" Evans A.	do.	do.	"
4142	Cpl. Shawyer H.V.	do.	do.	"
S. 4623	" Bissell J.C.	do.	do.	"
S. 16690	Rfn. Bradshaw F.	do.	do.	"
B. 200525	L/C. Clarke P.	do.	5. 10. 1917.	"
B. 200793	Rfn. Hall S.	do.	do.	"
S. 27083	" Catt A.E.	do.	do.	"
S. 27372	" Mowe E.	do.	do.	"
S. 2065	L/C. Richardson T.	do.	do.	"
6. 641	Sgt. Davis W.	do.	do.	"

Reported by O.C. 13th (S) Battn. The Rifle Brigade
6. 10. 1917.

✢ ✢ ✢ ✢ ✢ ✢ ✢ ✢ ✢ ✢ ✢ ✢ ✢ ✢ ✢ ✢

Verified.
O.R.S.

G.H.Q.
3rd Echelon.
11. 10. 1917.

Major for
Officer i/c Regular Infantry Section No. 2.

13TH (S) BATTALION THE RIFLES

District, Rifle Records, Winchester.   Daily Casualty Report.

Rank and Name.	C a s u a l t y.	P.R.

Reg. No.

S. 27467 Rfn. Schofield T.   Died of Wounds 6. 10. 1917. W. in Action
Gas. R. 11. 10. 17.
Reported by O.C. 1 Aus. C.C.S. 6. 10. 1917.

† † † † † † † † † † † † † † † † †

Verified.

O.R.S.

Officer i/c Regular Infantry Section No. 2.

Major for

G.H.Q.
3rd Echelon.
11. 10. 1917.

1st (S) BATTALION THE RIFLE BRIGADE.

District, Rifle Records, Winchester.   Daily Casualty Report.

Reg. No.   Rank and Name.   C a s u a l t y.   P.R.

S. 10417 L/C. Cain W.   Wounded in Action 2. 10. 1917. Nil.

Reported by O.C. 111th Trench Mortar Battery
                    6. 10. 1917.

+ + + + + + + + + + + + + +

1st (S) Bn Rifle Bde Verified.
                      O.R.S.

Officer I/c Regular Infantry Section No. 2.   Major for

G.H.Q.
3rd Echelon.
12. 10. 1917.

District, Rifle Records, Winchester.   Daily Casualty Report.

Reg. No.	Rank and Name.	Casualty.		P.R.
S. 23431	Rfn. Donoghy J.	Wounded in Action	5. 10. 17.	Nil.
374673	" Hewitt H.	do.	do.	do.

Amended Report.

S. 4392	R/S. Henderson H.A.	Wounded (Gas)	4. 10. 17.	W. in A.
S. 4623	Cpl. Bissell J.G.	do.	do.	do.
B.203171	Rfn. Arnold W.	do.	3. 10. 17.	do.

Cas. R. 11. 10. 17.

Reported by O.C. 13th (S) Batn. The Rifle Brigade,
8. 10. 1917.

+ + + + + + + + + + + + + + + +

Verified.
O.R.S.

Major for
Officer i/c Regular Infantry Section No. 2.

G.H.Q.
3rd Echelon.
14. 10. 1917.

13th (S) BAT͟T͟ⁿ ͟ ͟ ͟ T͟H͟E͟ R͟I͟F͟L͟E͟ B͟R͟I͟G͟A͟ ͟ ͟

District, Rifle Records, Winchester.   Daily Casualty Report.

Reg. No.	Rank and Name.	Casualty.		P. R.
S. 8?4	Rfn. Bampton F.	To Duty	5. 10. 1917.	W. in A.
B.200/91	" Gough F.	do.	2. 10. 1917.	do.
B.200782	" Statham E.J.A.	do.	5. 10. 1917.	do.
S. 3825	L/C. Watson R.	do.	do.	do.

Cas. R. 10. 10. 17.

Reported by O.C. 13th (S) Battn. The Rifle Brigade,
6. 10. 1917.

+ + + + + + + + + + + +

G.H.Q. 3rd Echelon.
14. 10. 1917.

Major for
Officer i/c Regular Infantry Section No. 2.

District, Rifle Records, Winchester.　　　Daily Casualty Report.

Amended Report.

Please cancel report of Missing in report C.1270 in the case of 6440 Rfn. Swindells A. This man has been reported by War Office as "Ad. General Hospital." D.A.A.G (2) B77L/6 dated 12. 10. 1917.

Verified.
C.R.S.

Major for
Officer i/c Regular Infantry Section No. 2.

G. H. Q.
3rd Echelon.
16. 10. 1917.

13TH (S) BATTN. THE RIFLE BRIGADE.

District, Rifle Records, Winchester.   Daily Casualty Report.

Reg. No.	Rank and Name.	Casualty.		P.R.
Z. 2766	CQMS Nethercott W.H.	Killed in Action	10. 10. 1917	Nil.
S. 34074	Rfn. Mansfield F.G.	do.	do.	do.
S. 34032	" Norton A.J.	do.	do.	do.
S. 33640	" Solomon G.	do.	do.	do.
S. 33738	" Webb F.	do.	do.	do.
S. 34082	" Bickmore L.E.J.	do.	do.	do.
S. 33773	" Draycott E.	do.	do.	do.
S. 33706	" Hector W.	do.	do.	do.
425715	" Young C.D.	do.	do.	do.
S. 20321	" Preston G.	do.	do.	do.
P. 137	" Mallett W.	Wounded in Action	9. 10. 1917	do.
S. 33687	" Barrie G.	do.	10. 10. 1917	do.
S. 31462	" Lambourne W.	do.	do.	do.
S. 4195	" Musk J.H.	do.	do.	do.
574108	" Cooper W.J.	Wounded (Gas).	12. 10. 1917	do.
4752	L/C. Turner D.	do.	do.	do.
B.200784	Rfn. Clarke S.	do.	do.	do.
304468	" Grimshaw W.J.	do.	do.	do.
B. 2406	" Smith C.	do.	do.	do.
304457	" Armsdon W.E.	do.	do.	do.
S. 21891	" Alderson C.	do.	do.	do.
S. 30986	" Tuffield A.	do.	do.	do.
374096	" Elston S.A.	do.	do.	do.
S. 28617	Cpl. Mayoh P.	do.	do.	do.
B.203371	Rfn. Hyslop W.	do.	do.	do.
S. 16120	" Johnson H.	do.	do.	do.
S. 26468	" Davey F.	do.	do.	do.
S. 15003	" Pawle H.E.	do.	do.	do.
S. 835	" Sharrett A.	do.	do.	do.
741193	Cpl. Pitt B.R.	do.	do.	do.
S. 24249	Rfn. Hurst F.G.	do.	do.	do.
S. 27382	" Clayden G.T.	do.	do.	do.
S. 19700	" Bennett H.	do.	do.	do.
B.200824	" Johnson J.	do.	do.	do.
S. 19810	" Middleton J.	do.	do.	do.
S. 27432	" Bailey R.	do.	do.	do.
572760	" Haver T.H.	do.	do.	do.
Z. 2756	A/C. Thompson H.	do.	do.	do.
S. 19884	" Martin J.	do.	do.	do.
S. 27442	L/S. Evans C.C.	do.	do.	do.
Z. 890	Rfn. Terry H.	do.	do.	do.
S. 27465	" Archer F.J.	do.	do.	do.

Reported by O.C. 13th (S) Battn. The Rifle Brigade
12. 10. 1917.

Verified.
O.R.S.

G.H.Q.
3rd Echelon.
18. 10. 1917.

Major for
Officer i/c Regular Infantry Section No. 2.

...TALION THE RIFLE BRIGADE.

District, Rifle Records, Winchester.   Daily Casualty Report.

Reg. No.	Rank and Name.	Casualty.			P. R.
S. 27092	Rfn. Mallett H.	Wounded at Duty	11. 10.	1917.	Nil.
304564	L/C. Edwards R.	To Duty	29. 9.	1917.	W. in A. C.1342.
S. 30790	Rfn. Babbs J.	do.	18. 10.	1917.	W. in A. C.1347
304512	" Conyer T.	do.	8. 10.	1917.	W. in A.
B.200793	" Hall S.	do.	12. 10.	1917.	do.
B.200425	L/C. Clarke P.	do.	16. 10.	1917.	do. C.1348.

Amended Report.

| 374673 | Rfn. Hewitt H. | Wounded at Duty | 5. 10. 1917. | W. in A. Cas. R. 14. 10. 17. |

Reported by O.C. 13th (S) Battn. The Rifle Brigade,
18. 10. 1917.

+ + + + + + + + + + + + + + +

Verified.
O.R.S.

G.H.Q.
3rd Echelon.
22. 10. 1917.

Major for
Officer i/c Regular Infantry Section No. 2.

District, Rifle Records, Winchester.   Daily Casualty Report.

| Reg. No. | Rank and Name. | C a s u a l t y . | P. R. |

S.30988   Rfn. Tesseyman J.   Killed in Action 28. 4. 1917. Missing.
                                            Cas. R. to W.O. 25.5.1.

Auth:- D.A.G. 3rd Echelon dated 18. 10. 1917.

++++++++++++++++++++

Verified.

O.R.S.

Major for
Officer i/c Regular Infantry Section No. 2.

G.H.Q.
3rd Echelon.
22. 10. 1917.

District, Rifle Records, Winchester.   Daily Casualty Report.

Reg. No.	Rank and Name.	Casualty.	P. R.
B. 2436	Rfn. Taylor J.	Died of Wounds NE 27. 7. 1917.	Nil.

Reported by O.C. 50th Field Ambulance 27. 7. 1917.

✢ ✢ ✢ ✢ ✢ ✢ ✢ ✢ ✢ ✢ ✢ ✢ ✢ ✢ ✢ ✢ ✢

Verified.
O.R.S.

G. H. Q.
3rd Echelon.   Major for
24. 10. 1917.   Officer i/c Regular Infantry Section No. 2.

Winchester Record Office Daily Casualty List dated 30.10.1917.

Regt.No.	Rank and Name.	Casualty.		PR.
S. 14088	L/C. Elsworthy J.	Missing 6.10.1917. "A" Coy. Reported by O.C. 111th T.M.B. 13.10.17.		Nil.
S. 27092	Rfn. Hallett H.J.	Wounded in Action 11.10.17.		Nil.
S. 27372	Rfn. Mowe E.	Returned to duty 14.10.17. Reported by O.C. Battalion 20.10.1917.		"W"

Verified.

ORS.

Major for,

30.10.17.   Officer i/c Infantry Section No.2.

SECRET

13th Bn The Rifle Brigade

WAR DIARY

From   1st Nov., 1917

To   30th Nov., 1917

Vol. No. 26.

Army Form C. 2118.

WAR DIARY
or
INTELLIGENCE SUMMARY.

(Erase heading not required.)

Instructions regarding War Diaries and Intelligence Summaries are contained in F. S. Regs., Part II. and the Staff Manual respectively. Title pages will be prepared in manuscript.

Place	Date	Hour	Summary of Events and Information	Remarks and references to Appendices

WAR DIARY
or
INTELLIGENCE SUMMARY.
(Erase heading not required.)

Army Form C. 2118.

Place	Date	Hour	Summary of Events and Information	Remarks and references to Appendices
STRAZEELE	1/11/17		The Battalion remained in rest billets at STRAZEELE until Novr. 8th. Training of every kind was continued. The Companies took part in Battalion, Brigade and Divisional Competitions. The Battalion Drill Competition was won by 'D' Coy. 'B' Coy., won the Brigade YUKON Pack Competition. In recreational encounters Sgt. GREGG, 'HQ' Coy., won the cross-country race. This was a most successful event; Officers and 400 other ranks starting on very heavy ground, and only a small number failing to complete the course in the given time. The barrel of beer for the Company shewing the greatest number finishing was won by 'A' Coy. The Brigade Commander inspected the Battn. Transport on the 2nd, and the Battalion on the 3rd, and expressed great approval with both parades. The scattered nature of the billets rendered it most difficult to collect the Battn., for amusement during the evenings, which nevertheless were most enjoyably spent in the various billets.	
KEMMEL SHELTERS.	8/11/17.		The Battalion moved from STRAZEELE on the morning of the 8th to hutments E. of LOCRE at KEMMEL SHELTERS. Ten days were spent here. Training and competitions were resumed, and much good work was done, the Battalion being noticeably improved. The health of all ranks was excellent.	
KLEINE ZILLEBEKE.	Nov. 17th/18th.		The Battalion took over the front line trenches N.E. of KLEINE ZILLEBEKE, on the night 17/18th Novr., relieving the 11th Battn. Royal Warwicks. The relief was carried out most satisfactorily on a dark night. Two Companies held the front shell-hole line, and one Coy. remained in Support, and one in Reserve. Four-day spells were made, the Support and Reserve Companies relieving the front line Companies on the night of 21/22nd Novr. Whilst holding this line the Battalion did good work in improving shell-holes and communications, an excellent signal service being maintained. All Companies being in telephonic communication with Battn. H.Qrs., during the whole period. Observation over the enemy was good, and much useful information of his movements was obtained. Sniping was brisk, and a bag of 8 was reported and confirmed.	

Army Form C. 2118.

WAR DIARY
or
INTELLIGENCE SUMMARY.
(Erase heading not required.)

Sheet 2.

Place	Date	Hour	Summary of Events and Information	Remarks and references to Appendices
RIDGE WOOD.	25/26th Novr.		On the night of the 25/26th Novr., the Battalion was relieved in the line by the 8th Battn. Somerset L.I., and proceeded into Brigade in Support hutments at RIDGE WOOD.) From this place numerous working parties were supplied. The Battalion continued to occupy these billets up to Novr. 30th 1917.	

	O.	O.R.
Effective strength of Battn., on 31/10/17.	35.	799.
Casualties during the month.	2.	49.
Reinforcements during the month.	5	31
Effective strength of Battn., on 30/11/17.	38.	781.

Commanding 13th Battalion The Rifle Brigade.
Lieut. Col.

1/12/1917.

Winchester Record Office Daily Casualty List dated 1.11.1917.

Regt.No.	Rank and Name.	Casualty.	PR.
S. 27065	L/C. Gurney E.W. *Amended*	"W" Shell Shock 4.10.1917. Reported by O.C. N.Z. Stat.Hsp. 15.10.1917. on A.F.W.3436.	Nil.
4142	Cpl. Shawyer H.V.	Wounded accidentally 4.10.17. Reported by G.O.C. 2nd Army dated 18.10.1917.	"W"
203	Rfn. Spiceley A.	Wounded in Action 24.10.17. Reported by O.C.Bn. 27.10.17.	Nil.

Verified. ORS.

Major for,

1.11.1917. Officer i/c Infantry Section No.2.

(   ) Battalion The Rifle Brigade

WINCHESTER RECORD OFFICE. DAILY CASUALTY LIST DATED 2.11.1917.

2nd LIEUT. W.M.SMITH.	WOUNDED IN ACTION 29.10.1917. Reported on A.G's.List No. 1155 dated 31.10.1917.	Nil.

Verified.
ORS.

Major for,
2.11.1917. Officer i/c Infantry Section No.2.

13th (Ser) Battalion The Rifle Brigade.

Winchester Record Office Daily Casualty List dated 12.11.17.

Regt.No.	Rank and Name.	Casualty.	PR.
S. 15847	Cpl. Mabbett F. *Amended*	Wounded Shell Shock 7.10.17. Reported by O.C. New Zealand Stationary Hospital 2.11.17.	Nil.
S. 27092	Rfn. Hallett H.J.	Reported Wounded in Action 11.10.17. on Casualty List No.C.1368 dated 2.11.17. Please cancel. Auth:- O.C.Battalion 6.11.1917.	

Verified.
ORS.

G. H. Qrs. 3rd Ech.
Nov. 12th. 1917.

Major for,
Officer i/c Infantry Section No.2.

13th (Ser) Battalion The Rifle Brig[ade]

Winchester Record Office. Daily Casualty List dated 13.11.17.

Regt.No.	Rank and Name.	Casualty.	OR.
Z. 2772	Rfn. Manning W.	"W" Shell Shock 4.10.17. Reported by O.C. 15 C.C.S. on A.F.W.3436 dated 1.11.17.	Nil.

Verified.

ORS.

G.H.Q. 3rd Ech.
Nov. 13th. 17.

Major for,
Officer i/c Infantry Section No.2.

Officer i/c Reg. Inf. Sec.⁴ No. 2
: Base.

Reference your memo overleaf:
(i) Rfn. HALLETT was reported W/a by O.C. 154: R.E. Field Coy. to which unit he was attached. A later report shewed that he remained "AT DUTY".

(ii) S. 27463 Rfn TYLER A returned to Batt.ⁿ 7/9/17. He will be reported on this week's A.F. B 213.

N. Roberts-Jones
Capt. + Adj
13: R.B.

[Stamp: ORDERLY ROOM No. C/871/... Date 6/11/17 13th BATT. RIFLE BRIGADE]

---

on The Rifle Brigade.

...STER.   Daily Casualty List.

Casualty   By Whom Reported   P.R.

Killed in Action,
31-5-1917.   O.C.Battn. on   "M"
                 memo d/- 9-11-17.   To W.O.
                                         22-8-17.

    -do-   -do-   -do-

...rified,
...ORS.
13th Bn R.Bde.   RJ

                                         Major for,
                        Officer i/c Infantry Section No.2.

[Stamp: A.G's G.H.Q. CASUALTIES]

13th (Service) Battalion The Rifle Brigade.

District Record Office. WINCHESTER.   Daily Casualty List.

Regtl No.	Rank & Name	Casualty	By Whom Reported	P.R.
B.203513	L/Sgt. Warner H.	Killed in Action, 31-5-1917.	O.C.Battn. on memo d/- 9-11-17.	"M" To W.O. 22-6-17.
S.6868	Rfm Clarke H.	-do-	-do-	-do-

Verified,
ORS.
13th Bn R.Bde.

General Headquarters,
3rd Echelon., 14-11-17.

Major for,
Officer i/c Infantry Section No.2.

O.C.
3rd Rifle Brigade

Reference. S/27092
Rfn Hallett H.J.
reported W in A 11/10/17
on A.F.B.213.
Kindly inform me
if this man has
since rejoined Bn
as no ambulance
report has been
received regarding
him, also if S/28643
Rfn Riley a has
rejoined Bn

R.J.Jenner
Major
O/C Infect No 2

13th (Service) Battalion The Rifle Brigade.

Winchester Record Office Daily Casualty List dated 23-11-17.

Regt.No.	Rank and Name.	Casualty.	PR.
423514	Rfn. Hallinan D.	Wounded (Gas) 2-10-1917. Reported by O.C.Battalion on A.F.B.213 dated 17-11-17.	Nil.

Verified.
ORS.

Major for.
23-11-17.   Officer i/c Infantry Section No.2.

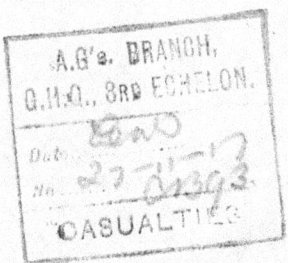

13th (Service) Battalion The Rifle Brigade.

Winchester Record Office. Daily Casualty List dated 24.12.1917.

Regt.No.	Rank and Name.	Casualty.	PR.
S.28620	A/Sgt. Drake E.	Wounded (Acc) 15.12.1917.	Nil.
B.200795	Rfn. Davies D.	Wounded in Action 17.12.1917.	Nil.
S. 359	Rfn. Gillham E.	ditto	Nil.

Reported by The Officer Commanding 13th (S) Bn. The Rifle Brigade dated 20.12.1917.

Verified.
ORS.

24.12.17.

Major for.
Officer i/c Infantry Section No.2.

13th (Ser) Bn. Rifle Bde
Dec 17

13th (Service............................

Winchester Record Office ..ily Casualty List dated 27-11-1917.
....

Regt.No.	Rank and Name.	Casualty.	PR.
S. 10075	Rfn. Vesey E.	KILLED IN ACTION. 22-11-1917.	Nil.
S. 29891	Rfn. Crowhurst J.	KILLED IN ACTION. 22-11-1917.	Nil.
S. 3666	Rfn. Thompson W.N.	Wounded in Action 23-11-1917.	Nil.
B. 200838	Rfn. Pooley A.	Wounded in Action 23-11-1917.	Nil.
S. 33609	Rfn. Corney W.J.	Wounded in Action 21-11-1917.	Nil.

Reported by O.C.Battn. 24-11-1917.
****
Verified.
ORS.

Major for.

27-11-1917.   Officer i/c Infantry Section No.2.

Daily Casualty List dated 27.12.17.

Regt.No.	Rank and Name.	Casualty.	PR.
S. 7129	Rfn. Margerison R.	Wounded in Action 19.12.1917. Reported by O.C.Battn. 22.12.17.	Nil.

Verified. ORS. *RH*

Major for.
O.i/c Infantry Section No.2.

27.12.17.

5/ Rn(S) Rifle Bde

Rec'd 28 DEC

13th (S) Bn. The Rifle Brigade.

Winchester District. Daily Casualty List dated 28-11-17.

Regt.No.	Rank and Name.	Casualty.	PR.
S. 14088	Rfn. Elsworthy J.W.	Killed in Action or Died of Wounds on or shortly after 6-10-1917. Burial reported by G.O.C. IX Corps dated 24-10-1917.	Missing. C.1368.

Verified.
ORS.
Major for.
28-11-17.   Officer i/c Infantry Section No.

SECRET

13th BATTALION THE RIFLE BRIGADE

WAR DIARY

From 1/12/1917

To   ..   .. 31/12/1917.

(Volume No 27)

WAR DIARY
or
INTELLIGENCE SUMMARY.
(Erase heading not required.)

Army Form C. 2118.

13 R.fc Bn.
Vol 28

Instructions regarding War Diaries and Intelligence Summaries are contained in F.S. Regs., Part II. and the Staff Manual respectively. Title pages will be prepared in manuscript.

Place	Date	Hour	Summary of Events and Information	Remarks and references to Appendices
RIDGE WOOD.	Dec.1 to Dec.4.		The Battalion remained in RIDGE WOOD CAMP, VIERSTRAAT, in the Support Area, until Decr. 4th. During the whole of this period. the Battn., was engaged in working and carrying in the reserve and front lines.	
CURRAGH CAMP.	Dec. 5th to Dec. 13th.		The Battn., moved to CURRAGH CAMP, Near LOCRE, in the Reserve Area, remaining there till Dec. 13th. During the week the usual programme of training was carried out. Recreational training, competitions and football matches took place during the afternoons. The morale of the troops during this period was excellent, and their health good.	
LOCRE				
FRONT LINE.	Dec. 13/14th to 21/22nd.		The Battn., relieved the 5th Bedfords in the front line, 1000 yards N.E. of KLEINE ZILLEBEKE; the shell-hole line extending from BITTER WOOD to NORTH FARM. The operations consisted of reconnoitring patrols on both sides of the BASSIVILLEBEEK, from which much valuable information was obtained. In the earlier part of the week the ground was muddy, and the nights extremely dark, rendering patrolling difficult. This was succeeded by a period of snow and intense frost. In spite of this the health of the troops was noticeably good, and in particular the number of cases of trench feet was negligible. In the course of the last 2 days the enemy frequently sent over mustard-gas shells, but no serious effects followed.	

Army Form C. 2118.

WAR DIARY
or
INTELLIGENCE SUMMARY.
(Erase heading not required.)

Instructions regarding War Diaries and Intelligence Summaries are contained in F. S. Regs., Part II. and the Staff Manual respectively. Title pages will be prepared in manuscript.

Place	Date	Hour	Summary of Events and Information	Remarks and references to Appendices

2353 Wt. W2544/1454 700,000 5/15 D.D.&L. A.D.S.S./Forms/C. 2118.

Army Form C. 2118.

13 Rifle B? [?]
VII 28

WAR DIARY
or
INTELLIGENCE SUMMARY.
(Erase heading not required.)

Instructions regarding War Diaries and Intelligence Summaries are contained in F. S. Regs., Part II. and the Staff Manual respectively. Title pages will be prepared in manuscript.

Place	Date	Hour	Summary of Events and Information	Remarks and references to Appendices
RIDGE WOOD.	Dec. 1 to Dec. 4.		The Battalion remained in RIDGE WOOD CAMP, VIERSTRAAT, in the Support Area, until Decr. 4th. During the whole of this period the Battn., was engaged in working and carrying in the reserve and front lines.	
CURRAGH CAMP, LOCRE.	Dec. 5th to Dec. 13th.		The Battn., moved to CURRAGH CAMP, Near LOCRE, in the Reserve Area, remaining there till Dec. 13th. During the week the usual programme of training was carried out. Recreational training, competitions and football matches took place during the afternoons. The morale of the troops during this period was excellent, and their health good.	
FRONT LINE.	Dec. 13/14th to 21/22nd.		The Battn., relieved the 6th Bedfords in the front line, 1000 yards N.E. of KLEINE ZILLEBEKE; the shell-hole line extending from BITTER WOOD to NORTH FARM. The operations consisted of reconnoitring patrols on both sides of the BASSEVILLEBEEK, from which much valuable information was obtained. In the earlier part of the week the ground was muddy, and the nights extremely dark, rendering patrolling difficult. This was succeeded by a period of snow and intense frost. In spite of this the health of the troops was noticeably good, and in particular the number of cases of trench feet was negligible. In the course of the last 2 days the enemy frequently sent over mustard-gas shells, but no serious effects followed.	

2353 Wt. W2544/1454 700,000 5/15 D. D. & L. A.D.S.S./Forms/C. 2118.

Army Form C. 2118.

WAR DIARY
or
INTELLIGENCE SUMMARY.
(Erase heading not required.)

Instructions regarding War Diaries and Intelligence Summaries are contained in F. S. Regs., Part II. and the Staff Manual respectively. Title pages will be prepared in manuscript.

Place	Date	Hour	Summary of Events and Information	Remarks and references to Appendices
RIDGE WOOD.	21/22–29th.		The Battalion returned to RIDGE WOOD CAMP.) As before, the troops were employed in working and carrying parties in the reserve line and front line.	
CURRAGH CAMP.	29th–31st.		The Battalion moved to CURRAGH CAMP. Working parties and carrying parties were continued in the reserve and front lines. Parties were formed for wiring the reserve line. Active preparations were in progress for a Christmas dinner and entertainment to be held in the Cinema Hall, LOCRE, on Jan. 1st. During the month the following mentions in Dispatches were notified:–	

T/Lieut. Col. W.R.STEWART, M.C.
T/Capt. E.B.PUGHE.
Capt. C.NICHOLSON, M.B. R.A.M.C.
No.S.3749 L/Sgt. Capern F.
" S.4432 L/Cpl. Kirkpatrick H.

	O.	O.R.
Total Effective Strength on 1/12/17	38	781
Casualties during month	1	35
	37	746
Reinforcements during month.	4	22
Total Effective strength on 31/12/17	41	768

[signature]
Capt.
Commanding 13th Battn. The Rifle Brigade.

13th Rifle Brigade
January to December
1918

Index..........................

SUBJECT.

8/3

No.	Contents.	Date.

(41,365). Wt.9392—94. 2000. 6/19.   **Gp.164.** A.&E.W.
(44,173).   „   21,613—105. 500. 10/19.   „

CONFIDENTIAL

13th (S) Batt.n The Rifle Brigade

War Diary

From ... ... 1st Jan., 1918
To ... ... 31st Jan., 1918

Vol. 28.

Army Form C. 2118.

WAR DIARY
or
INTELLIGENCE SUMMARY

(Erase heading not required.)

Instructions regarding War Diaries and Intelligence Summaries are contained in F. S. Regs., Part II. and the Staff Manual respectively. Title Pages will be prepared in manuscript.

Place	Date	Hour	Summary of Events and Information	Remarks and references to Appendices

Army Form C. 2118.

WAR DIARY
or
INTELLIGENCE SUMMARY.
(Erase heading not required.)

Instructions regarding War Diaries and Intelligence Summaries are contained in F.S. Regs, Part II and the Staff Manual respectively. Title pages will be prepared in manuscript.

Place	Date	Hour	Summary of Events and Information	Remarks and references to Appendices
LOCRE.	Jan.1st/18.		The Battalion Xmas Dinner was held in the Cinema Hall at LOCRE.	
CURRAGH CAMP.	Jan. 1st to Jan. 5th.		The Battalion was in CURRAGH CAMP. Large working parties were found daily for work on the Reserve Line. A raiding party of 4 Officers and 70 O.R., was trained.	
BULGAR & BITTER WOODS.	Jan. 5/6th.		The Battalion relieved the 11th Bn. Royal Warwickshire Regt., in BULGAR and BITTER WOODS. From the 6th to the 9th much patrolling was carried out preparatory to the raid, which took place on the 9th/10th Jan.	
do.	Jan.9/10th.		The Battalion carried out a successful raid on some enemy dug-outs. Although no identification was secured, severe casualties are known to have been inflicted. Our casualties were 1 Officer and 2 men wounded, and 3 men missing.	
	11/12th.		Throughout this tour in the line the weather was exceptionally bad. The Battalion was relieved and proceeded by light railway to RIDGEWOOD CAMP.	
	Jan.12th.		The Battalion moved by train to EBELINGHEM, and marched to rest billets in LA SABLONIERE. During the rest period, extensive training was carried out.	
	Jan. 31st.		The Battalion Sports were held on this date.	

Army Form C. 2118.

WAR DIARY
INTELLIGENCE SUMMARY.
(Erase heading not required.)

Instructions regarding War Diaries and Intelligence Summaries are contained in F. S. Regs., Part II. and the Staff Manual respectively. Title pages will be prepared in manuscript.

Place	Date	Hour	Summary of Events and Information	Remarks and references to Appendices
			- 2 -	

			O. OR.
			Total effective strength on 1/1/18 .... 41 768
			Casualties during month 4 47
			                                                          37. 721
			Reinforcements during month. .... 5 46.
			Total effective strength on 31/1/18. .... 42 767
			
			During the month the following Honours and Awards were notified :-
			
			D.S.O. Lieut. Col. W.R.STEWART, M.C.
			
			Mentioned in Despatches: Capt. G.Nicholson, R.A.M.C.
			                                    2nd Lieut. E.McD.CAMPBELL (Killed in Action)
			
			Military Medal: No.S.27421 Cpl. Blackmore F.
			                   " P. 4365 L/Cpl. Martin C.
			                   " B200425 L/Cpl. Clarke P.J.
			                   " B200393 Rfn. Wood L.
			
			                                                                                                 Lieut. Col.
			3/2/18. Commanding 13th Battalion The Rifle Brigade.	

13th (Ser) Battan, The Rifle Brigade.

Winchester Record Office. Daily Casualty List dated 31.1.1918.

```
                                                    Previously
                                                    reported.
S. 21897  Cpl.  Waines E.  MISSING 10.1.1918. "D" Coy   Nil.
S. 27408  Rfn.  Quin P.            -ditto-    "D" Coy   Nil.
S. 27772  Rfn.  Robinson W.        -ditto-    "D" Coy   Nil.
```

Reported by O.C. 13th Rifle Brigade 12.1.1918.

Major for.

G.H.Q. 3rd Echelon.
January 31st.1918.   Officer i/c Infantry Section No.2.

Secret.

13th Battalion. The Rifle Brigade.

— WAR DIARY. —

From February 1st 1918

To February 28th 1918.

— Vol: 29. —

Army Form C. 2118.

WAR DIARY
or
INTELLIGENCE SUMMARY.
(Erase heading not required.)

Instructions regarding War Diaries and Intelligence Summaries are contained in F. S. Regs., Part II. and the Staff Manual respectively. Title pages will be prepared in manuscript.

Place	Date 1918	Hour	Summary of Events and Information	Remarks and references to Appendices
	Feb. 1		The Battalion in rest billets at LA SABLONNIERE where training, sports and concerts took place.	
	" 2		Brigade Sports were held, the Battalion easily winning the Cup by scoring more points than the other Units in the Brigade put together.	
At LA SABLONNIERE.	" 3			
	" 4		The Battalion moved on this day to FORRESTER and SCOTTISH WOOD Camps, in the DICKEBUSCH Area.	
At FORRESTER and SCOTTISH WOOD CAMPS.	5-9			
	" 10		The Battalion moved forward to MANAWATU Camp, S. of YPRES.	
At MANAWATU CAMP.	" 11-15			
	" 16		The Battalion moved to SCOTTISH WOOD CAMP.	
At SCOTTISH WOOD CAMP.	" 17-20		During the period 5th to 20th February, day and night working parties were provided. Work consisted of construction of Strong points and company R.E. material, General Duties under	

Army Form C. 2118.

WAR DIARY
or
INTELLIGENCE SUMMARY.
(Erase heading not required.)

Place	Date	Hour	Summary of Events and Information	Remarks and references to Appendices
	1/18		took place.	
	26.2.1		The Battalion moved into Brigade Support, Battalion H.Q. in HOOGE CRATER. The Battalion provides day working parties on excavation of Divisional Reserve Line, and at night, parties for the carrying of rations to the Battalions in the front line.	
	27-27		The Battalion moved into the front line.	
ypes(north)			During the month the following Honours Award were received :-	
			7871. F.P. BATT. CHEVALIER de l'ORDRE de la COURONNE (with CROIX de GUERRE)) Belgian decorations
			Z.2822. SGT. BALCHIN N. - CROIX de GUERRE.	
			A/Capt E.WOOD - MILITARY CROSS.	
			30420 4/Cpl. ANTHONY F. - D.C.M.	
			Total effective strength 1/2/18 42 769 oc.	
			Total casualties = 2 69	
			40 697	
			" Reinforcements - 7 186	
			Total effective strength 28/2/18. 49 883	

J.B.Right Capt.
a/Col,
Commanding 13: Battalion The Rifle Brigade.

WAR DIARY or INTELLIGENCE SUMMARY

Army Form C. 2118.

13 Rfl Bde Vol 31

Place	Date 1918	Hour	Summary of Events and Information	Remarks and references to Appendices
	Feb 28/9 Mar 1/		Battalion moved from support in HOOGE CRATER to front line – POLDERHOEK sector; relieving 10th Royal Fusiliers.	
	6/7th (night)		Battalion relieved by the 8th. On the evening of the 8th the enemy attacked in the POLDERHOEK sector, and the Battalion moved up to support, but were not called upon to counter-attack and returned to MANAWATU Camp on the 9th.	
	11/12 (night)		Battalion relieved 13 K.R.R.C. in front line; his days this time spent in the front line and 6 days in support. Batt. H.Qrs in GLENCORSE WOOD and HOODE CRATER respectively.	
	23/24 (night)		Battalion returned to MANAWATU Camp where two days and spent.	
	25/26 (night)		Battalion relieved 13th Royal Fusiliers (112. Bde) in front line astride MENIN Road.	
	27/28 (night)		Battalion relieved by 1/4th K.O.Y.L.I, and returned to huts in the WIPPENHOEK area.	
	29th		In the early morning the Battalion entrained at HOPOUTRE siding near POPERINGHE; detraining at BOUQUEMAISON about 3.0 p.m. on the	
	30th		where the Battalion marched to DOULLENS, and entrained about 6.0 p.m.	

Army Form C. 2118.

WAR DIARY
or
INTELLIGENCE SUMMARY

(Erase heading not required.)

Instructions regarding War Diaries and Intelligence Summaries are contained in F. S. Regs., Part II. and the Staff Manual respectively. Title Pages will be prepared in manuscript.

Place	Date	Hour	Summary of Events and Information	Remarks and references to Appendices
	30/3/18		The Battalion arrived at a suburb of AMIENS at 11.0 p.m. and then marched to PONT NOYELLES, arriving there at 4.0 a.m. 31st.	
	31st.		Battalion entrained at 12 noon for MARIEUX, 4 miles from DOULLENS, and spent the remainder of the day billeted in an aerodrome.	
			Total effective strength 1/3/18. O. 49 O.R. 887
			Total casualties: 3 94
			46 793
			Total reinforcements: - 101
			Total effective strength 31/3/18 46 894

W. Mount
Lt. Col.
Comdg. 13. Batt. The Rifle Brigade.

Army Form C. 2118.

WAR DIARY
or
INTELLIGENCE SUMMARY.

(Erase heading not required.)

Instructions regarding War Diaries and Intelligence Summaries are contained in F. S. Regs., Part II. and the Staff Manual respectively. Title pages will be prepared in manuscript.

Place	Date	Hour	Summary of Events and Information	Remarks and references to Appendices

111th Inf.Bde.
37th Div.

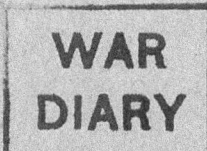

13th BATTN. THE RIFLE BRIGADE.

A P R I L

1 9 1 8

Attached:
Casualty Lists.

SECRET

13th (Service) Battⁿ The Rifle Brigade.

WAR DIARY

From .. .. 1st April 1918
To .. .. 30th April 1918

Vol. No 31

Army Form C. 2118.

WAR DIARY
or
INTELLIGENCE SUMMARY

(Erase heading not required.)

Instructions regarding War Diaries and Intelligence Summaries are contained in F. S. Regs., Part II. and the Staff Manual respectively. Title Pages will be prepared in manuscript.

Place	Date	Hour	Summary of Events and Information	Remarks and references to Appendices

INTELLIGENCE SUMMARY

(Erase heading not required.)

Instructions regarding War Diaries and Intelligence Summaries are contained in F. S. Regs., Part II. and the Staff Manual respectively. Title Pages will be prepared in manuscript.

Place	Date 1918	Hour	Summary of Events and Information	Remarks and references to Appendices
MARIEUX	April 1st		The Battalion was billeted for the day in the Aerodrome near MARIEUX. The same night (1st/2nd) the Battalion relieved the 7th Bn. MANCHESTER Regt. in the Reserve Line at GOMMECOURT. Whilst in Reserve, night carrying parties for the Front Line were provided.	
GOMMECOURT	5th/6th		On the night of the 5th/6th the Battalion went into the Front Line, GOMMECOURT Sector, relieving the 8th LINCOLNS and the 1st MIDDLESEX. Three Companies were in the Front Line and one Company in Support.	
	"8th"		In the evening the Commanding Officer, Lt. Col. W. R. STEWART, D.S.O., M.C. while going round the Front Line trenches, was killed by an enemy sniper.	
	"10th"		The burial of the late Lt. Col. STEWART took place in the British Cemetery at COUIN, with full military honours.	
	"12th"		Lt. Col. H.S.C. RICHARDSON (Rifle Brigade) assumed command of the Battalion.	
	"13th"		On the night of the 12th/13th the Battalion was relieved in the Front Line by the 6th BEDFORDS and 13th R. FUSILIERS, and went into the Reserve Line behind HEBUTERNE	
HEBUTERNE	13th/14th		On the night of the 13th/14th the Battalion relieved the 13th Bn. AUSTRALIAN IMPERIAL FORCE in HEBUTERNE - 3 Companies in the Front Line and one in Support.	
	16th/17th		On the night of the 16th/17th the Battalion was relieved by the 7th MANCHESTERS afterwards	

INTELLIGENCE SUMMARY

(Erase heading not required.)

Instructions regarding War Diaries and Intelligence Summaries are contained in F.S. Regs., Part II. and the Staff Manual respectively. Title Pages will be prepared in manuscript.

Place	Date 1918	Hour	Summary of Events and Information	Remarks and references to Appendices
HÉBUTERNE	Apl.16/17th		afterwards proceeding to Bivouac near COIGNEUX.	
COIGNEUX	" 17th		On the morning of the 17th the Battalion marched to Billets in LOUVENCOURT.	
LOUVENCOURT	" 20th		On the 20th. Lt. Col. A.C. RICHARDSON left the Battalion on being posted to command of 2nd Bn. The Rifle Brigade.	
	23rd		Lt. Col. R.A. MOSTYN-OWEN (Rifle Brigade) assumed command of the Battalion. During the period spent in LOUVENCOURT (17th to 23rd) the Battalion carried out the usual training.	
	" 24th		In the afternoon of the 24th the Battalion proceeded in motor lorries from LOUVENCOURT to SOUASTRE, and the same night marched to the trenches, relieving the 8th W. YORKS in the Front Line opposite ABLAINZEVELLE.	
ABLAINZEVELLE	" 28th/29th		On the night of the 28th/29th the Battalion was relieved in the Front Line by the 10th L. FUSILIERS - taking the place of that Unit in the Support Line, BUCQUOY.	
	29th and 30th		The Battalion remained in the Support Line during these 2 days.	

	Officers	Other Ranks
Effective Strength of Battalion on 1/4/18	47	897
Casualties during month	10	201
	37	696
Reinforcements during month	9	64
Effective Strength of Battalion on 30/4/18	46	760

Rhorty Owen

Lt. Colonel
Commdg. 13th (S.) Bn. 1st Rifle Brigade

CASUALTY LISTS.

Winchester Record Office. Daily Casualty List dated 2.4.1918.

Regt.No.	Rank and Name.	C a s u a l t y.
	Amendment	Now Rapid
S. 28620	A/Sgt. Drake E.	Wounded(negligently self-inflicted) Cancel Rept 15.12.1917. Reported by G.O.C. Wounded (acc) Second Army 27.3.18. to W.O. 28.12.17.

Major for.
Officer i/c Infantry Section No.2.

2.4.1918.

WINCHESTER RECORD OFFICE. DAILY CASUALTY LIST DATED 2.4.18.

| Regt.No. | Rank and Name. | C a s u a l t y. | PR. "W" |

2474   L/Sgt. Blandford F.   Died of Wounds, received in action 30.3.1918. Reported by O.C. No.2.Aust. General Hospital 30.3.18.

Major for.
Officer i/c Infantry Section No.2.

2.4.1918.

Winchester Record Office Daily Casualty List dated 4.4.1918.

Regt.No.	Rank and Name.	Casualty.		PR.
B. 200801	Rfm. Baker J.W.	Killed in Action	27.3.1918.	Nil.
S. 28625	L/C. Atterton G.	Wounded	25.3.1918.	Nil.
S. 33696	Rfm. Dimond G.H.	Wounded	25.3.1918.	Nil.
B. 3167	Rfm. Smith F.W.	Wounded	25.3.1918.	Nil.
S. 4565	L/C. Sheesmith H.	Wounded	27.3.1918.	Nil.

Reported by Officer Commanding 13th Rifle Brigade 30.3.1918.

Major for.
Officer i/c Infantry Section No.2.

4.4.18.

P.R.

N11.

13th (Service) Battalion The Rifle Brigade.

Winchester Record Office Daily Casualty List dated 4.4.18.

2ND. LIEUT. M.A.STAPLETON.   WOUNDED   24.3.1918.

Reported by Officer Commanding 13th Rifle Brigade 30.3.1918.

RH Major for.
Officer I/C Infantry Section No.2.

4.4.18.

Winchester Record Office. Daily Casualty List dated 5.4.18.

Regt.No.	Rank and Name.	Casualty.	PR.
B. 200835	Rfm. Martin F.	Wounded (AT DUTY) 25.3.1918.	Nil.
S. 30821	Rfm. Holloway H.	Wounded (AT DUTY) 25.3.1918.	Nil.
S. 33696	Rfm. Diamond G.	Rejoined Unit 30.3.1918.	"W"
		Reported by O.C. Battalion. 30.3.18.	
3737795	Rfm. Greenfield E.G.	Wounded 21.3.18. Reported by O.C. 49th F.A. 23.3.1918.	Nil.

5.4.18.   *R\[?\]*   MAJOR for,
Officer i/c Infantry Section No.2.

- 5 APR

****

Winchester Record Office Daily Casualty List dated 10-4-1918.

Regt.No.	Rank and Name	Casualty		PR.
S. 27461	L/C. Jones I.	Killed in Action	5-4-1918.	Nil.
S. 37794	Rfn. Thomas W.J.F.	ditto	5-4-1918.	Nil.
S. 31489	Rfn. Wilkins A.	ditto	5-4-1918.	Nil.
O/ 52	Rfn. Dicker J.	Wounded	28-3-1918.	Nil.
S. 31517	Rfn. Owen	Wounded	5-4-1918.	Nil.
S. 31685	Rfn. Bell J.W.	Wounded	5-4-1918.	Nil.
B. 2033251	Rfn. Worrilow S.	Wounded	5-4-1918.	Nil.
S. 21854	Rfn. Simmonds W.	Wounded	5-4-1918.	Nil.
S. 2897	Sgt. Rutter J.H.	Wounded	5-4-1918.	Nil.
S. 30755	Rfn. Greenfield A.	Reported Wounded 22-3-18 in Casualty List C./S/S.		

Cancel Rept. to War Office dated 29-3-1918. Please delete.

Reported by Officer Commanding Battalion 6-4-1918.

Amendment.

| S. 28625 | L/C. Atterton G. | Now reported Wounded (Gas) 25-3-18. Cancel Rept of Wounded |
| B. 3167 | Rfn. Smith F.W. | ditto |

Reported by O.C.50th Field Ambulance 30-3-1918.

****

Major for,
Officer i/c Infantry Section No.2.

10-4-18.

...th (Ser) Battalion The Rifle Brigade.

...(Service) Battalion Daily ...

Winchester Record Office Daily Casualty List dated 10-4-1918.

2nd Lieut. H.Beaumont MM. Wounded 5-4-1918.   Nil.
2nd Lieut. T.Campbell. Wounded 5-4-1918.   Nil.
Reported by O.C.Battn. 6-4-18.

****

Major for,

10-4-18.   Officer i/c Infantry Section No.2.

...ce, ...ach, ...fle Brigade.

Winchester Record Office Daily Casualty List dated 11-4-1918.

Regt.No.	Rank and Name.	Casualty.	PR.
S. 27414	Rfm.L/C. Ward G.	Killed in Action 6-4-1918.	Nil.
O/ 38	Rfn. Chamberlein S.W.	Wounded 6-4-1918.	Nil.
S. 4564	L/S. Lindop F.D.	ditto	Nil.
S. 4023	Rfn. Turness W.S.	ditto	Nil.
B. 202334	L/C. Harrison J.	ditto	Nil.
S. 31550	Rfn. Stringer S.	ditto	Nil.
B. 203281	Rfn. Hardiker J.	ditto	Nil.
5845	Rfn. Watts J.	ditto	Nil.

Reported by O.C.Battn 8-4-18.

Capt. for,
Officer i/c Infantry Section No.2.

11-4-1918.

Winchester 13   ord Office Daily Casualty List dated

Regt.No.	Rank and Name.	C a s u a l t y.	PR.
S. 21897	Cpl. Wines, E.	Killed in Action 10-1-18.	{ Missing, to W.O.
S. 27408	Rfn. Quin P.	Killed in Action 10-1-18.	{ C.146a d/-
			{ 3-2-1918.

Reported by O.C.Battalion 3-4-1918.

****

Capt. for,
Officer i/c Infantry Section No.2.

11-4-1918.

13th (Ser) Battalion The Rifle Brigade.

WINCHESTER RECORD OFFICE. DAILY CASUALTY LIST DATED 12.4.1918.

PR. Nil.

LIEUT)COLONEL. W.R.STEWART. DSO. MC. KILLED IN ACTION. 8.4.1918.
2ND. LIEUT. J.F.BARR. WOUNDED. 7.4.1918. Nil.

Reported by O.C. 13th Rifle Brigade 9.4.1918.

Major for,
Officer i/c Infantry Section No. 2.

12.4.1918.

13TH RIFLE BRIGADE.
List No. 1320. 13.4.18.

2/LIEUT   BATTEN   J.   Wounded(acc.)12.4.18.
8th Bn. Scottish Rifles attd.

th (Ser) Battalion The Rifle Brigade

Winchester Record Office. Daily Casualty List dated 12.4.1918.

Regt.No.	Rank and Name.	Casualty.	PR.
S. 1690	Sgt. Osell G.	Wounded 6.4.1918.	Nil.
1517	Rfn. Chiddy S.	Wounded 6.4.1918.	Nil.
S. 27370	L/C. Bradford A.	Wounded 7.4.1918.	Nil.
346	Rfn. Tillett W.	Wounded 8.4.1918.	Nil.
O/ 304489	L/C. Spreadbury P.	Wounded 6.4.1918.	Nil.
	Reported by O.C.Battalion 9.4.1918.		
O/ 147	Rfn. Stevens C.W.	Died of Wounds 9.4.1918.	"W"
		Reported by O.C. 4 General Hospl 9.4.1918.	

Major for,
Officer i/c Infantry Section No.2.

12.4.18.

Winchester Record Office Daily Casualty List dated 13-4-18.

Regt.No.	Rank and Name.	Casualty	PR.
6178	Rfn. Biggs A.	Wounded 5-4-1918.	Nil.
S.2043	Cpl. Earp H.	" 5-4-1918.	Nil.
B.200860	Rfn. Peck J.	" 8-4-1918.	Nil.
S.28079	L/S. Kirby A.	" 8-4-1918.	Nil.
S.37787	Rfn. Pegg L.	" 8-4-1918.	Nil.
S.57756	Rfn. Marriott R.	" 8-4-1918.	Nil.

Reported by O.C. Battalion 11-4-1918.

Amendments

S.27370	c.Rfn. Bradford A.	Wounded (Gas) 7-4-18.	Cancel-report. Wounded. in
S.4023	Rfn. Turness W.	ditto 8-4-18.	Wounded. Gas.
B.203281	Rfn. Hardiker J.	ditto 8-4-18.	Wounded.
S.4564	L/S. Lindop F.	ditto 8-4-18.	Wounded.
S.1690	Sgt. Osell G.	ditto 8-4-18.	Wounded.

Reported by O.C. 49th F.A. 7-4-18.

****

MAJOR for,
Officer i/c Infantry Section No.3.

15-4-1918.

Army Form W.3745

To D.A.G. BASE

I regret to inform you of the undermentioned deaths.

(Unit) H.Q. 13th Rifle Brigade

Date 15/4/18

Number	Rank	Name	Unit	Religion and Age	Date and Time of Death	Cause of Death
S/1569	L/C	CALIP	H.I. 13 RIFLE BRIGADE	C E	14/4/18 9.0 p.m.	DIED of WOUNDS at 48 FIELD AMB OF A.D.S.

O.C.

13th (S(er) Battalion The Rifle Brigade.

Winchester Record Office, Daily Casualty List dated 18.4.1918.

2nd Lieut. J.Batten.   Wounded (Acc) 12.4.1918.   Nil.
                        Reported by O.C. Battn. 15.4.1918.

R/G   Major for.
Officer i/c Infantry Section No.2.

18.4.1918.

15th (Service) Battalion The Rifle Brigade.

Winchester Record Office. Daily Casualty List dated 18.4.1918.

Regt.No.	Rank and Name.	Casualty.	PR.
423478	Rfn. Barman G.	Wounded 10.4.1918.	Nil.
45040	Rfn. Porter W.A.	Wounded 12.4.1918.	Nil.
O/344	Rfn. Turner C.H.	Wounded 11.4.1918.	Nil.
S.30829	Rfn. Gibbons W.	Wounded 8.4.1918.	Nil.
S.37799	Rfn. Whitehorn H.H.	Wounded 11.4.1918.	Nil.
B200830	Rfn. Kirk W.	Wounded 9.4.1918.	Nil.

Reported by O.C.Battalion 13.4.1918.

Major for.
Officer i/c Infantry Section No.2.

18.4.1918.

War ...cord Office Daily Casualty List dated 19.4.1918.

Regt.No.	Rank and Name.	Casualty.	PR.
S. 1569	L/Cpl. Calip H.	Died of Wounds 14.4.1918. Reported by O.C. 49th F.A. 15.4.18.	Nil.
O/ 134	Rfn. Read H.G.	Killed in Action 14.4.1918.	Nil.
S. 27449	Rfn. Marks R.W.	Wounded 13.4.1918.	Nil.
S. 318036	Rfn. Dalton A.	Wounded 13.4.1918.	Nil.
S. 37765	Rfn. Pullen H.J.	Wounded 13.4.1918.	Nil.

Reported by O.C.Battalion 15.4.1918.

Major for,
Officer i/c Infantry Section No.2.

19.4.1918.

13th (Ser...) Battalion The ...le Brigade.

Winchester Record Office. Daily Casualty List dated 20.

Regt.No.	Rank and Name.	Casualty.
O/ 65	Rfn. Field T.	Died of Wounds. 16.4.1918. Reported by O.C. 24 G.H. 17.4.18.

Major for.
Officer i/c Infantry Section No.2.

20.4.1918.

Regt.No	Rank and Name.	Casualty.	PR.
S. 3893	L/C. Holloway G.	Killed in Action. 14.4.1918.	Nil.
S. 16637	Rfn. Hamilton J.	Killed in Action. 14.4.1918.	Nil.
S. 25836	Rfn. Lewis E.	Killed in Action. 14.4.1918.	Nil.
S. 4765	Rfn. Buckler R.	Wounded 14.4.1918.	Nil.
S. 23778	Rfn. Edney A.	Wounded 14.4.1918.	Nil.
S. 31481	L/C. Pearce H.	Wounded 14.4.1918.	Nil.

Reported by O.C.Battalion 16.4.1918.

MAJOR for,

Officer I/c Infantry Section No.2.

22.4.1918.

W... ...cord Office. Daily Casualty List dated 23.4.1918.

Regt.No.	Rank and Name.	Casualty.	PK.
3531	Rfn. Dark H.	Killed in Action 16.4.1918.	Nil.
O/93	Rfn. Jeffries A.	Killed in Action 16.4.1918.	Nil.
S. 32523	Rfn. Clarke H.	Wounded 15.4.1918.	Nil.
S. 27747	Rfn. Cable J.	Wounded 16.4.1918.	Nil.
S. 21386	Rfn. Edwards W.	Wounded 16.4.1918.	Nil.
S. 17591	Rfn. Graves A.	Wounded 15.4.1918.	Nil.
S. 23533	Sgt. Lidbury A.	Wounded 16.4.1918.	Nil.
S. 27486	L/C. Medley A.	Wounded 16.4.1918.	Nil.
S. 25240	Rfn. Pink W.	Wounded 15.4.1918.	Nil.
S. 31481	L/C. Pearce H.	Rejoined Battn. 16.4.1918.	"W"
S. 30013	Rfn. Pink A.	Wounded 15.4.1918.	Nil
B. 203338	Rfn. Skelly W.	Wounded 16.4.1918.	Nil.
S. 23561	Rfn. Tetlow J.	Wounded 16.4.1918.	Nil.

Reported by O.C.Battalion. 20.4.1918.

Major for.
Officer i/c Infantry Section No.2.

23.4.13.

...chester Record Office. Daily Casualty List dated 27.4...

Regt.No.	Rank and Name.	Casualty.	PR.
423478	Rfn. Bannan G.	Wounded 'Gas' 10.4.1918.	"W"
S. 30829	Rfn. Gibbons W.	Wounded 'Gas' 8.4.1918.	"W"
B. 200830	Rfn. Kirk W.	Wounded 'Gas' 9.4.1918.	"W"
304489	L/C. Spreadbury P. Wounded 'Gas' 6.4.1918.		"W"

Reported by O.C. 49th F.A. 22.4.18.

Major for,
Officer i/c Infantry Section No.2.

27.4.1918.

SECRET

13th (Service) Battn. The Rifle Brigade.

WAR DIARY

From   1st May 1918
To   31st May 1918

Vol. 32

Army Form C. 2118.

WAR DIARY
INTELLIGENCE SUMMARY.
(Erase heading not required.)

Instructions regarding War Diaries and Intelligence Summaries are contained in F. S. Regs., Part II. and the Staff Manual respectively. Title pages will be prepared in manuscript.

Place	Date 1918	Hour	Summary of Events and Information	Remarks and references to Appendices
BUCQUOY	May 1st		On this date the Battalion was in Support Trenches behind BUCQUOY and ABLAINZEVELLE	
"	2nd/3rd	Night	The Battalion relieved the 13th K.R.R.C. in the Front Line at BUCQUOY	
"	8th		The Battalion carried out a minor operation, narrative of which is attached	
"	9th/10th	Night	The Battalion was relieved in the Front line by the 8th Lincolns Regt. and proceeded to Billets in SOUASTRE	
SOUASTRE	10th to 13th		During this period the Battalion carried out training and re-fitted	
ESSARTS	13th/14th	Night	The Battalion moved up into trenches and dug-outs in ESSARTS relieving the 13th K.R.R.C.	
"	14th to 16th		During the stay in ESSARTS the Battalion provided daily working-parties	
"	17th/18th	Night	The Battalion was relieved by the 8th W. Yorks Regt. and moved into Camp at AUTHIE	
AUTHIE	18th to 30th		While encamped at AUTHIE, Training was carried out each day. On the 25th the Battalion was inspected by the G.O.C. 111th Infantry Brigade. A certain amount of Recreational Training was carried out, and on	

Army Form C. 2118.

WAR DIARY
or
INTELLIGENCE SUMMARY.
(Erase heading not required.)

Place	Date	Hour	Summary of Events and Information	Remarks and references to Appendices
	1918 May.			
SAILLY-AU-BOIS	30th		the 30th the Battalion beat the 10th R. FUSILIERS (4-0) in the First Round of the Divisional Football Competition	
	31st		The Battalion, being in Corps Reserve, moved up into trenches between SAILLY-AU-BOIS and HEBUTERNE.	
			Officers Other Ranks	
			Effective Strength of Battalion on 1/5/18 47 782	
			Casualties during month 10 180	
			31 602	
			Reinforcements during month 1 334	
			Effective Strength of Battalion on 31/5/18 38 936	

R. W. Orr
Lt. Colonel
Comdg. 13th (S) Bn. The RIFLE BRIGADE

SECRET

13th (Service) Battalion The Rifle Brigade

War Diary

From 1/6/18

To 30/6/18

Vol. 33.

Army Form C. 2118.

WAR DIARY
or
INTELLIGENCE SUMMARY.
(Erase heading not required.)

Instructions regarding War Diaries and Intelligence Summaries are contained in F. S. Regs., Part II. and the Staff Manual respectively. Title pages will be prepared in manuscript.

Place	Date	Hour	Summary of Events and Information	Remarks and references to Appendices

WAR DIARY

INTELLIGENCE SUMMARY.

(Erase heading not required.)

Army Form C. 2118.

Instructions regarding War Diaries and Intelligence Summaries are contained in F. S. Regs., Part II. and the Staff Manual respectively. Title pages will be prepared in manuscript.

Place	Date	Hour	Summary of Events and Information	Remarks and references to Appendices
SAILLY AU BOIS.	June 1st.		Battalion in Reserve Line, HEBUTERNE -- SAILLY AU BOIS.	
AUTHIE.	Night 4/5th.		Relieved by New Zealanders, and spent 5th in Camp in BOIS DU WARNIMONT, near AUTHIE.	
BOUVELLES.	6th.		Battalion moved by motor buses to BOUVELLES on the night 5/6th, arriving there at 9 a.m. on the 6th; early in the evening marched to GUINEMICOURT.	
GUINEM-ICOURT.	6th.-- 9th.		The Battalion remained in this place in G.H.Q. Reserve, training being carried out every available day.	
RUMIGNY.	10th.		Embussed and moved to RUMIGNY, being there until the 15th as part of Reserve to French Army. Training was carried out and football matches were played.	
SAINS-EN-AMIENOIS.	Night 15/16th.		The Battalion marched to SAINS-en-AMIENOIS--remaining there until the 19th.	
NAMPTY.	Night 19/20th.		Marched to NAMPTY--remaining there 2 days. The river was taken advantage of and Aquatic sports were held on the morning of 21st.	
HENU.	Night 21/22nd.		Marching to LOEUILLY Station, the Battalion entrained for MONDICOURT, arriving there at 2 a.m. on the 22nd, thence marching to HENU, where Battalion remained in Camp until night 24/25th.	
BUCQUOY.	Night 24/25th.		Battalion proceeded to the Line in BUCQUOY Sector, relieving the 2/4th Battn., Duke of Wellington's Regt.	

Army Form C. 2118.

WAR DIARY
INTELLIGENCE SUMMARY.
(Erase heading not required.)

Place	Date	Hour	Summary of Events and Information	Remarks and references to Appendices
BUCQUOY.	June 26th.		Notification was received that No. S.6522 Sgt. W.GREGG, D.C.M., M.M., and No.B. 203174 Rfn. W.BEESLEY had been awarded the VICTORIA CROSS for valour in the Field, during operations carried out by the Battalion at BUCQUOY on 8th May 1918.	
do.	30th.		The Battalion still in the line in the BUCQUOY Sector.	
			During the month the undermentioned Honours & Rewards were notified:-	
			THE VICTORIA CROSS. No.S. 6522 Sgt. W.GREGG, D.C.M., M.M. " B203174 Rfn. W.BEESLEY.	
			DISTINGUISHED CONDUCT MEDAL. No.S.20479 L/Cpl. Lewis R. " S.14454 Rfn. Barton F.	
			MILITARY CROSS. A/Capt. P.F.DAVY. 2/Lieut. A.C.W.GEORGE. " " W.WALLACE. " " J.FORRESTER.	
			MENTIONED IN DISPATCHES. A/Capt. W.S.BASCOMBE, M.M. No.5/9714 L/Sgt. Quilty F.	
			MERITORIOUS SERVICE MEDAL. S.4566 CSM. T.JOLLY. S.4362 Sgt. S.RENTON.	

Army Form C. 2118.

WAR DIARY
INTELLIGENCE SUMMARY.
(Erase heading not required.)

Place	Date	Hour	Summary of Events and Information	Remarks and references to Appendices
	1/7/18.		- 3 -	
			THE MILITARY MEDAL. THE MILITARY MEDAL.	
			S.28656 Rfn. Frankish A. S.17271 L/C. Hunt J.	
			S.28935 " Ely F. S.33323 Rfn. White V.	
			S.14216 Cpl. Collins T. S.6649 L/C. Wright A.	
			O/61. L/C. Farnfield R. S.34075 Rfn. Post A.	
			P.4850 Rfn. Couzens F. S.16030 L/S. Crook G.	
			S.27464 L/C. Craston G. O/122 L/C. Peters P.	
			B.203236 " Scott W. S.20413 " Sherwin M. n	
			S.31675 Rfn. Eaglestone A. S.33434 " Pankhurst J.	
			425696 " Douglas P. S.31018 " Beard T.	
			S.4729 " Gladman L. Z.2478 " Gilbert J.	
			S.4420 " Seager J. S.4375 Rfn. Jackson J.	
			S.7065 " Waller G. S.15079 " Messenger A.	
			O. OR.	
			Effective strength on 1/6/18 38 936	
			Casualties during month 3 83	
			35 853	
			Reinforcements during month 8 34	
			Effective strength on 30/6/18. 43 - 887.	
			[signature]	
			Lieut. Colonel,	
			Commanding 13th Battalion The Rifle Brigade.	

<u>Secret.</u>

<u>War Diary</u>

<u>July 1918.</u>

<u>Volume 34.</u>

<u>13: Bn. The Rifle Brigade.</u>

Army Form C. 2118.

WAR DIARY

(Erase heading not required.)

July 1918.

Place	Date	Hour	Summary of Events and Information	Remarks and references to Appendices
BUCQUOY	July 1st		Battalion remained in the line S. of BUCQUOY until 2nd July, being relieved there on the night 2nd/3rd July by 13th Royal Fusiliers. The Battalion proceeded to SOUASTRE,	
SOUASTRE	3rd		to Reserve Billets, where baths were opened and specialist training carried out. On the night 7/8th July	
BUCQUOY	8th		the Battalion again went into the line N. of BUCQUOY, remaining there until night of 13/14th July. Battalion relieved 8th Lincolns. The usual trench warfare was waged. Nothing of special interest can be mentioned in connection with this tour.	
ESSARTS	14th		The Battalion was relieved by the 10th Royal Fusiliers on the night 13/14th July, and proceeded to support positions at ESSARTS. The night of the 20th/21st July saw the Battalion in Reserve trenches in PIGEON WOOD. From the latter place	
PIGEON WOOD	21st		bathing parties went daily to SOUASTRE. Battalion remained in PIGEON WOOD until night of 26/27th July, when the front line was again taken over S. of BUCQUOY, Battn. H.Q. being at PETTEMOY	
BUCQUOY	31st		FARM. The remaining four days were spent in this portion of the line during ideal weather.	

```
                                             O.    O.R.
         Total strength, 30/6/18    =       42    884
         Decreases during month     =        5     99
                                             37   785
         Increases during month     =        8    134
         Total strength, 31/7/18    =       45    919
```

Chunfur Twee
Lt.Col.,
Commanding 13th Battalion, The Rifle Brigade.

SECRET.

WAR DIARY

August 1918.

Volume 35.

13th Battalion The Rifle Brigade.

13th. BATTN. THE RIFLE BRIGADE   SECRET.

WAR DIARY   AUGUST 1918

1st. AUGUST - Battalion in the Line: Headquarters at RETTEMOY FARM. Much good work in reconnoitring enemy positions and his probable movements was done here, and five congratulatory messages on patrols were received from the Divisional General.

The Battalion was relieved by the 1/1st HERTS Regt. on the night 9th/10th. and proceeded to rest Billets SOUASTRE remaining there until night 17th/18th. when it relieved 8th. SOMERSETS in the Support Line at ESSARTS. Whilst out of the Line a very successful Rifle Meeting was held.

On the night 20th/21st the Battalion moved forward to front line trenches in front of ABLAINZVELLE preparatory to taking part in a general attack. The Battalion held the Left Sector of the Divisional Line with ROYAL FUSILIERS on the Right, and in touch with troops of the 2nd. Division on Left.

APPENDIX "A"   The Objective given to the Battalion was Line running N.E. to S.W. on the E. side of the Village.

The orders were to advance, take the Trenches in front of them, sweep round the flank N. of the Village, reach their objective line and consolidate. The whole advance being, on the Right 1,700 yards and on the Left 2,000 yards.

At ZERO hour (4.50a.m.) a dense mist prevailed. At the opening of the Barrage it was scarcely possible to see more than 50 yards ahead. A good knowledge of the ground however, enabled the Battalion to move forward and reach their objective with little trouble.

The order of Advance was "D" and "B" Companies in front, "D" Company on the Right and "B" Company on the Left, "A" Company in Support and "C" Company in Reserve. By 7.20a.m. a message was received that Companies had reached their objectives and were consolidating.

Headquarters then moved forward and established themselves in Trench N.E. of the Village and 500 yards behind final objective.

According to orders the 63rd.(R.N.) Division moved through the Battalion at ZERO plus 50 minutes crossing over our objective Line went forward to the attack of LOGEAST WOOD and ACHIET LE GRAND. LOGEAST WOOD was captured by them but they were held up on the high ground in front of ACHIET LE GRAND. The close of the day found the Line running roughly due EAST of LOGEAST WOOD.

The following day the front Line was thoroughly reconnoitred by Officers and other ranks concerned in a further advance.

On the night 22nd/23rd orders were received for the Division to advance and take ACHIET LE GRAND and BIHUCOURT. The enemy at the former place having successfully resisted the attempts of the 63rd.(R.N) Division to take it on the 21st., and having great natural defences including the Railway Embankment, added to the fact that it was known to be a Line which the enemy had instructions to hold and defend at all costs, it will be seen that the task to be accomplished was a heavy one. All preparations for the attack were completed by the early hours of the morning and at 11a.m. under cover of heavy Barrage the troops advanced over the hill and down a 1,500 yards slope. Half an hour later the position had been stormed and won. Prisoners were coming back in large parties. A fierce hand to hand struggle took place on the Railway Embankment; here the enemy had massed Machine Guns both light and heavy, light Field Guns and Trench Mortars, but the speed of our attack and surprise of the enemy gave us success.

By one o'clock the Battalion had consolidated the Line 1,000 yards EAST of the Railway Embankment and were pushing on to the capture of BIHUCOURT. This Village was in our hands and the Line consolidated EAST of it, by 2.15p.m. Prisoners to the number of 500 were captured by the Battalion also 40 heavy M.G's, 70 light M.G's, 20 Trench Mortars, 10 Tank Guns, one 4.2c.m. Gun and one 77m.m. Gun, Material, R.E. Stores, Equipment etc. in great bulk were also brought in. The Line then ran SAPIGNIES (exclusive) - BIHUCOURT - BIEFVILLERS - AVESNES les BAUPAUME, forming an acute salient into our LINE.

At 4a.m. on the 24th. orders were received to move forward and straighten this salient and to occupy the high ground N. of BIEFVILLERS and N.E. of BIHUCOURT. This advance was accomplished and by 7a.m. on the morning of the 25th. the Line had been thoroughly straightened out.

Having received instructions to exploit our successes, strong patrols were again pushed forward, crossing the ARRAS - BAPAUME road S. of SAPIGNIES and moving on towards FAVREUIL. By 2p.m. the high ground immediately EAST of FAVREUIL was held by patrols, these being in touch with the New Zealanders who were quickly advancing on our Right.

The situation on the Left was obscure but SAPIGNIES although not held by the Division on the Left appeared clear of the enemy. ✢ It was decided to attack and take FAVREUIL and orders were received for the 111th. Infantry Brigade to carry out this operation.

✢APPENDIX"B"

At 6p.m. the Battalion had moved forward to a position of assembly under the cover of banks 800 yards EAST of FAVREUIL the order of battle being thus:- 13th. Rifle Brigade on the Right, K.R.R.C on the Left, Royal Fusiliers in Support, ZERO hour at 6.30p.m. At 6p.m. enemy put down a heavy counter preparation Barrage in front of the Village and along the Valley of approach.

At 6.30p.m. troops moved forward to the attack. It was seen that the enemy were advancing in force to counter attack. 400 yards from the Village our advancing troops came in conflict with enemy forces in considerable numbers. The fight was not of long duration and by ZERO plus five minutes, 400 prisoners had laid down their arms. The advance proceeded. At ZERO plus ten minutes our troops were entering the Village on the Right.

A message was then received that the K.R.R.C were held up by heavy M.G. fire from N.W. outskirts of the Village. A Company of the Support Battalion was deflected to press home attack, meanwhile the Rifle Brigade pushed through the Village taking prisoners and machine guns and reached their objective an enemy trench 150 yards EAST of the Village.

Orders were then given by O.C. Rifle Brigade that a defensive flank be formed by the Royal Fusiliers and

3.

Details of the K.R.R.C who had penetrated into the Village in the centre but had not reached objective. The line then ran along EAST edge of Village to about Centre then due WEST through Centre of the Village passing the Church to about 200 yards WEST of the Village then NORTH to a point WEST of N.W. corner of the WOOD yards from it. The position was secure.

Orders were given to clear the village of machine gun crews and remaining enemy. This was effected in spite of dense undergrowth and difficult terrain by the Rifle Brigade in conjunction with small parties of the Royal Fusiliers and K.R.R.C. during the night. By 11p.m. the Village was clear, the enemy having been captured or killed and the Brigade Line ran the whole length of the EAST front of the Village.

This most successful operation, unfortunately claimed rather heavy casualties owing to the hard fight put up by a fresh counter attack regiment the enemy had thrown in specially for this operation.

At 4.30a.m. on the morning of the 26th. The Brigade was relieved by a Battalion of the K.O.S.B's and returned to LOGEAST WOOD to rest, remaining there until the end of the month

APPENDIX "C"

++++++++++++++++++++++++++++++++++

	Officers	O.R.
STRENGTH ON 31/7/18............	40	551
DECREASE during Month...........	14	406
	31	315
INCREASE during Month...........	9	156
	40	601

Lieut. Colonel,
Commanding 13: Batt" The Rifle Brigade.

APPENDIX A.

1. Information has not yet been received as to whether the attack on GOMIECOURT has succeeded. "C"Company will watch their flank as they advance and on reaching the vicinity of the RAILWAY EMBANKMENT will be prepared to form a defensive flank if necessary facing NORTH.

2. One Platoon of "A"Company and one of "C" Company are already in position in the out-post line. 2 leading platoons of "B"Company on the Right and "D" on Left will leave SUNKEN ROAD at ZERO and push through the out-post line at 100 yards interval by their Support platoons: their objective will be RAILWAY G.4.c.4.4. to Bridge over RAILWAY G.4.c.5.3. The cemetry will be inclusive to "B" Company. On reaching RAILWAY "B" and "D" Companies will push patrols about 100 yards beyond the RAILWAY.

3. As soon as barrage goes on, "A"Company on Right and "C"Company on Left will pass through and capture BLUE TRENCH from G.10.d.90.30 to G.11.c.95.90. "B"Company will follow close behind "A"Company and mop up. O.C. "B"Company will detail a small party to follow behind "C"Company. "A"Companies Right will be line just on crossing over RAILWAY on to cross roads G.10.c.7.9. and thence to G.10.d.99.20. "D"Company will move forward about 200 yards behind "B"Company and will support the attack where required at discretion of O.C.Company. After capturing the BLUE XXXXTRENCH two Companies 10th.Royal Fusiliers will come

2.

through the 13th.Rifle Brigade and go on and capture BIHUCOURT consolidating approx.200 yards EAST of village. "B"Coy will not go beyond BLUE TRENCH, but "A","C" and "D" Companies will move forward behind 10th.Royal Fusiliers and mop up and help consolidate on objective.

5. Artillery barrage will open at ZERO on line BRICKWORKS G.9.b.5.0.-CEMETRY G.3.d.5.3. at ZERO plus 8 barrage will advance at the rate of 25 yards a minute to ACHIET - GOMIECURT Rd.

Leading platoons have approximately 1,200 yards to go to above barrage line, so they must push on <u>as quickly as possible</u> to catch up our barrage.

Barrage will stand on ACHIET - GOMIECOURT Rd. for 12 minutes and will stand in front of BLUE TRENCH for one hour

6. It is probable that considerable artillery fire will be directed on SUNKEN ROAD so support Companies must get over the road as quickly as possible and then correct their XXXXX distances after.

7. ZERO will be 11a.m.

(Sgd) R.MOSTYN-OWEN Lt.Col.
Cmndg.The 13th.Rifle Brigade.

23/8/18
9a.m.

APPENDIX 16

Urgent Operations Priority.
Handed in at RUJE.

To:- M O T U

G.127   25/8/18

RUJE in cooperation with LEKA will attack
FAVREUIL this evening Aug.25 AAA Dividing
line between RUJE and LEKA H.15.b.0.0 -
H.15b.0.2 - H.15.b.3.1. and from then due
East from FAVREUIL AAA West of Barrage line
no troops of RUJE will be within 200 yds.of
BIHUCOURT - FAVREUIL Road forming up line
RUJE H.15.central - H.9.b.50.00 AAA Dividing
line between SAPIGNIES - FAVREUIL Road inclusive
to right Batth.AAA MOTU on right VOGU on Left
MONA in support LOGE will be at the disposal of
G.O.C. RUJE AAA Advance will be made Arty.
Barrage opening at a line H.15.H.30.95 -
H.10.a.00 at ZERO plus 6 mins AAA At ZERO
plus 12mins.barrage will roll forward at the
rate of 100 yds. in 3 mins.to a line due East
of main N. and S.Road through SAVREUIL where
it will stand for 10 mins.AAA It will then
advance at the rate of 100 yds in 3 mins.to
protective barrage on a line H.10.b.8.0 -
H.10.c.5.0. when it will remain for 15 mins.and
then cease AAA Heavy Arty.are bombarding
SAVREUIL from 4 p.m.onwardAAA After capturing
village the leading Batths.will consolidate
trench East of FAVREUIL AAA When barrage has
ceased MONA will push forward patrols right of
high ground West of BEUGNATRE and establish an

2.

outpost line pushing forward into the village
AAA Brigade report centre H.8.b.30.40 shrine
where all reports are to be sent AAA ZERO
hour will be at 6.30p.m. AAA Acknowledge.

       R U J E   4.30p.m.

C O P Y.   APPENDIX "B"

1. N.Z.Div. and 111th.Bde. will advance this evening and capture FAVREUIL. N.Z.Div on the Right 111th.Bde.on Left AAA Road running East and West through H15 and 16 central is inclusive to N.Z.Div.

2. 13th.R.B. on Right.
   13th.K.R.R.C on Left
   Road H15.b.98 church in centre of village and road running East from there will be inclusive to 13th.R.B.

3. "A"Coy on Left,"C"Coy on Right will be in front "D"Coy in close support.

4. Positions of Assembly. "C"&"A"Coys under bank between H.15.a.30.00 and H.15.a.20.80 "D"Coy along road and bank between H.15.a.10.00 and H.15.a.00.80.

5. Objective. Trench H.16.b.30.15 to H.16.b.10.75. On reaching this line 10th.R.F. will pass through and form an outpost line 500 yards in front 13th.R.B.and 13th.K.R.R.C will consolidate objective as far as possible.

6. Artillery Barrage. at ZERO plus 6 mins will open on line H.15 central to H.10.a.00.00. It will stand on line till ZERO plus 12 mins. Barrage will advance 100 yds every 3mins.It will stand for 10 mins.200 yds.East of main road running North and South in H.16.a.20 and for 15 mins 200 yds beyond objective.

7. "B" and "C"Coys will withdraw their outposts to behind bank in line to be in assembly positions at ZERO.

8. Zero Hour. 6.30p.m. Coys will filter into assembly positions in small parties.
   N.Z. barrage opens at ZERO.

2.

9. <u>Batth.H.Q.</u> will be at H.D.P.30.30. All reports will be sent here R.A.P. here also.

Acknowledge.

<u>Copies sent to:</u> No 1. "A" Coy.
                       2 "B" "
                       3 "D" "
                       4. War Diary
                       5. File

By runner 8.15p.m.

                               G.G.H. IRVING Capt A/Adjt.
25/8/18.   13th. Battn. Rifle Brigade.

Copy No..........

THE 13th. BATTN. THE RIFLE BRIGADE.

APPENDIX "C"

NARRATIVE OF OPERATIONS - FAVREUIL - AUG.25/26th.1918.

1. At 6p.m. on the 25th.AUG., the enemy, either preparatory to counter-attacking, or by means of aeroplanes, saw troops advancing in Artillery Formation up Valley H.8.c.and d., put down a heavy H.E. barrage. At 6.20p.m. British 18 pdrs., firing from N.W. over SAPIGNIES, fell on main road from H.8.d.6.4., to 5.7. and on lengthening fell along bank in H.9.c.4.2., and so onwards towards FAVREUIL causing numerous casualties. It appeared to be one Battery firing as shells were falling in 8's and 4's. At ZERO plus 6 the 2 leading Companies crawled forward to crest on getting upto get forward they were met by heavy M.G.and Rifle fire from trench H.15.b.00.70., N.W. corner of Village, and from H.10.a., causing many casualties on the left. "D"Coy., and Right Company., of the 10th.R.Fus., were then deflected to the right and worked forward under covering fire from the left flank. During this phase enemy reinforcements were seen debouching from the wood to reinforce their firing line. Eventually "C"Coy., on the right succeeded in getting round and getting into Huts about H.15.b.8.5., thus taking enemy in flank. As soon as the enemy realised that they were out flanked their fire ceased and at least 150 surrendered. "A"and "C"Companies, reinforced by "B" Company, then pushed on through the village, meeting little opposition and astablished themselves in trench on East of Village in touch with N.Z's on right. Patrols of "A"and "C"coys. pushed forward and captured 60 to 70 prisoners in the Huts at H.16.b.5.3., (N.of Road). There were not many Germans in the Village, some 30 or 40 only surrendered, but the trench E of the Village was strongly held and between 60 and 70 prisoners were taken here. All this time enemy M.G's were still active in the N.of the wood - efforts were made to get in touch on the left, but the K.R.R.C., were held up outside the Village, so a defensive flank was formed on the line H.16.b.3.7.,-CHURCH - H.10.c.10.30., at which latter place were about 40 men of 10th.R.F. During the night enemy evacuated the Village, some 20 being captured endeavouring to make their way back to their own lines. During the night one of our patrols scuppered a M.G. and crew at N.E. corner of Village.

2. During the afternoon Officers reconnoitred the ridge immediately West of the Village, and it appared that the Village was only lightly held.
At 8p.m. the fact that the enemy put down a heavy barrage West

2.

of Village and also held the front edge of Village very strongly, supports the assumption that troops were assembling for counter attack. This assumption is supported by Officer prisoners statement to Battalion Intelligence Officer.

3. At 6.15p.m. hearing that the K.R.R.C were held up I endeavoured to direct the Support Company 10th.R.F., to work via H.9.central round left flank to support K.R.R.C. At 7.25 p.m., I ordered Capt Goddard, West Riding Regt., to work round left flank and get in touch with flank of next Division. This officer had previously received instructions to co-operate on left of N.Z., Division.

4. About 400 prisoners were sent back by this Battalion. Over 350 being counted at Battn.H.Q.(H.o.c.3.3). From here they were sent back, in the majority of cases without escort, along the main road into SAPIGNIES. A number of the prisoners had GIBRALTAR on the sleeves of their tunics.

(Sgd) R.MOSTYN - OWEN Lt.Col.
Cmmdg. The 13th.Battn.Rifle Brigade.

27/8/18.

13th Battalion, The Rifle Brigade.

WINCHESTER RECORD OFFICE.   **DAILY CASUALTY LIST.**

Regt.No.	Rank & Name	Casualty & Date	Prev.Report
B203236	Cpl Scott, W.	Killed in action 25-8-18.	Nil.
B200837	Rfn Moorse, E.	do. " do. 25-8-18.	"
B201625	Rfn Davies, F.	do. " do. 23-8-18.	"

The above casualties reptd by O.C. 13th Rif. Bde dated 29-8-18.

Regt.No.	Rank & Name	Casualty	Date	Prev.Report
S.27847	L/C Atkinson, J.	Wounded,	23-8-18.	Nil.
B201292	Rfn Askew, E.	"	"	"
B200668	" Archer, H.	"	"	"
S. 6696	L/C Allen, R.	"	25-8-18.	"
S.21943	Rfn Applebe, H.	"	24-8-18.	"
S. 4217	Sgt Artlett, G.	"	23-8-18.	"
S.32244	Rfn Archer, G.	"	"	"
48600	Cpl Barnard, P.	"	23-8-18.	"
B203322	Rfn Brett, E.	"	"	"
S.24285	" Bennett, A.	"	"	"
S.23458	" Bartlett, R.	"	25-8-18.	"
S. 5901	" Brighten, H.	"	23-8-18.	"
P. 1507	" Bessell, E.	"	25-8-18.	"
S.9522	" Bean, W.	"	23-8-18.	"
S. 6938	L/S Johnston, B.	"	"	"
48433	Rfn Bradshaw, T.	"	"	"
S.10088	Sgt Bailey, H.	"	"	"
S.30708	Rfn Baker, W.	"	"	"
S.27077	" Baldwin, A.	"	"	"
S.37680	" Brown, W.	"	"	"
S.30856	" Brooks, J.	"	"	"
49011	" Barden, E.	"	"	"
B203233	" Bull, A.	"	24-8-18.	"
49015	" Butler, A.	"	25-8-18.	"
S.34110	L/C Brown, H.	"	23-8-18.	"
41387	Rfn Bassett, T.	"	"	"
S.27849	" Bowhill, W.	"	"	"
S.36891	" Brady, B.	"	"	"
318431	" Chivers, G.	"	"	"
B203265	Cpl Curtlin, H.	"	"	"
O. 43	Rfn Cullen, A.	"	24-8-18.	"
S.32725	" Coe, W.	"	23-8-18.	"
S.13652	" Calnon, G.	"	21-8-18.	"
S.16711	" Curson, H.	"	23-8-18.	"
B. 698	" Connelly, G.	"	25-8-18.	"
P. 1390	Sgt Clarke, F.	"	23-8-18.	"
Z. 284	" Craig, R.	"	"	"
P. 4250	Rfn Couzens, P.	"	"	"
S.20611	" Cox, F.	"	"	"
48438	" Callery, T.	"	25-8-18.	"
S. 3792	" Cook, W.	"	21-8-18.	"
S.16030	Sgt Crook, G.	"	23-8-18.	"
S.27763	Rfn Cox, G.	"	"	"
41389	L/C Chapman, A.	"	"	"
B201384	Rfn Cooper, F.	"	"	"
374117	" Coldrick, W.	"	"	"
374684	" Connor, T.	"	21-8-18.	"
48601	Cpl Corkhill, E.	"	24-8-18.	"
S.14216	" Collins, T.	"	"	"
B200800	L/C Davey, F.	"	25-8-18.	"
S.32933	Rfn Dunks, J.	"	"	"
B203693	" Davison, J.	"	23-8-18.	"
S. 6160	" Day, W.	"	"	"
S.8148	L/C Dutfield, W.	"	"	"
S. 2121	Rfn Davis, J.	"	25-8-18.	"
S.4468	" Dunkley, H.	"	23-8-18.	"
O. 54	L/C Doust, H.	"	"	"
445053	Rfn Dawkins, W.	"	"	"
45899	" Dommett, W.	"	"	"

Cont.

13th Battalion, The Rifle Brigade. Sheet, 2.

WINCHESTER RECORD OFFICE.   DAILY CASUALTY LIST.

Regt.No.	Rank & Name.	Casualty & Date.	Prev.Report.
425695	Rfn Drew, C.	Wounded 21-8-18.	
B203191	" Draper, A.	" 25-8-18.	
S.37714	" Ellum, C.	" 23-8-18.	
S.31675	" Eaglestone, A.	" 24-8-18.	
S.35040	" Eustace, C.	" "	
5758	" East, W.	" 25-8-18.	
41320	" Ellis, G.	" 23-8-18.	
S.3230	L/C Evans, A.	" "	
S.25465	Rfn Evans, C.	" "	
S.32928	" Ferne, H.	" "	
O.66	" Fairbrass, E.	" 25-8-18.	
S.1842	" Foster, J.	" 23-8-18.	
O.61	L/C Farnfield, R.	" 21-8-18.	
S.31345	Rfn Green, W.	" 23-8-18.	
B203277	Cpl Gatehouse, E.	" 23-8-18.	
S.15421	Rfn Griss, R.	" 24-8-18.	
S.13051	" Green, E.	" 23-8-18.	
48614	" Goldstein, B.	" "	
B203202	L/C Goldstein, S.	" "	
B200451	L/C Harpes, W.	" "	
S.28633	Rfn Hughes, T.	" 25-8-18.	
41392	" Hall, H.	" 23-8-18.	
41406	" Hastler, F.	" 24-8-18.	
S.27718	" Hammond, A.	" 25-8-18.	
45930	" Hare, A.	" "	
S.18349	L/C Hackett, G.	" 23-8-18.	
O.88	Rfn Holden, H.	" "	
S.3114	" Hardstaff, H.	" "	
41405	" Henry, W.	" "	
S.27705	" Haddock, B.	" "	
B200770	L/C Hookem, F.	" 25-8-18.	
S.15628	" Hall, W.	" 23-8-18.	
49034	Rfn Harvey, A.	" 25-8-18.	
48603	Cpl Harpp, A.	" 23-8-18.	
S.37651	Sgt Hill, F.	" "	
S.33668	Rfn Hutton, W.	" "	
S.34080	" Hardy, G.	" "	
S.26861	" Halcox, G.	" "	
421808	" Herbert, J.	" "	
49031	" Hicks, H.	" "	
49029	" Harper, S.	" "	
B202336	" Ingram, A.	" "	
304474	" Jordan, G.	" "	
O.94	" Jones, C.	" 25-8-18.	
B200828	" Jardine, J.	" "	
S.30955	" Johnson, J.	" 23-8-18.	
S.31283	" King, J.	" "	
S.10190	" King, T.	" "	
B.1394	Sgt Knock, A.	" 21-8-18.	
O.101	L/C Lake, W.	" 24-8-18.	
B200832	Rfn Leverton, P.	" 23-8-18.	
S.16793	" Lee, D.	" 25-8-18.	
S.11919	" Long, J.	" 23-8-18.	
S.5519	Cpl Lees, J.	" "	
49036	Rfn Lawrence, J.	" "	
P.104	" Love, H.	" "	
O.710	" Leeke, J.	" "	
O.103	" Lloyd, R.	" "	
O.107	" Lambert, G.	" 24-8-18.	
S.37752	" Marshall, R.	" 23-8-18.	
422943	" Mainhood, J.	" 25-8-18.	
A.45036	" Mitchell, A.	" 23-8-18.	
S.31010	" Mole, G.	" "	
S.35035	" Moseley, S.	" 25-8-18.	
6599	A/C Marsom, J.	" 24-8-18.	
S.14961	L/C Marshall, S.	" 23-8-18.	

Cont.

13th (S) Battalion, The Rifle Brigade.   Sheet 3.

District:- Rifle Records, Winchester.   Daily Casualty List.

Regt. No.	Rank & Name.	CASUALTY.		Prev. Reptd.
S.32929	Rfn.Miles W.	Wounded.	23.8.18.	"
P. 209	Sgt.Manning A.	"	"	
S.20609	Rfn.Milan F.	"	"	
S.13723	" Mills H.	"	"	
B200919	" Mortlock G.	"	"	
B202227	" McLaughlin P.	"	"	
B202103	L/c.Mercer W.	"	"	
S.15847	Cpl.Mabbott F.	"	"	
S. 6029	Rfn.Millburn H.	"	"	
B200685	Cpl.Nichol T.	"	25.8.18.	
49048	Rfn.Noakes G.	"	"	
S.20377	" Newton F.	"	23.8.18.	
D. 120	" Nash J.	"	24.8.18.	
O. 118	" Nutkins W.	"	23.8.18.	
573365	" Norris J.	"	"	
48608	" Osborne F.	"	"	
B200089	" Oakley T.	"	"	
S.23866	" Odd S.	"	"	
Z. 906	" Oldham W.	"	21.8.18.	
48961	" Powlesland V.	"	24.8.18.	
S.33751	" Pepperdine E.	"	25.8.18.	
49051	" Purvis W.	"	23.8.18.	
S.14103	L/c.Payne W.	"	"	
S.21286	Rfn.Payne W.	"	24.8.18.	
O. 660	" Pomp A.	"	25.8.18.	
B. 379	" Parry F.	"	"	
O. 356	Sgt.Pollard F.	"	23.8.18.	
571660	Rfn.Peak M.	"	"	
5739	" Parker W.	"	"	
S.31488	" Payne F.	"	"	
S.37765	" Pullen H.	"	24.8.18.	
S.37763	" Pell A.	"	23.8.18.	
S.37761	" Pocock H	"	"	
B202329	" Rollins, J.	"	"	
S.30494	" Ruffles, G.	"	25-8-18.	
B201740	" Rogers, W.	"	24-8-18.	
B200469	L/C Rolt, A.	"	25-8-18.	
O. 132	Rfn Rant, E.	"	23-8-18.	
P. 215	" Ramsden, F.	"	"	
49054	" Rendall, R.	"	"	
49056	" Rushbrooke, W.	"	"	
S.17631	Sgt Reed, L.	"	24-8-18.	
S.16719	Rfn Smith, F.	"	23-8-18.	
S.37789	" Stannard, W.	"	25-8-18.	
S.29908	" Sullivan, J.	"	23-8-18.	
S.36546	" Sampson, E.	"	"	
S.37777	" Soame, H.	"	"	
41410	" Stevens, W.	"	24-8-18.	
S.30655	" Sheppard, E.	"	23-8-18.	
S.31520	" Smith, T.	"	"	
48613	" Southgate, E.	"	"	
B203338	" Skelly, W.	"	24-8-18.	
5194	" Shearman, C.	"	"	
S.30789	" Sharrod, J.	"	23-8-18.	
S.17998	" Shipman, R.	"	24-8-18.	
5636	" Sebrof, R.	"	23-8-18.	
S. 9272	L/C Smith, W.	"	"	
48618	Rfn Smith, J.	"	"	
B200782	Sgt Statham, E.	"	"	
422064	Rfn Sullivan, D.	"	"	
423901	" Stokes, G.	"	"	
S.32775	" Talbot, C.	"	22-8-18.	
45052	" Terry, A.	"	23-8-18.	
B201751	" Tilley, G.	"	"	

Cont.

13th Battalion, The Rifle Brigade.

Sheet, 4.

WINCHESTER RECORD OFFICE.   DAILY CASUALTY LIST.

Regt.No.	Rank & Name.	Casualty & Date.	Prev.Report.
B201048	Rfn Thomson, W.	Wounded 25-8-18.	
S.10127	" Tabor, W.	" "	
S.24972	" Thrasher, C.	" 23-8-18.	
S.16633	" Teeling, C.	" "	
Z. 8124	Cpl Tillett, W.	" "	
45051	Rfn Thompson, W.	" "	
S. 3897	Sgt Thurston, F.	" "	
41029	Rfn Taylor, C.	" "	
S.37791	" Thurston, S.	" "	
S.23561	" Tetlow, J.	" "	
48969	" Upton, E.	" "	
41002	" Venns, L.	" 24-8-18.	
S.19701	" Vale, A.	" 23-8-18.	
S.19570	" Vanhinsbergh, P.	" "	
S.17259	" Wilkes, E.	" "	
S. 4502	" Wheeler, H.	" 22-8-18.	
O. 169	" Waterton, H.	" 23-8-18.	
S.22051	" Weedon, H.	" "	
45861	" Wilkinson, G.	" "	
45966	" White, W.	" "	
S.32660	" Wornes, F.	" 21-8-18.	
S.32967	" Webster, D.	" 25-8-18.	
48970	" Walker, A.	" "	
S.26570	" Williams, E.	" "	
B201369	" Weavers, W.	" 24-8-18.	
41398	" Wiltshire, C.	" 23-8-18.	
S.17202	" Wilmot, J.	" "	
P. 1515	L/C Webb, W.	" "	
S.37657	Rfn White, W.	" "	
O. 658	" West, J.	" 24-8-18.	
41030	" Wade, S.	" 23-8-18.	
S.25156	" Wright, C.	" "	
48971	" Warren, E.	" "	
48972	" Watson, F.	" "	
S.32171	" Warwick, E.	" "	
48612	" Williams, D.	" "	
S. 6649	L/C Wright, A.	" 21-8-18.	
S.12043	" Young, R.	" 23-8-18.	

The above casualties reported by O.C. 13th Rif. Bde dated 27-8-18.

2nd Sept., 1918.

Major for,
Officer i/c No.2 Infantry Section.

SECRET.

13th BATTALION THE RIFLE BRIGADE.

WAR DIARY

for

SEPTEMBER

1918.

VOLUME No. 36.

13th Battalion The Rifle Brigade.

WAR DIARY.

Sept. 1918.

1st & 2nd. At LOGEAST WOOD in rest billets. Reorganisation after recent operations and specialist training carried out.

3rd. Moved to HUTS North of FAVREUIL.

4th to 9th. Remained in HUTS North of FAVREUIL. Training carried out.

Night 9/10th. Battalion moved up to take over defence of Main Line of Resistance West of HAVRINCOURT WOOD.

10th. Holding Main Line of Resistance.

11th. On the afternoon of the 11th September the Battalion moved forward from BERTINCOURT and concentrated in HAVRINCOURT WOOD, preparatory to taking up Assembly positions for an attack upon TRESCAULT SPUR.

Although HAVRINCOURT WOOD was subjected to very heavy shell fire, probably as a result of the attack which was taking place N., of our Sector, our casualties during the concentration were relatively light.

An Outpost Line running approximately round the edge of the Wood on the Battalion front was thrown out by the Reserve Company ('A' Coy.—Capt. E.A.HARVEY, M.C.). This Company suffered several casualties from shell-fire, and, (during the night) was attacked by a strong enemy Patrol, which bombed one of their Posts, wounding an Officer and two men.

In spite of the fact that gas shells continually fell in the WOOD, little difficulty was experienced in taking up Assembly Positions, which operation was completed by 4-45 a.m., on the 12th September.

12th. At 5-25 a.m., the barrage opened, and was very satisfactory on the whole, but one or two casualties were sustained owing to the proximity of the barrage to the Assembly Positions, which rendered the inevitable percentage of "shorts" more dangerous than usual.

The attack was launched with two Companies in the Front Line, 'B' Company on the Right (Capt. G.H.FAIRBAIRN, M.C.), 'D' Company (Capt. P.F.DAVY, M.C.), on the Left, 'C' Company (Capt. E.W.WOOD, M.C.), were in Support, and 'A' Company (Capt. E.A.HARVEY, M.C.), in Reserve, afforded considerable assistance with Lewis Gun fire from the edge of the WOOD.

The advance was momentarily checked by heavy M.G., fire from Strong Points in the TRANSVAAL System. The prompt and skilful manner in which the strong points were silenced, was probably the most outstanding feature of the whole action.

At 7 a.m., messages were received stating that the Front Companies had reached their first objective, and that the Support Company was consolidating in the TRANSVAAL System. About this time the first batch of prisoners passed through.

At 8 a.m., the T.M., attached to the Battalion went forward to assist in the consolidation.

An hour later the Intelligence Officer (2/Lieut. J.C.H.MATHAMS, M.C.), returned and reported that all objectives were gained, that Companies were in touch on the flanks, and that sound liaison had been established with the Battalions on the right and left.

At 6-35 p.m., after a comparatively quiet day, there was a marked increase in enemy harassing fire, and much enemy movement was seen, and almost immediately a determined counter-attack was launched against our Left Coy.

Sept. 12th. (Cont.).	At 6-55 p.m., in answer to our S.O.S., our Artillery put down a good barrage of 15 minutes duration. This effectively cut off the enemy's retreat and contributed largely to the fiasco in which his attack culminated. Although several parties of the enemy succeeded in making their way into our lines, they were immediately ejected, leaving behind them a large number of dead. Our captures included six Machine Guns, one T.M., many boxes of ammunition, and a complete telephone outfit. The rest of the night was normal.
13th.	At 6 a.m., an inter-Company relief was carried out; 'A' Company relieving 'C' Company, who, in turn, relieved 'D' Company on the Left. This Company had suffered heavy casualties, having only one Officer (Capt. P.F.DAVY, M.C.), and one N.C.O., (Cpl. Faggeter) above the rank of Lance Corporal left, and were withdrawn to Reserve. Except for a persistent and spiteful bombardment of the Sunken Road, and the forward edge of the WOOD, the day offered nothing of special interest, but the enemy brought a repetition of the previous counter-attack, on very much the same lines, with the exception of an intense bombardment. The S.O.S., went up at 5-47 p.m., but was not seen. Fortunately, however, Artillery retaliation was asked for by telephone at the same time, and at 5-56 p.m., a slow barrage was put down by our guns. Shortly after this the enemy approached our Right Company's Front from the direction of CHARING CROSS, but were driven off by Lewis Gun and rifle fire. Almost at the same time a determined attack was made against our Left Company, during which about fifteen of the enemy succeeded in gaining a footing in our trench. They were immediately ejected, and the survivors, becoming entangled in our wire, were promptly shot down. By 8-50 p.m., the situation was completely restored, and all Companies reported everything everything quiet on the Battalion front. Throughout the whole of the 13th September, and during the night of the 13/14th September, the enemy maintained a continuous bombardment of the Eastern edge of the WOOD with gas shells.

14th.	At 5-20 a.m., our barrage opened in support of an attack by the 62nd Division and 10th Royal Fusiliers on our Left.
	At 8 a.m., the 10th R.F., were reported to have gained their objective in CHAPEL WOOD Switch, and established Posts.
	At 1-25 p.m., our Left Company reported that the S.O.S., had been put up by the 10th R.F. The H.Qrs., of this Battalion, having been informed of this by telephone, replied that the situation was being dealt with.
	At 2-20 p.m., the enemy having been located in DERBY TRENCH, and reported by the 10th R.F., to be advancing towards TRESCAULT, our Support Company threw out two Platoons to form a defensive flank, in which operation our Reserve Company co-operated.
	At 4 p.m., the 10th R.F., reported the situation restored and the line strongly held in statu quo ante..
	At 5-30 p.m., the relief by the 13th R.F., commenced and was completed by 10-45 p.m.
	Casualties. The casualties from 11th September to 14th September (inclusive) were:-
	    Killed .... 2 Officers and 26 O.R.
	    Wounded .... 2 " " 98 "
	    Missing .... Nil " " 12 "
	Supplies. The supply of water and ammunition of all kinds was excellent throughout, and much praise is due to the Transport, under charge of Lieut. M.G.S.HOPSON, for the very good work in bringing it forward to advanced Dumps under most trying circumstances. The pack-mule system

Sept. 14th. (Cont.).	of bringing up rations was employed and proved most satisfactory. Rations were delivered at TRANSVAAL Post daily without a casualty to mules or drivers.
Night 14/15th.	The Battalion came back to a position W., of HAVRINCOURT WOOD in the vicinity of VELU.
15th.	The Battalion moved back to LEBECQUIERE where it remained until
18th,	when, after short notice, it again moved forward to a position West of HAVRINCOURT WOOD. The Battalion returned to LEBECQUIERE the same evening.
19th.	At LEBECQUIERE.
20th.	The Battalion moved to LIGNY---THILLOY.
21st.	At LIGNY---THILLOY.
22nd.	The Battalion moved to PYS Area---in Corps Reserve.
23rd to 28th.	In PYS Area; billetted in Huts and Bivouacs. Training carried out, and preparations made for Battalion Sports on the 30th, in celebration of 25th September.
29th.	The Battalion moved forward, after short notice, to vicinity of VILLERS-AU-FLOS
30th.	Moved forward to relieve 95th Infantry Brigade of 5th Division, N.E., of GONNELIEU. Sports cancelled.

The following Rewards were notified during the month:-

Distinguished Service Order.
Lieut. Col. R.MOSTYN-OWEN.

Bar to Military Cross.
Capt. A.W.RAYMOND, M.C. (R.A.M.C.).
2/Lieut. A.L.COOPER, M.C.

Military Cross.
Capt. L.G.N.LANGMEAD.
"   G.G.H.IRVING.
Lieut. E.R.PIDSLEY.
2/Lieut. A.A.B.McDONALD.
2/Lieut. W.T.KERRUISH.

Distinguished Conduct Medal.
S.7972 Sgt. Ellington M.
7720   "   Mitchell J.
24207   "   Sanders C.
S.7196 CSM. Crane T.,M.M.

Military Medal.
S.13202 Rfn. Tombs V.
O/710   "   Leake J.
41394   "   Last J.
S.11905 "   Callery T.
304455   "   Rowe W.
S.27364 "   Vincent B.
S.4620   "   Balkwill W.
S.19979 Cpl. Gaze H.
B203255 L/C. Walker E.
48617   "   Forth T.
S.14206 "   Cousins W.
S.19576 Rfn. Nurse T.
S.18410 Sgt. Harris A.
1001   "   Sando F.
S.15627 L/C. Allen H.
S.2035   "   Hancock J.

Honours and Rewards. (Cont.).

Military Medal.

B.203208	Sgt.	Higgins O.
S.9751	"	Woods S.
S.37094	L/C.	Hewitt A.
S.37663	Rfn.	Curtis W.
S.4433	"	Mackey J.
8533	Cpl.	Lee A. (Leinster Regt., attached).
S.4088	CSM.	Patterson H.
B.203253	L/S.	Champion N., D.C.M.
S.17234	Cpl.	Otley G.
Z.2788	Rfn.	Sharp N.
49024	"	Ward J.
S.31976	"	Lear M.
B.2397	CSM.	Stenning C.

	Off.	O.R.
Total strength of Battalion on Aug. 31st.	40	682
" decrease during September.	8	235
	32	447
Total Reinforcements during September.	6	430
	38	877

[signature]

Lieut. Colonel,
Commanding 12th Battalion The Rifle Brigade.

3/10/18.

13th Battalion The Rifle Brigade.

11/9/18.

1. On 12th Sept. 1918:-
   (a) The New Zealand Division on the Right and the 37th Division on the Left are to attack the TRESCAULT SPUR from Q.29.central to K.35. central.
   (b) The 62 Division on the Left of the 37th Division are to attack HAVRINCOURT and the HINDENBURG System in K.34 and 35 from the S.W.

2. **Southern Divisional Boundary.**
   P.1.c.0.10.- P.3.c.0.3.-P.10.b.6.0.-P.11.d.0.8.-Q.7.c.0.9.-
   Q.9.c.0.0.- Q.16.c.0.6.-Q.17.a.0.6.-Q.11.c.6.0.-and thence due East.

3. Objectives will be as follows:-
   First Objective (RED).
   SNAP RESERVE and junction with BUNG ALLEY, thence North West along TRESCAULT Road,
   Second Objective (GREEN).
   Q.11.d.0.0.-Q.5.c.8.8.-thence by DERBY TRENCH to Q.4.a.7.7.
   Final Objective (DOTTED GREEN).
   CHAPPEL WOOD Switch to K.35.d.2. ., thence to K.35.c.8.9.

4. The attack on the 37th Divisional Front will be carried out by 111th Infantry Brigade—
   13th Rifle Brigade will attack on the Right
   13th K.R.R.C., are attacking on the Left.
   Inter-Battalion Boundary will be from Q.15.b.7.6.-Q.5.c.80.30.
   10th Royal Fusiliers will be in Support.

5. **ASSEMBLY.** The head of the Battalion will move off at 4-30 p.m.
   Order of march:- 'HQ', 'B', 'D', 'C' and 'A' Companies.
   Platoons at 200 yards interval. Limbers will be with Companies.
   Route: Railway Crossing, P.2.d.5.1.- ROUYAULCOURT - P.17.d.5.5.,
   along track to Q.1.d.30.30., where guides will meet Companies, and guide them to new locations in Q.8.c., Q.14.b., Q.15.a.
   Companies will pass starting point-P.2.d.5.1.-at following times:-

'HQ' Coy.	....	4-30 p.m.	
'B' "	....	4-40 "	
'D' "	....	4-50 "	
'C' "	....	5-0 "	
'A' "	....	5-10 "	

6. **OUTPOSTS.** 'A' Coy., will detail 1 Platoon to take up line of observation alongside of Wood in Q.9.c., at dusk. They will be pushed forward about 200 to 300 yards to positions from which they can cover the advance at Zero with fire. They will withdraw after first objective is gained.

7. **JUMPING-OFF POSITIONS.** 'B' Company on Right — 'D' Company on Left, between Q.15.c.6.9., and Q.15.b.8.8.
   'C' Company in Support will be in Q.15.b., and move down to Sunken Road at Zero.
   'A' Company will remain in Battalion Reserve in Q.15.a.
   Companies will be in position by 4-40 a.m.

8. After the first objective is gained 'C' Company will move up to and consolidate Strong Points, Q.10.central and Q.10.d.

9. In event of attack being held up Os.C. 'B' and 'D' Companies may call on 'C' Company as a final resort.
   In event of enemy counter-attacking O'C' 'C' Company will act on his own initiative.

10. **BARRAGE.** Barrage will open at ZERO on line Q.15.central to Q.9.d.5.5., and stand on that line from ZERO to ZERO plus 3 mins. It will then advance 100 yards in 3 minutes; it will stand for 10 minutes at 300 yards in front of first objective.

2.

11. **CONSOLIDATION.** The final objective (GREEN LINE) is the approximate line that will be consolidated. Protective patrols only will be pushed forward.

12. **T.M.** One Light Trench Mortar is attached to Battalion H.Qrs., and will be held in Reserve.

13. **M.G.** One Section of Machine Gun Company is attached to the Battalion and will accompany 'B' Company in the attack.

14. **ADMINISTRATIVE** arrangements have been issued separately.
    R.A.P., — Q.8.d.4.6.
    Headquarters — Position of Battalion H.Qrs., will be notified later.

15. **ZERO.** ZERO hour will be notified later.

                                        G.G.H. IRVING.   Capt. & A/Adjt.,
                                        13th Battalion The Rifle Brigade.

Issued at 3 p.m.,(by Runner.).

Copy No. 1, O.C. 'A' Coy.
   "   2.   "   'B' "
   "   3.   "   'C' "
   "   4.   "   'D' "
   "   5. War Diary.
   "   6. File.

13th Battalion, The Rifle Brigade.

WINCHESTER RECORD OFFICE.   **DAILY CASUALTY LIST.**

Regt.No.	Rank	Name	Casualty & Date		Prev.Report.
S. 8006	Sgt	Bumstead, G.	Killed in action	12-9-18.	Nil.
B201238	Rfn	Broadley, W.	" " "	12-9-18.	"
48443	"	Corns, J.	" " "	13-9-18.	"
S.15721	"	Cutting, H.	" " "	13-9-18.	"
Z. 2793	"	Cowell, G.	" " "	12-9-18.	"
1248	Sgt	Woof, T.	" " "	13-9-18.	"
S.33748	Rfn	Collier, W.	" " "	12-9-18.	"
S. 8885	"	Davies, H.	" " "	12-9-18.	"
S.30300	L/C	Driver, C.F.	" " "	13-9-18.	"
S.18341	Rfn	Fisher, W.	" " "	12-9-18.	"
B203208	Sgt	Higgins, O.	" " "	12-9-18.	"
S. 5682	Rfn	Hinson, J.	" " "	12-9-18.	"
S.21073	"	Hankins, H.	" " "	12-9-18.	"
Z. 817	"	Judd, F.	" " "	12-9-18.	"
S.32651	"	Jarvis, H.	" " "	12-9-18.	"
S.27456	"	Key, H.	" " "	12-9-18.	"
B201380	"	Lawrence, W.	" " "	12-9-18.	"
S.32041	"	Phillips, F.	" " "	12-9-18.	"
B200966	"	Round, J.	" " "	12-9-18.	"
S.28645	"	Riley, A.	" " "	12-9-18.	"
41034	"	Streeter, F.	" " "	14-9-18.	"
S.10101	"	Smith, F.	" " "	12-9-18.	"
S.24207	Sgt	Sanders, C.	" " "	12-9-18.	"
S.14986	Rfn	Scheurmier, F.	" " "	12-9-18.	"
P. 1049	"	White, A.	" " "	15-9-18.	"

The above casualties reptd by O.C. 13th Rif.Bde dated 17-9-18.

23rd Sept., 1918.

Officer i/c No.2 Infantry Section.

Major for,

13th Battalion, The Rifle Brigade.

WINCHESTER RECORD OFFICE.   **DILY CASUALTY LIST.**

Regt.No.	Rank & Name.	Casualty & Date.	Prev.Report.
S.21952	Rfn Fossett, S.	Died of wounds 13-9-18.	Nil.
S.30355	Rfn Addison, W.	Wounded 12-9-18.	
S.28625	L/S Atterton, G.	" 12-9-18.	
49233	Rfn Bull, F.	" "	
315100	" Bond, T.	" "	
41399	L/C Blythe, J.	" "	
46247	Rfn Boxall, R.	" 13-9-18.	
S.8664	" Bampton, F.	" "	
S.2426	" Bamford, W.	" "	
S.1171	" Babb, E.	" 15-9-18.	
S.5802	L/C Bachelor, A.	" 12-9-18.	
374659	Rfn Cameron, R.	" 13-9-18.	
B201252	" Clark, G.	" "	
445062	" Currell, H.	" "	
S.35102	" Cooling, J.	" 12-9-18.	
S.32647	" Chilton, A.	" "	
48905	" Caspell, S.	" "	
5209	Cpl Carter, J.	" "	
S.7196	CSM Crane, T.	" 13-9-18.	
6589	Rfn Critcher, G.	" "	
6056	L/C Carter, F.	" 12-9-18.	
B.2480	Cpl Crawford, C.	" "	
Z.979	Rfn Carroll, C.	" "	
O.46	" Colby, J.	" 13-9-18.	
B201956	" Dale, D.	" "	NIL.
S.31510	" Doncaster, G.	" "	
O.413	" Delloche, T.	" 12-9-18.	
B200530	Cpl Eade, G.	" "	
B202123	Rfn Eighteen, W.	" 13-9-18.	
45581	" Edwards, R.	" "	
S.27442	Cpl Evans, C.	" 12-9-18.	
S.29807	Rfn Edmonds, W.	" "	
B201290	" Forrester, W.	" "	
S.24742	Cpl Ford, G.	" 13-9-18.	
O.70	Rfn Fagg, A.	" 12-9-18.	
445080	" Gennings, A.	" "	
S.10768	L/S Glynn, S.	" "	
S.29861	Rfn Gardiner, B.	" 13-9-18.	
S.26038	" Gibbs, J.	" 12-9-18.	
S.5341	Cpl Gale, C.	" "	
S.14678	Rfn Godwin, A.	" 13-9-18.	
B201371	" Harvey, M.	" 12-9-18.	
B201636	" Hawes, L.	" 15-9-18.	
46697	" Hoey, G.	" 12-9-18.	
S.28736	" Holloway, F.	" "	
S.27094	L/C Hewitt, A.	" "	
Z.774	Rfn Holt, L.	" "	
Z.2443	" Hunt, J.	" "	
S.18251	" Hitchen, J.	" 14-9-18.	
S.4791	Sgt Jones, J.	" 12-9-18.	
4017	Rfn James, W.	" "	
S.28372	" Kelvey, H.	" 13-9-18.	
45845	" Lee, R.	" "	
45623	" Lister, H.	" "	
46641	" Luff, C.	" 12-9-18.	
S.17181	" Lewis, C.	" "	
S.3696	" Lincoln, W.	" 13-9-18.	
B202098	" Mankertz, C.	" "	
B201265	" Martin, W.	" "	
445064	" Moore, R.	" 12-9-18.	
S.37753	" McCarthy, C.	" "	
45500	" Murphy, H.	" 13-9-18.	
S.29410	" Morris, G.	" 12-9-18.	

Cont.

13th Battalion, The Rifle Brigade. Sheet, 2.

Winchester Record Office.   Daily Casualty List.

Regt.No.	Rank & Name	Casualty & Date	Prev.Report.
S.11437	Rfn Marks, J.	Wounded 14-9-18.	
S.15079	" Messenger, A.	" 12-9-18.	
Z. 2794	L/S Marshall, T.	" "	
O. 116	Rfn Mortby, F.	" "	
O. 110	" Mitchell, J.	" "	
45953	" Nichols, F.	" 13-9-18.	
49050	" Pettitt, C.	" "	
S.37766	" Prior, G.	" 12-9-18.	
S.31647	" Parkes, A.	" 13-9-18.	
S.18427	" Power, H.	" 12-9-18.	
S.10160	" Powell, W.	" "	
Z. 675	" Porter, S.	" "	
S.1235	Sgt Price, G.	" "	
S.3658	L/C Ralph, C.	" "	
50929	Rfn Read, J.	" 14-9-18.	
S.37774	" Redgrave, G.	" 12-9-18.	
S.30642	" Rowe, B.	" "	
S. 7455	L/C Remant, C.	" "	
48122	Rfn Struys, C.	" 14-9-18.	NIL.
S.31393	" Sanders, F.	" 12-9-18.	
S.32922	" Smithson, A.	" 13-9-18.	
S.25997	" Smith, J.	" 12-9-18.	
O. 366	" Stebbings, E.	" 17-9-18.	
O. 339	" Smith, W.	" "	
B. 2397	CSM Stenning, C.	" 12-9-18.	
S. 28391	Rfn Todd, W.	" 14-9-18.	
S.32448	Rfn Thompson, R.	" 13-9-18.	
48967	" Turner, W.	" "	
S.1572	" Turner, R.	" 12-9-18.	
48968	" Underwood, W.	" "	
O. 561	L/C Waugh, R.	" 14-9-18.	
49235	Rfn Webb, G.	" 12-9-18.	
374252	" West, L.	" 15-9-18.	
41065	" Woolley, F.	" 12-9-18.	
48974	" Wells, D.	" 13-9-18.	
48611	" Wells, J.	" "	
S.37804	" White, C.	" "	
45967	" Wildman, B.	" "	
S.17527	" Wood, S.	" "	
S.28033	" Warne, E.	" 12-9-18.	
S. 9419	" Wheatley, E.	" "	
Z. 2761	" Wells, E.	" "	
S. 3825	Cpl Watson, R.	" "	
S.21010	Rfn Young, T.	" 13-9-18.	
S. 5714	" Young, A.	" 12-9-18.	

The above casualties reptd by O.C. 13th Rif.Bde dated 17-9-18.

24th Sept., 1918.

Officer i/c No.2 Infantry Section.
Major for,

13th Battalion, The Rifle Brigade.

WINCHESTER RECORD OFFICE.   **DAILY CASUALTY LIST.**

Regt.No.	Rank & Name.	Casualty & Date.	Prev.Report.
O. 116	Rfn Mortby, F.	To duty 18-9-18.	"W" (D.C.L.24-9-18
	Reptd by O.C. 13th Rif. Bde dated 21-9-18.		
S.14865	Rfn Coyston, C.	Wounded 12-9-18.	Nil.
Z. 2478	Cpl Gilbert, J.	" 19-9-18.	"
S.16442	Rfn Ram, A.	" 12-9-18.	"
S.16502	" Munday, J.	" 12-9-18.	"
B201635	" Davis, R.	" 12-9-18.	"
S.15848	Cpl Sheehan, A.	" 12-9-18.	"
45621	Rfn Hedges, A.	" 12-9-18.	"
S.23512	" Cross, E.	" 12-9-18.	"
48436	" Coyle, C.	" 12-9-18.	"
B201219	" Webb, J.	" 13-9-18.	"

The above casualties reptd by O.C. 13th Rif.Bde dated 17-9-18.
                                                            19

AMENDED REPORT.

| 45623 | Rfn Lister, H. | Killed in action 13-9-18. | Cancel report of "W" in D.C.List d/24-9-18. |

Reptd by O.C.13th Rif.Bde dated 22-9-18.

C1699
29/9/18

25th Sept.,1918.   Major for,
                    Officer i/c No.2 Infantry Section.

13th Battalion, The Rifle Brigade.

WINCHESTER RECORD OFFICE.   **DAILY CASUALTY LIST.**

Regt.No. Rank & Name.	Casualty & Date.	Prev.Report.
49021 Rfn Wood, S. Reptd by O.C. 13th Rif.Bde dated 23-9-18.	Wounded 12-9-18.	Nil.
S. 4195 Rfn Musk, J. Auth:- BURIAL; Reptd by V.Div.B.O. through IV.C.B.O. G/1153/13 dated 10-9-18. (Extract,51700.)	Killed in action or died of wounds on or shortly after 8-5-18.	"M" (C.1577.)
~~S.37789 Rfn Stannard, W.~~ * ~~Auth:- BURIAL;~~ ~~Reptd by 62nd Div.B.O. through VI Corps,~~ ~~G/1155/47 undated.~~	~~Killed in action or died of wounds on or shortly after 25-8-18.~~	~~"W"~~ ~~(C.1674.)~~

* See memo.

27th Sept., 1918.

Major for,
Officer i/c No.2 Infantry Section

SECRET

13th. BATTALION THE RIFLE BRIGADE.

WAR DIARY

50th Month of

OCTOBER 1918

VOLUME 37.

13th. Battalion The Rifle Brigade.

WAR DIARY - - OCTOBER 1918.

1st. Oct. The Battalion moved forward and took over Front Line West of Canal at VAUCELLES from 2nd. CANTERBURYS' (N.Z), with Battalion Headquarters at BLEAK HOUSE.

2nd. and 3rd. Oct. were spent in reconnoitring and preparing for the crossing of the CANAL.

4th. Oct. from information gained by Patrols and observers, proved that the enemy had evacuated his Posts on CANAL. "A" and "B" Companies at once pushed forward Patrols, and with the Companies behind, followed up the retreating enemy, crossing the CANAL at 1000 hours, and establishing themselves on the high ground W., of BELAISE FARM. The enemy was then holding MESNIERES - BEAUREVOIR Line.

On 6th & 7th Oct. the line was held and improved, and strong patrols were made towards entrenched enemy. Three thick belts of wire and a well organised trench system were facing us.

On night 7/8th. Oct. the 10th. R.F., moved up to an Assembly Position behind the Battalion preparatory to passing through and taking the MESNIERES - BEAUREVOIR line at 4.30a.m. of the 8th.
The Battalion provided 3 Platoons (less L.G. Sections) as escort for 3 Tanks which were accompanying attacking Infantry.
"C" Company was attached to 10th. R.F. as Support Company, but was not used.
The attack was successfully launched: one Tank only being successful in crossing the wire and breaking through enemy line. Good work was done by parties attached, 80 prisoners being taken by the Party attached to this Tank.
By evening the attack had advanced to general line BOUT de PRE' - GUILLMIN.
The 112th. Infantry Brigade, having leap-frogged over the 111th. Infantry Brigade, the Battalion, with the remainder of the Brigade, advanced as Brigade in Reserve.

Night 9/10th. Oct. The Battalion bivouacked in GUILLEMIN FARM

Morning 10th. Oct. Brigade Headquarters were established in LIGNY-en-CAMBRESIS on the morning of the 10th., and the Battalion moving up also established its Headquarters in this Village.

10th to 21st. Oct. were spent at LIGNY, where the Battalion supplied working parties for the filling in of craters, shell holes, etc., A successful Battalion Concert was held there at the LICHSPIELER.

On 21st. Oct. The Battalion moved to BETHINCOURT.

22nd. Oct. The Battalion moved from BETHINCOURT to BRIASTRE prior to making an attack in conjunction with the 5th. Division.

23rd. Oct. The Battalion left the Railway in front of BRIASTRE at 0430 hours and moved up into positions behind the 5th. Division Assembly Positions.
By 0600 the Battalion was in position.
Owing to the temporary failure of the 5th. Division to advance, it was not until 0907 that the Battalion was able to move forward.
The Barrage opened at 1000 hours and stood for 15 mins. after which the Battalion closely followed the Barrage to their objective in the following formation:-
Two Companies leading ("A" on the Left and "C" on the Right) One Company in Support, and one Company in Reserve.

2.

23rd.Oct. (contd)
As soon as the objective was reached Patrols were furnished by the Reserve Company ("B"), and contact having been obtained with Patrols of the K.R.R.C., on our Right, the Line of the River was reported clear of the enemy by 1527 hours.

This line was then consolidated and the ESSEX Regt passed through us at 1715 hours.

The Battalion moved to Billets in BEAURAIN.

24th.Oct.
The Battalion moved to NEUVILLE, and remained in Billets there until the 31st.October.

GGGGGGGGGGGGGGGGGGGG

The following awards were notified during the month:-

Bar to Military Cross.
2/Lieut.J.C.H.Mathams. M.C.

Military Cross.
Lieut.G.S.Hunter.(A.S.C)
2/Lieut.F.Simpson
2/Lieut.J.F.Thoburn.
B2397 CSM.Stenning. M.M.

Bar to Military Medal
B2399   Cpl.Pattinson.A.M.M.
S3826   Rfn.Stacey.R.   M.M.
S32484   Cpl.Pankhurst.   M.M.

Military Medal
3470   Sgt.Dennis.J.
741231   CQMS.Croxford.B.
S1715   Rfn.Maughan.J.
1248   Sgt.Woof.T.
B1191   "   Orger.J.
S7146   Cpl.Roberts.E.
S34657   Rfn.Clark.J.
S3788   Cpl.Bacon.J.
S27442   L/S Evans.C.
S31642   Rfn.Dillon.J.
45845   "   Lee.R.
S20627   "   Cramp.E.
S20476   "   Thorndick.W.
O/   "   Stevens.T.
S13859   L/S Titley.F.
3474   Sgt.Saunders.W.
S3981   Cpl.Johnson.C.
P1336   Rfn.Fowler.J.
S16617   "   Trigg.C.
6646   "   Bradley.F.
45967   "   Wildman.B.
48987   "   Turner.W.
B200688 "   Hemsley.W.
3420   Sgt.Goodwin.P.

GGGGGGGGGGGGGGGGGGGGGGG

	O.	O.R.
Strength on 30/9/18	38	877
Decrease during October	8	170
	30	707
Increase during October	8	146
	38	853

R Mostyn Owen

Lieut.Col.
Commanding 13th.Battalion The Rifle Brigade.

2/11/18.

13th Battalion, The Rifle Brigade.

WINCHESTER RECORD OFFICE.   **DAILY CASUALTY LIST.**

Regt.No.	Rank	& Name.	Casualty & Date.	Prev.Report.
Amendment				
S. 6060	L/C	Ayling, W.	Killed in action 8-10-18.	Cancel rep. of "W" in D.C.L. 15-10-18.
				C.1719
B201572	Rfn	Pepperell, F.	Wounded 8-10-18.	Nil.
46716	"	Norris, H.	do. "	"
47822	"	Ferrara, A.	do. "	"
445056	"	Rea, H.	do. "	"

The above casualties reptd by O.C. 13th Rif.Bde dated 15-10-18.

| S.37789 | Rfn | Stannard, W. | K.in A. or D.of W. on or shortly after 25-8-18. | "W" (C.1674.) |

Auth:- Reptd "W.& Missing 25-8-18" by O.C. Battn dated 15-10-18.
Burial reptd by 62nd D.B.O. through VI Corps Undated.

S.27763	Rfn	Cox, G.	"B"Coy.	W.& Missing	23-8-18.	"W" (C.1674.)
S. 6160	"	Day, W.	"D" "	-do-	23-8-18.	- do -
B200451	L/C	Harper, W.	"D" "	-do-	23-8-18.	- do -
421808	Rfn	Herbert, J.	" "	-do-	23-8-18.	- do -
422943	"	Mainhood, J.	"B"Coy.	-do-	25-8-18.	- do -
B202103	L/C	Mercer, W.	"A"Coy.	-do-	23-8-18.	- do -
O. 356	Sgt	Pollard, F.	"D" "	-do-	23-8-18.	- do -
5739	Rfn	Parker, W.	" "	-do-	23-8-18.	- do -
S.37763	"	Pell, A.	" "	-do-	23-8-18.	- do -
P. 215	"	Ramsden, F.	" "	-do-	23-8-18.	- do -
45052	"	Terry, A.	" "	-do-	23-8-18.	- do -
S.24972	"	Thrasher, C.	" "	-do-	23-8-18.	- do -
S.19570	"	Vanhinsbergh, P.	"B"Coy.	-do-	23-8-18.	- do -

The above casualties reptd by O.C. 13th Rif.Bde dated 15-10-18.

19th Oct.,1918.

Officer i/c No.2 Infantry Section.
Major for,

13th Battalion, The Rifle Brigade.

WINCHESTER RECORD OFFICE. DAILY CASUALTY LIST.

Regt.No.	Rank	Name	Casualty & Date	Prev.Report.
49463	Rfn	Bruce, A.	Wounded 26-10-18.	Nil.
S.26085	"	Burge, W.	" 23-10-18.	"
5436	"	Butchers, F.	" "	"
445043	"	Barnes, T.	" "	"
423637	"	Bull, E.	" "	"
49013	L/C	Bish, E.	" "	"
S. 3788	Cpl	Bacon, J.	" "	"
S.17233	L/S	Chambers, R.	" "	"
B. 1205	Rfn	Cannons, J.	" "	"
318429	"	Curtis, W.	" "	"
O. 696	"	Chapman, J.	" "	"
O. 37	"	Copping, W.	" "	"
O. 52	"	Dicker, J.	" "	"
425695	"	Drew, C.	" "	"
O. 68	Cpl	Field, D.	" "	"
O. 79	Rfn	Gowers, E.	" "	"
O. 76	"	Giddings, L.	" "	"
S. 31192	"	Gagette, H.	" "	"
S.28299	"	Healey, G.	" "	"
B201195	"	Hardy, R.	" 27-10-18.	"
S.37728	"	Hanson, T.	" 23-10-18.	"
O. 82	"	Harmer, E.	" "	"
S.15401	"	Hardinan, A.	" "	"
45584	"	Jackson, H.	" 26-10-18.	"
O. 98	"	Kempster, A.	" 22-10-18.	"
S. 3696	"	Lincoln, W.	" 23-10-18.	"
S.33234	"	Lawricks, W.	" 22-10-18.	"
49035	"	Lane, H.	" 23-10-18.	"
S.32739	"	Marston, W.	" 27-10-18.	"
O. 112	"	Morrison, C.	" 23-10-18.	"
41407	"	Motts, H.	" 23-10-18.	"
S.35111	"	Moyse, J.	" "	"
574462	"	Newey, W.	" "	"
45813	"	Newton, E.	" "	"
41120	"	Oakley, K.	" "	"
S. 8574	"	Osland, E.	" "	"
S.30001	"	Powell, S.	" "	"
S. 7146	Cpl	Roberts, E.	" "	"
P. 450	Rfn	Ransom, W.	" "	"
Z. 2757	"	Sheppard, E.	" "	"
S.10769	"	Stone, J.	" 26-10-18.	"
S. 5183	L/C	Smedes, C.	" 23-10-18.	"
S. 3690	Cpl	Shaill, W.	" 27-10-18.	"
S.29897	Rfn	Sparks, J.	" 23-10-18.	"
48962	"	Smith, E.	" "	"
S. 5365	"	Taylor, A.	" "	"
S.15091	"	Thomas, J.	" "	"
45963	"	Tomlin, G.	" "	"
41002	"	Venns, L.	" "	"
B200212	"	Vandersteen, J.	" 22-10-18.	"
S.28823	"	White, R.	" 23-10-18.	"
3218	Cpl	Wood, A.	" "	"
S.10520	Rfn	Whitaker, E.	" "	"
6623	"	Williamson, M.	" "	"
49022	"	Young, A.	" 27-10-18.	"

The above casualties reptd by O.C. 13th Rifle Brigade dated 27-10-18.

2nd Nov., 1918.

Major for,
Officer i/c No.2 Infantry Sect.

13th Battalion The Rifle Brigade Order No. 29.

22/10/18.

INFORMATION. On ZERO day extensive operations will be undertaken on this Front.

The 5th Division on the Right of the Corps Front, and the 42nd Division on the Left are advancing at ZERO hour to capture the RED and BLUE Lines.

At ZERO plus 3 hours and 20 minutes—
13th K.R.R.C., on Right,
13th R.Bde., on Left,
will pass through the 5th Division and capture and consolidate the GREEN Line.

At ZERO plus 3 hours and 52 minutes—
10th R.Fus., on Right, and
1st Essex on Left, are passing through GREEN LINE and capturing GREEN DOTTED LINE, throwing out an Outpost Line to the BROWN LINE.

All inter-Brigade, Battalion and Company Boundaries are shewn on attached map.

INTENTION. 13th R.Bde., will attack with two Companies in Front Line.

'C' Company on Right.
'A' Company " Left.
'D' Company and L.T.M.B., will be in Support.
'B' Company will be in Reserve.

INSTRUCTIONS. At ZERO hours the Battalion will move into preliminary positions on line E.15.d.5.0. – E.21.b.5.4.

At ZERO plus 2 hours 20 minutes the Battalion will move forward to Assembly Positions on line

'D' Company will be about 400 yards in rear of 'A' and 'C' Companies.

'B' Company will be about 400 yards in rear of 'D' Coy.

'A' and 'C' Companies will advance so as to pass through 5th Division BLUE LINE at ZERO plus 5 hours 20 minutes.

'D' Company will advance in Supprt at 400 yards distance and will be prepared to offer any assistance which may be asked for by the leading Companies.

'B' Company will move under orders from O.C., Battalion.

On reaching objective 'A' and 'C' Companies will at once consolidate and offer all assistance possible to the Battalions on the Flanks by bringing fire to bear on any targets which may offer themselves on the low ground in front of them and on their Flanks.

L.T.M. O.C. L.T.M., will select a position from which he can bring fire to bear on hostile counter-attacks.

MOPPING-UP O.C., Reserve Company will detail two Platoons to follow in rear of 1st Essex at ZERO plus 3 hours 52 minutes and assist in mopping-up SALESCHES – Main Road through SALESCHES, (excl.).

As soon as this has been completed to the satisfaction of O.C., 1st Essex these two Platoons will return and report to their Company.

SYNCHRONISATION OF WATCHES. Watches will be synchronised at Battn., H.Qrs., at 18.00 hours tonday and again by Runner at ZERO minus 2 hours.

HEADQUARTERS and R.A.P.

ADMINISTRATIVE.
1. Six pack mules will accompany Reserve Company with S.A.A., and L.G., magazines.
2. In addition to tools carried by Coys., a limber will bring

13th Battn. The Rifle Brigade.   SECRET

WAR DIARY.   NOVEMBER 1918

NOVEMBER 1st -3rd. Battalion at NEUVILLE carrying out usual training.

November 4th. The Battalion, having moved up during the night of November 3/4th 1918, was in position by 04.45 hours.

'A' 'C' and 'D' Companies were in jumping off positions on BLACK LINE (in accordance with appendix "A" attached) and 'B' Company (Reserve) in cellars in CHISSIGNES.

At ZERO plus 4 minutes (05.34 hours) the leading Companies moved forward.

The right Company ("D") closely supported by 2 Platoons of 'A' Company, reached the Railway, which, after a fierce struggle and much hand to hand fighting, they captured, taking about 12 Machine Guns and 50 prisoners. Pushing forward towards the BLUE LINE they overcame all enemy opposition and reached this objective well up to time. During this advance they encountered considerable opposition from Machine Guns and Trench Mortars which were reduced and captured by various small operations, in several cases by individual men.

Meanwhile, the Left Company moving forward to the Railway met with fierce opposition. The right flank of this Company was temporarily held up, but the left two platoons (plus one Platoon of 'A' Company) pushed forward and continued the advance joining up with 'D' Coy on the BLUE LINE, well up to schedule time. This advance was also ~~~~~ contested by the enemy and many Machine Gun Nests and Trench Mortars were captured, and 30 to 40 prisoners taken.

The Support Company ('B') left CHISSIGNIES at 06.00 hours and moved forward to the Railway. The Company Commander seeing that the advance was held up by Machine Gun fire from X.5.a.4.5., (approx), organised an attack by two platoons from the south, astride the Railway, and with the co-operation of a Tank and a Trench Mortar Section thus cleaned up the pockets of Germans by 07.15 hours. Several Machine Guns and 70 prisoners were in these pockets.

'B' Company, and the remainder of 'C' and 'A' Companies then quickly advanced to the BLUE LINE.

In the attack on the Railway the casualties sustained were considerable, including two Company Commanders and several Platoon Commanders.

At 08.00 hours the advance was continued from the BLUE LINE to the BLUE DOTTED LINE under heavy shell fire.

The enemy opposition was now broken, and prisoners were giving themselves up freely. only one or two isolated posts offered resistance, and these were quickly mopped up by Platoons or Sections being detached to deal with them.

The BLUE DOTTED LINE was reached by 08.50 hours, and by 10.30 hours Companies had been reorganised and the line consolidated

By 09.30 hours the 112th Brigade had passed through continuing the attack.

The Battalion muched reduced ~~by the attack~~ in strength, continued to hold the consolidated BLUE DOTTED LINE, until withdrawn at 20.00 hours.

Signal communication during this operation was rendered impossible owing to shell fire. Linesmen worked continuously throughout the day, but were unable to establish communication until long after the BLUE DOTTED LINE had been captured. Visual signalling was rendered quite impossible owing to the mist. In addition the country between Battalion Headquarters and the line until a late hour, was heavily shelled, so that several runners became casualties and messages subsequently lost.

CASUALTIES.   Killed...........3 Officers   ..27. O.R.
                   Wounded..........5.   "   ..90   "
                   Missing..........-   "   ..14   "

Sheet 2.

November 5th The Battalion moved back to BEURAIN, where it remained till the 10th carrying out the usual training.

November 11th. The Battalion moved to CAUDRY. The Armistice was declared on the same day. Remained at CAUDRY till the end of the month carrying out usual training. Divisional and Brigade inspections during this period.

	Officers	O.R.
STRENGTH ON 31/10/18.	38.	845.
DECREASE during month............	8.	260.
INCREASE during month.......	10.	188.
	40.	773.

R. Martyn Owen.
Lieut. Col.
13th Battalion The Rifle Brigade.

2 Sheets.
(1)

13th Battalion, The Rifle Brigade.

WINCHESTER RECORD OFFICE. **DAILY CASUALTY LIST.**

Regt.No.	Rank & Name.	Casualty & Date.	Prev.Report.
56564	L/C Hutchinson, P.	Died of wounds 6-11-18. Reptd by O.C. No.19, C.C.S. dated 7-11-18.	Nil.
S.32446	Rfn Timbers, F.	Killed in action 4-11-18.	Nil.
45587	" Plowman, F.	" " " 4-11-18.	"
S.27392	L/C Budd, A.	Wounded at duty 4-11-18.	Nil.
S.37702	Rfn Cox, H.	" " " "	"
49038	" Laws, B.	" " " "	"
45490	" Martin, T.	" " " "	"
S. 4433	Cpl Mackey, J.	" " " "	"
46653	Rfn Nash, W.	" " " "	"
S.18627	" Risbridger, E.	" " " "	"
B200955	Rfn Applebee, J.	Wounded 4-11-18.	Nil.
49232	" Anderson, P.	" "	
S.27047	L/C Atkinson, J.	" "	
S. 9268	Cpl Bayliss, F.	" "	
S.17255	L/C Bickell, E.	" "	
S.30421	Rfn Brackenbury, F.	" "	
48433	" Bradshaw, T.	" "	
S.35039	" Busby, W.	" "	
S. 4620	" Balkwell, W.	" "	
49012	" Beck, M.	" "	
S.31470	" Bassett, A.	" "	
B202088	" Bates, A.	" "	
B201286	L/C Collett, G.	" "	
S. 3659	Rfn Crimp, W.	" "	
49017	" Clarke, R.	" "	
318431	" Chivers, G.	" "	
S.37707	" Draper, S.	" "	
B203693	" Davison, J.	" "	
374102	" Dean, W.	" "	
319017	" Doughty, M.	" "	
O. 415	" Dunster, E.	" "	
S.28440	Cpl Dunkling, G.	" "	
S.24287	Rfn Eversfield, F.	" "	NIL.
S. 4041	Cpl Finnegan, J.	" "	
S.23540	L/C Freedman, S.	" "	
48617	Cpl Forth, T.	" "	
S.34708	Rfn Farey, W.	" "	
S.14678	Rfn Godwin, A.	" "	
46150	" Goldsmith, J.	" "	
50002	" Green, R.	" "	
45476	Cpl Glass, R.	" "	
S.30525	L/C Harris, J.	" "	
49028	Rfn Hall, H.	" "	
S.17724	" Hawkes, J.	" "	
S.18410	Sgt Harris, A.	" "	
S.12869	L/C Hodson, E.	" "	
S.37725	Rfn Hassell, J.	" "	
S.21214	" Jones, H.	" "	
40871	" Kennedy, L.	" "	
S.37655	" Lewis, F.	" "	
41394	" Last, J.	" "	
6616	A/C Lamport, G.	" "	
40947	Rfn Lewis, E.	" "	
S.26057	" Morgan, A.	" "	
5125	L/C Mills, A.	" "	
S. 4054	Rfn Morgan, E.	" "	
Z. 1715	L/C Maughan, J.	" "	
S.21867	Rfn May, J.	" "	
S.37750	" Mason, H.	" "	

Continued.

13th Battalion, The Rifle Brigade.

WINCHESTER RECORD OFFICE. **DAILY CASUALTY LIST.**

Regt.No.	Rank	Name	Casualty & Date	Prev.Report.
45515	Rfn	Mackintosh, M.	Wounded 4-11-18.	Nil.
47751	"	MacDonald, J.	" "	
B200733	"	Mullens, C.	" "	
B200961	"	Newton, F.	" "	
B201179	"	Norfolk, S.	" "	
50125	"	Northway, R.	" "	
6439	"	Payne, C.	" "	
S.10160	"	Powell, V.	" "	
S.30449	"	Pretty, E.	" "	
48112	"	Pope, S.	" "	
S.32484	L/S	Pankhurst, E.	" "	
S.32530	Rfn	Perry, B.	" "	
49053	"	Partridge, A.	" "	
48961	"	Powlesland, V.	" "	
S. 2697	Sgt	Rutter, J.	" "	
B. 1209	Rfn	Reed, J.	" "	
O. 138	"	Rogers, R.	" "	
6156	L/C	Redman, O.	" "	
S.31960	Rfn	Rider, A.	" "	NIL.
B201388	"	Rutter, J.	" "	
S.27941	"	Rodway, G.	" "	
B201616	"	Stones, J.	" "	
B201283	"	Sproll, J.	" "	
B201639	"	Simpson, J.	" "	
46628	"	Surrey, J.	" "	
S.31652	"	Sutton, R.	" "	
S.33915	"	Shaw, T.	" "	
48965	"	Swindells, T.	" "	
S.28321	L/C	Simonds, W.	" "	
B. 2397	CSM	Stenning, C.	" "	
S.15979	L/C	Saunders, B.	" "	
S.28179	Rfn	Softley, H.	" "	
S.24624	"	Smith, A.	" "	
574735	"	Taylor, A.	" "	
S.16617	"	Trigg, C.	" "	
Z. 8124	Cpl	Tillett, W.	" "	
5647	Rfn	Trott, J.	" "	
S.27364	"	Vincent, B.	" "	
S.31312	"	Wenn, E.	" "	
45591	"	Wyatt, G.	" "	
S. 4303	L/C	Wyatt, W.	" "	
S.14673	"	Watling, H.	" "	
S.17488	L/S	Winfield, H.	" "	
S.24123	Rfn	Wallis, T.	" "	

The above casualties reptd by O.C. 13th Rifle Bde dated 6-11-18.

AMENDED REPORT.

S.16010 Rfn Brown, W.   CANCEL REPORT OF "K. in A. 4-11-18" in
                        D.C.List dated 13-11-18.
        Now reported:- Wounded 4-11-18.

Reptd by O.C. 13th Rifle Bde dated 9-11-18.

15th Nov., 1918.

Major for,
Officer i/c No.2 Infantry Section.

13th Battalion, The Rifle Brigade.

WINCHESTER RECORD OFFICE. **DAILY CASUALTY LIST.**

Regt.No.	Rank & Name.	Casualty & Date.	Prev.Report.
S.34730	Rfn Brewer, G.	Killed in action 23-10-18.	Nil.
	Reptd by O.C. 13th Rifle Bde dated 5-11-18.		
47748	Rfn Cunningham, H.	Adm.38 C.C.S.Wounded 24-10-18.	Nil.
	Reptd by O.C. 38 C.C.S. dated 26-10-18.		
S.14454	Rfn Barton, R.	Died of wounds 6-11-18.	Nil.
	Reptd by O.C. No.3 C.C.S. dated 6-11-18.		
41392	Rfn Hall, H.	Killed in action 4-11-18.	Nil.
S.37766	" Prior, G.	" " " "	"
45964	" Wace, F.	" " " "	"
49235	" Webb, G.	" " " "	"
B200813	" Cooper, H.	" " " "	"
B201657	" Sutherland, F.	" " " "	"
O. 436	" Hall, H.	" " " "	"
S. 2985	Sgt Cotter, A.	" " " "	"
S. 3826	Rfn Stacey, R.	" " " "	"
S. 1547	L/C Burford, G.	" " " "	"
S. 6465	Rfn Williams, D.	" " " "	"
S.27303	Cpl Davison, H.	" " " "	"
S.18254	Rfn Mould, R.	" " " "	"
S.16174	L/C Saltoun, A.	" " " "	"
S.20487	Rfn Lewis, D.	" " " "	"
S.24836	" Saunders, S.	" " " "	"
S.16010	" Brown, W.	" " " "	"
S.27629	" McLeod, S.	" " " "	"
S.28528	" Lansdown, S.	" " " "	"
S.25365	" Webster, G.	" " " "	"
S.20598	" Bird, J.	" " " "	"
S.37663	" Curtis, W.	" " " "	"
S.34704	" Allam, R.	" " " "	"
46205	" Ware, W.	" " " "	"
41410	L/C Stevens, W.	" " " "	"
41391	" Field, E.	" " " "	"
45582	Rfn Gardner, A.	" " " "	"
S.35093	" Scholes, J.	" " " "	"
S.37800	" Worrall, J.	" " " "	"
B201167	" Clarke, E.	" " " "	"
315491	" Cracknell, T.	" " " "	"

The above casualties reptd by O.C. 13th Rifle Bde dated 6-11-18.

| 741939 | Rfn Still, F. | Died of wounds 5-11-18. | Nil. |
| | Reptd by O.C. 48th F.Amb. dated 5-11-18. | | |

13th Nov., 1918.

Major for,
Officer I/c No.2 Infantry Section.

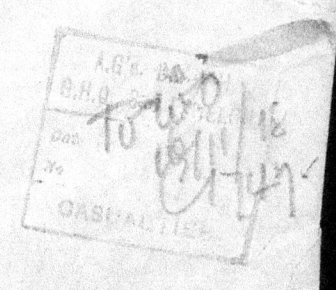

CONFIDENTIAL
****

W A R   D I A R Y

of

13th (S) Battn. RIFLE BRIGADE

from Dec.1st to Dec.31st, 1918.

(VOLUME 40)

SECRET

13th Battalion, The Rifle Brigade.

WAR DIARY

DECEMBER 1918.

The month of December was partially taken up by the Divisional move into Belgium.

December 1st. the Battalion moved to CAPPELLE and thence on the 2nd. to PREUX AU SART where the Battalion remained till 13th carrying out usual training etc.

On the 14th the Battalion moved to HOUDAIN and thence to LOUVROIL where the Battalion rested till the 17th.

The Battalion moved next to ESQUELMES on the 17th and moved the following day to MERBES ST MARIE, on the 19th the Battalion marched to FONTAINE L'EVECQUE and moved the following morning to final destination of JUMET arriving about 13.00 hours.

The average days march was 10 miles and on one day, the 15th, 13 miles.

During the whole of the march not a man fell out.

STRENGTH. On 30th November 1918	42 Officers.	761 Other Ranks.
DECREASE DURING MONTH	1 Officer	39 Other Ranks.
INCREASE " "	1 Officer	138 Other Ranks.

HONOURS AND AWARDS DURING MONTH
Bar to Distinguished Conduct Medal

No.B.203252 Cpl.(L/Sgt)(Sgt)Champion, D.C.M., M.M.
"H.Q." Company.

The Distinguished Conduct Medal

No.S.27088 C.S.M.,W.D.Martin, "C" Company.
B.2818 Sgt.C.Wilson, "C" Coy.

(Authy 3rd Army R.O.d/3.12.18.

Lieut.Col.,
1.1.19.   Commanding 13th Battalion, The Rifle Brigade

111/37

13th Rifle Brigade

January & February
1919

Index............................

SUBJECT.

No.	Contents.	Date.

(41,365). Wt.9392—94. 2000. 6/19. **Gp.164.** A.&E.W.
(44,173). ,, 21,613—105. 500. 10/19. ,, ,,

MESSAGE FORM.   Series No. of Message _____

In		Recd. At ___ By ___	Army Form C 2128
CALL	v	Sent At ___ By ___	(pads of 100)
Out	v		Date Stamp

PREAMBLE _____

M.M. Offices: Delivery _____ v
Origin _____

PREFIX _____   Words _____

TO: 37 Division O

FROM & Place: 111 Infantry Bde

Originator's Number	Day of Month	In reply to Number
X16	4	

Herewith duplicate copy of 13" R Bde War Diary for Jany

TIME OF ORIGIN _____ TIME OF HANDING IN (For Signal use only)

Originator's Signature (Not Telegraphed) Capt

SECRET   13th Battalion The Rifle Brigade.

WAR DIARY   JANUARY 1919

The month of January was spent at JUMET, the Battalion periodically furnishing guards at JUMET, LODLINENSART and ROUX. etc.

The Battalion entered for and won the Brigade Cross Country Run by over 1,000 points.

Demobilization proceeded favourably during the month.

	O.R.	O.R.
Decrease during the month.	6.	193.
Increase during the month.	2.	37.

Barraclough
Capt for
O.C. 13th Battalion The Rifle Brigade.

6.2.19

SECRET.

13th Battalion The Rifle Brigade.

WAR DIARY.   FEBRUARY 1919.

The Battalion was billeted at JUMET during this month.

During the month the Battalion furnished Guards at ROUX, LODELINSART, DIVISIONAL H.Q and BRIGADE H.Q.

Sports and entertainments were organised and proved very successful. A Race Meeting organised by Lt.Col.R.A.Mostyn-Owen.D.S.O. for the Division proved a great success.

During the month Demobilization proceeded rapidly both in Officers and men.

	Offs.	O.R.
Total Decrease during the month	8.	239.
Total Increase during the month.	2.	10.

R. Mostyn Owen.

Lieut.Col.
Comdg 13th Battalion The Rifle Brigade

www.ingramcontent.com/pod-product-compliance
Lightning Source LLC
Chambersburg PA
CBHW080802010526
44113CB00013B/2311